Real-Resumes For Firefighting Jobs

...including real resumes used to change careers
and gain federal employment

Anne McKinney, Editor

PREP PUBLISHING

FAYETTEVILLE, NC

PREP Publishing
1110 ½ Hay Street
Fayetteville, NC 28305
(910) 483-6611

Library of Congress Cataloging-in-Publication Data

Real resumes for firefighting jobs : --including real resumes used to change careers and gain federal employment / Anne McKinney, editor.
        p. cm. -- (Real-resumes series)
   ISBN 978-1475093605; 1475093608 (alk. paper)
   1. Fire extinction--Vocational guidance. 2. Fire fighters. 3. Resumes (Employment) I. Title: Real resumes for fire fighting jobs. II. McKinney, Anne, 1948- III. Series.

   TH9119.R43 2004
   650.14'2--dc22   2004041422

Printed in the United States of America

PREP Publishing

Contents

Real-Resumes For Firefighting Jobs

Anne McKinney, Editor

A WORD FROM THE EDITOR:
ABOUT THE REAL-RESUMES SERIES

Welcome to the Real-Resumes Series. The Real-Resumes Series is a series of books which have been developed based on the experiences of real job hunters and which target specialized fields or types of resumes. As the editor of the series, I have carefully selected resumes and cover letters (with names and other key data disguised, of course) which have been used successfully in real job hunts. That's what we mean by "Real-Resumes." What you see in this book are *real* resumes and cover letters which helped real people get ahead in their careers.

We hope the superior samples will help you manage your current job campaign and your career so that you will find work aligned to your career interests.

The Real-Resumes Series is based on the work of the country's oldest resume-preparation company known as PREP Resumes. If you would like a free information packet describing the company's resume preparation services, call 910-483-6611 or write to PREP at 1110½ Hay Street, Fayetteville, NC 28305. If you have a job hunting experience you would like to share with our staff at the Real-Resumes Series, please contact us at preppub@aol.com or visit our website at www.prep-pub.com.

The resumes and cover letters in this book are designed to be of most value to people already in a job hunt or contemplating a career change. If we could give you one word of advice about your career, here's what we would say: Manage your career and don't stumble from job to job in an incoherent pattern. Try to find work that interests you, and then identify prosperous industries which need work performed of the type you want to do. Learn early in your working life that a great resume and cover letter can blow doors open for you and help you maximize your salary.

Introduction:
The Art of
Changing
Jobs...
and Finding
New Careers

As the editor of this book, I would like to give you some tips on how to make the best use of the information you will find here. Because you are considering a career change, you already understand the concept of managing your career for maximum enjoyment and self-fulfillment. The purpose of this book is to provide expert tools and advice so that you *can* manage your career. Inside these pages you will find resumes and cover letters that will help you find not just a job but the type of work you want to do.

Overview of the Book

Every resume and cover letter in this book actually worked. And most of the resumes and cover letters have common features: most are one-page, most are in the chronological format, and most resumes are accompanied by a companion cover letter. In this section you will find helpful advice about job hunting. Step One begins with a discussion of why employers prefer the one-page, chronological resume. In Step Two you are introduced to the direct approach and to the proper format for a cover letter. In Step Three you learn the 14 main reasons why job hunters are not offered the jobs they want, and you learn the six key areas employers focus on when they interview you. Step Four gives nuts-and-bolts advice on how to handle the interview, send a follow-up letter after an interview, and negotiate your salary.

The cover letter plays such a critical role in a career change. You will learn from the experts how to format your cover letters and you will see suggested language to use in particular career-change situations. It has been said that "A picture is worth a thousand words" and, for that reason, you will see numerous examples of effective cover letters used by real individuals to change fields, functions, and industries.

The most important part of the book is the Real-Resumes section. Some of the individuals whose resumes and cover letters you see spent a lengthy career in an industry they loved. Then there are resumes and cover letters of people who wanted a change but who probably wanted to remain in their industry. Many of you will be especially interested by the resumes and cover letters of individuals who knew they definitely wanted a career change but had no idea what they wanted to do next. Other resumes and cover letters show individuals who knew they wanted to change fields and had a pretty good idea of what they wanted to do next.

Whatever your field, and whatever your circumstances, you'll find resumes and cover letters that will "show you the ropes" in terms of successfully changing jobs and switching careers.

Before you proceed further, think about why you picked up this book.
- Are you dissatisfied with the type of work you are now doing?
- Would you like to change careers, change companies, or change industries?
- Are you satisfied with your industry but not with your niche or function within it?
- Do you want to transfer your skills to a new product or service?
- Even if you have excelled in your field, have you "had enough"? Would you like the stimulation of a new challenge?
- Are you aware of the importance of a great cover letter but unsure of how to write one?
- Are you preparing to launch a second career after retirement?
- Have you been downsized, or do you anticipate becoming a victim of downsizing?
- Do you need expert advice on how to plan and implement a job campaign that will open the maximum number of doors?
- Do you want to make sure you handle an interview to your maximum advantage?

- Would you like to master the techniques of negotiating salary and benefits?
- Do you want to learn the secrets and shortcuts of professional resume writers?

Using the Direct Approach

As you consider the possibility of a job hunt or career change, you need to be aware that most people end up having at least three distinctly different careers in their working lifetimes, and often those careers are different from each other. Yet people usually stumble through each job campaign, unsure of what they should be doing. Whether you find yourself voluntarily or unexpectedly in a job hunt, the direct approach is the job hunting strategy most likely to yield a full-time permanent job. The direct approach is an active, take-the-initiative style of job hunting in which you choose your next employer rather than relying on responding to ads, using employment agencies, or depending on other methods of finding jobs. You will learn how to use the direct approach in this book, and you will see that an effective cover letter is a critical ingredient in using the direct approach.

Lack of Industry Experience Not a Major Barrier to Entering New Field

"Lack of experience" is often the last reason people are not offered jobs, according to the companies who do the hiring. If you are changing careers, you will be glad to learn that experienced professionals often are selling "potential" rather than experience in a job hunt. Companies look for personal qualities that they know tend to be present in their most effective professionals, such as communication skills, initiative, persistence, organizational and time management skills, and creativity. Frequently companies are trying to discover "personality type," "talent," "ability," "aptitude," and "potential" rather than seeking actual hands-on experience, so your resume should be designed to aggressively present your accomplishments. Attitude, enthusiasm, personality, and a track record of achievements in any type of work are the primary "indicators of success" which employers are seeking, and you will see numerous examples in this book of resumes written in an all-purpose fashion so that the professional can approach various industries and companies.

The Art of Using References in a Job Hunt

You probably already know that you need to provide references during a job hunt, but you may not be sure of how and when to use references for maximum advantage. You can use references very creatively during a job hunt to call attention to your strengths and make yourself "stand out." Your references will rarely get you a job, no matter how impressive the names, but the way you use references can boost the employer's confidence in you and lead to a job offer in the least time.

You should ask from three to five people, including people who have supervised you, if you can use them as a reference during your job hunt. You may not be able to ask your current boss since your job hunt is probably confidential.

A common question in resume preparation is: "Do I need to put my references on my resume?" No, you don't. Even if you create a references page at the same time you prepare your resume, you don't need to mail, e-mail, or fax your references page with the resume and cover letter. Usually the potential employer is not interested in references until he meets you, so the earliest you need to have references ready is at the first interview. Obviously there are exceptions to this standard rule of thumb; sometimes an ad will ask you to send references with your first response. Wait until the employer requests references before providing them.

The "direct approach" is the style of job hunting most likely to yield the maximum number of job interviews.

Using references in a skillful fashion in your job hunt will inspire confidence in prospective employers and help you "close the sale" after interviews.

An excellent attention-getting technique is to take to the first interview not just a page of references (giving names, addresses, and telephone numbers) but an actual letter of reference written by someone who knows you well and who preferably has supervised or employed you. A professional way to close the first interview is to thank the interviewer, shake his or her hand, and then say you'd like to give him or her a copy of a letter of reference from a previous employer. Hopefully you already made a good impression during the interview, but you'll "close the sale" in a dynamic fashion if you leave a letter praising you and your accomplishments. For that reason, it's a good idea to ask supervisors during your final weeks in a job if they will provide you with a written letter of recommendation which you can use in future job hunts. Most employers will oblige, and you will have a letter that has a useful "shelf life" of many years. Such a letter often gives the prospective employer enough confidence in his opinion of you that he may forego checking out other references and decide to offer you the job on the spot or in the next few days.

With regard to references, it's best to provide the names and addresses of people who have supervised you or observed you in a work situation.

Whom should you ask to serve as references? References should be people who have known or supervised you in a professional, academic, or work situation. References with big titles, like school superintendent or congressman, are fine, but remind busy people when you get to the interview stage that they may be contacted soon. Make sure the busy official recognizes your name and has instant positive recall of you! If you're asked to provide references on a formal company application, you can simply transcribe names from your references list. In summary, follow this rule in using references: If you've got them, flaunt them! If you've obtained well-written letters of reference, make sure you find a polite way to push those references under the nose of the interviewer so he or she can hear someone other than you describing your strengths. Your references probably won't ever get you a job, but glowing letters of reference can give you credibility and visibility that can make you stand out among candidates with similar credentials and potential!

The approach taken by this book is to (1) help you master the proven best techniques of conducting a job hunt and (2) show you how to stand out in a job hunt through your resume, cover letter, interviewing skills, as well as the way in which you present your references and follow up on interviews. Now, the best way to "get in the mood" for writing your own resume and cover letter is to select samples from the Table of Contents that interest you and then read them. A great resume is a "photograph," usually on one page, of an individual. If you wish to seek professional advice in preparing your resume, you may contact one of the professional writers at Professional Resume & Employment Publishing (PREP) for a brief free consultation by calling 1-910-483-6611.

Part One: Some Advice About Your Job Hunt

What if you don't know what you want to do?

Your job hunt will be more comfortable if you can figure out what type of work you want to do. But you are not alone if you have no idea what you want to do next! You may have knowledge and skills in certain areas but want to get into another type of work. What *The Wall Street Journal* has discovered in its research on careers is that most of us end up having at least three distinctly different careers in our working lives; it seems that, even if we really like a particular kind of activity, twenty years of doing it is enough for most of us and we want to move on to something else!

That's why we strongly believe that you need to spend some time figuring out *what interests you* rather than taking an inventory of the skills you have. You may have skills that you simply don't want to use, but if you can build your career on the things that interest you, you will be more likely to be happy and satisfied in your job. Realize, too, that interests can change over time; the activities that interest you now may not be the ones that interested you years ago. For example, some professionals may decide that they've had enough of retail sales and want a job selling another product or service, even though they have earned a reputation for being an excellent retail manager. We strongly believe that interests rather than skills should be the determining factor in deciding what types of jobs you want to apply for and what directions you explore in your job hunt. Obviously one cannot be a lawyer without a law degree or a secretary without secretarial skills; but a professional can embark on a next career as a financial consultant, property manager, plant manager, production supervisor, retail manager, or other occupation if he/she has a strong interest in that type of work and can provide a resume that clearly demonstrates past excellent performance in *any* field and *potential* to excel in another field. As you will see later in this book, "lack of exact experience" is the last reason why people are turned down for the jobs they apply for.

How can you have a resume prepared if you don't know what you want to do?

You may be wondering how you can have a resume prepared if you don't know what you want to do next. The approach to resume writing which PREP, the country's oldest resume-preparation company, has used successfully for many years is to develop an "all-purpose" resume that translates your skills, experience, and accomplishments into language employers can understand. What most people need in a job hunt is a versatile resume that will allow them to apply for numerous types of jobs. For example, you may want to apply for a job in pharmaceutical sales but you may also want to have a resume that will be versatile enough for you to apply for jobs in the construction, financial services, or automotive industries.

Based on more than 20 years of serving job hunters, we at PREP have found that your best approach to job hunting is **an all-purpose resume** and **specific cover letters tailored to specific fields** rather than using the approach of trying to create different resumes for every job. If you are remaining in your field, you may not even need more than one "all-purpose" cover letter, although the cover letter rather than the resume is the place to communicate your interest in a narrow or specific field. An all-purpose resume and cover letter that translate your experience and accomplishments into plain English are the tools that will maximize the number of doors which open for you while permitting you to "fish" in the widest range of job areas.

Figure out what interests you and you will hold the key to a successful job hunt and working career. (And be prepared for your interests to change over time!)

"Lack of exact experience" is the last reason people are turned down for the jobs for which they apply.

Your resume will provide the script for your job interview.

When you get down to it, your resume has a simple job to do: Its purpose is to blow as many doors open as possible and to make as many people as possible want to meet you. So a well-written resume that really "sells" you is a key that will create opportunities for you in a job hunt.

This statistic explains why: The typical newspaper advertisement for a job opening receives more than 245 replies. And normally only 10 or 12 will be invited to an interview.

But here's another purpose of the resume: it provides the "script" the employer uses when he interviews you. If your resume has been written in such a way that your strengths and achievements are revealed, that's what you'll end up talking about at the job interview. Since the resume will govern what you get asked about at your interviews, you can't overestimate the importance of making sure your resume makes you look and sound as good as you are.

So what is a "good" resume?

Very literally, your resume should motivate the person reading it to dial the phone number or e-mail the screen name you have put on the resume. When you are relocating, you should put a local phone number on your resume if your physical address is several states away; employers are more likely to dial a local telephone number than a long-distance number when they're looking for potential employees.

If you have a resume already, look at it objectively. Is it a limp, colorless "laundry list" of your job titles and duties? Or does it "paint a picture" of your skills, abilities, and accomplishments in a way that would make someone want to meet you? Can people understand what you're saying? If you are attempting to change fields or industries, can potential employers see that your skills and knowledge are transferable to other environments? For example, have you described accomplishments which reveal your problem-solving abilities or communication skills?

How long should your resume be?

One page, maybe two. Usually only people in the academic community have a resume (which they usually call a *curriculum vitae*) longer than one or two pages. Remember that your resume is almost always accompanied by a cover letter, and a potential employer does not want to read more than two or three pages about a total stranger in order to decide if he wants to meet that person! Besides, don't forget that the more you tell someone about yourself, the more opportunity you are providing for the employer to screen you out at the "first-cut" stage. A resume should be concise and exciting and designed to make the reader want to meet you in person!

Should resumes be functional or chronological?

Employers almost always prefer a chronological resume; in other words, an employer will find a resume easier to read if it is immediately apparent what your current or most recent job is, what you did before that, and so forth, in reverse chronological order. A resume that goes back in detail for the last ten years of employment will generally satisfy the employer's curiosity about your background. Employment more than ten years old can be shown even more briefly in an "Other Experience" section at the end of your "Experience" section. Remember that your intention is not to tell everything you've done but to "hit the high points" and especially impress the employer with what you learned, contributed, or accomplished in each job you describe.

Your resume is the "script" for your job interviews. Make sure you put on your resume what you want to talk about or be asked about at the job interview.

The one-page resume in chronological format is the format preferred by most employers.

Once you get your resume, what do you do with it?

You will be using your resume to answer ads, as a tool to use in talking with friends and relatives about your job search, and, most importantly, in using the "direct approach" described in this book.

When you mail your resume, always send a "cover letter."

A "cover letter," sometimes called a "resume letter" or "letter of interest," is a letter that accompanies and introduces your resume. Your cover letter is a way of personalizing the resume by sending it to the specific person you think you might want to work for at each company. Your cover letter should contain a few highlights from your resume—just enough to make someone want to meet you. Cover letters should always be typed or word processed on a computer—never handwritten.

Never mail or fax your resume without a cover letter.

1. Learn the art of answering ads.

There is an "art," part of which can be learned, in using your "bestselling" resume to reply to advertisements.

Sometimes an exciting job lurks behind a boring ad that someone dictated in a hurry, so reply to any ad that interests you. Don't worry that you aren't "25 years old with an MBA" like the ad asks for. Employers will always make compromises in their requirements if they think you're the "best fit" overall.

What about ads that ask for "salary requirements?"

What if the ad you're answering asks for "salary requirements?" The first rule is to avoid committing yourself in writing at that point to a specific salary. You don't want to "lock yourself in."

There are two ways to handle the ad that asks for "salary requirements."

First, you can ignore that part of the ad and accompany your resume with a cover letter that focuses on "selling" you, your abilities, and even some of your philosophy about work or your field. You may include a sentence in your cover letter like this: "I can provide excellent personal and professional references at your request, and I would be delighted to share the private details of my salary history with you in person."

What if the ad asks for your "salary requirements?"

Second, if you feel you must give some kind of number, just state a range in your cover letter that includes your medical, dental, other benefits, and expected bonuses. You might state, for example, "My current compensation, including benefits and bonuses, is in the range of $30,000-$40,000."

Analyze the ad and "tailor" yourself to it.

When you're replying to ads, a finely tailored cover letter is an important tool in getting your resume noticed and read. On the next page is a cover letter which has been "tailored to fit" a specific ad. Notice the "art" used by PREP writers of analyzing the ad's main requirements and then writing the letter so that the person's background, work habits, and interests seem "tailor-made" to the company's needs. Use this cover letter as a model when you prepare your own reply to ads.

Date

Exact Name of Person
Title or Position
Exact Name of Company
Address (no., street)
City, State, Zip

Dear Exact Name of Person (or Dear Sir or Madam if answering a blind ad):

I look forward to having the opportunity to talk with you soon about how I could contribute to the City of Colorado Springs as an experienced firefighter who offers outstanding technical, motivational, and communication skills.

Employers are trying to identify the individual who wants the job they are filling. Don't be afraid to express your enthusiasm in the cover letter!

As you will see from my resume, I have gained extensive expertise in firefighting techniques while answering over 250 calls yearly with one of the nation's busiest volunteer fire departments. Known for my ability to lead in stressful conditions, I was unanimously elected to be a part of this team serving 40,000 people. With a Colorado I and II Level firefighting certification, I offer expert skills related to equipment utilization and maintenance, rescue and firefighting techniques, and fire safety. Soon I will be completing my Level III certification and I am pursuing a National Firefighter certification.

A proven leader, I earned rapid promotion to "middle management" while supervising a team of ten mechanics in the U.S. Army. While expertly diagnosing and repairing automobiles and trucks, I was chosen for supervisory roles ahead of my peers and earned numerous commendations for my technical and leadership skills.

You would find me to be a dedicated and energetic professional with the ability to lead in life-or-death situations. Known for giving unselfishly of my time, I volunteer my time working for the Special Olympics.

I would appreciate your giving me the opportunity for us to meet to discuss your current and future needs and how I might serve them. I can provide outstanding references at the appropriate time. Thank you in advance for your time.

Sincerely yours,

Michael Hess

2. Talk to friends and relatives.

Don't be shy about telling your friends and relatives the kind of job you're looking for. Looking for the job you want involves using your network of contacts, so tell people what you're looking for. They may be able to make introductions and help set up interviews.

About 25% of all interviews are set up through "who you know," so don't ignore this approach.

3. Finally, and most importantly, use the "direct approach."

The "direct approach" is a strategy in which you choose your next employer.

More than 50% of all job interviews are set up by the "direct approach." That means you actually mail, e-mail, or fax a resume and a cover letter to a company you think might be interesting to work for.

To whom do you write?

In general, you should write directly to the *exact name* of the person who would be hiring you: say, the vice-president of marketing or data processing. If you're in doubt about to whom to address the letter, address it to the president by name and he or she will make sure it gets forwarded to the right person within the company who has hiring authority in your area.

How do you find the names of potential employers?

You're not alone if you feel that the biggest problem in your job search is finding the right names at the companies you want to contact. But you can usually figure out the names of companies you want to approach by deciding first if your job hunt is primarily geography-driven or industry-driven.

In a **geography-driven job hunt,** you could select a list of, say, 50 companies you want to contact **by location** from the lists that the U.S. Chambers of Commerce publish yearly of their "major area employers." There are hundreds of local Chambers of Commerce across America, and most of them will have an 800 number which you can find through 1-800-555-1212. If you and your family think Atlanta, Dallas, Ft. Lauderdale, and Virginia Beach might be nice places to live, for example, you could contact the Chamber of Commerce in those cities and ask how you can obtain a copy of their list of major employers. Your nearest library will have the book which lists the addresses of all chambers.

In an **industry-driven job hunt,** and if you are willing to relocate, you will be identifying the companies which you find most attractive in the industry in which you want to work. When you select a list of companies to contact **by industry,** you can find the right person to write and the address of firms by industrial category in *Standard and Poor's, Moody's,* and other excellent books in public libraries. Many Web sites also provide contact information.

Many people feel it's a good investment to actually call the company to either find out or double-check the name of the person to whom they want to send a resume and cover letter. It's important to do as much as you feasibly can to assure that the letter gets to the right person in the company.

On-line research will be the best way for many people to locate organizations to which they wish to send their resume. It is outside the scope of this book to teach Internet research skills, but librarians are often useful in this area.

What's the correct way to follow up on a resume you send?

There is a polite way to be aggressively interested in a company during your job hunt. It is ideal to end the cover letter accompanying your resume by saying, "I hope you'll welcome my call next week when I try to arrange a brief meeting at your convenience to discuss your current and future needs and how I might serve them." Keep it low key, and just ask for a "brief meeting," not an interview. Employers want people who show a determined interest in working with them, so don't be shy about following up on the resume and cover letter you've mailed.

STEP THREE: Preparing for Interviews

It pays to be aware of the 14 most common pitfalls for job hunters.

But a resume and cover letter by themselves can't get you the job you want. You need to "prep" yourself before the interview. Step Three in your job campaign is "Preparing for Interviews." First, let's look at interviewing from the hiring organization's point of view.

What are the biggest "turnoffs" for potential employers?

One of the ways to help yourself perform well at an interview is to look at the main reasons why organizations *don't* hire the people they interview, according to those who do the interviewing.

Notice that "lack of appropriate background" (or lack of experience) is the *last* reason for not being offered the job.

The 14 Most Common Reasons Job Hunters Are Not Offered Jobs (according to the companies who do the interviewing and hiring):

1. Low level of accomplishment
2. Poor attitude, lack of self-confidence
3. Lack of goals/objectives
4. Lack of enthusiasm
5. Lack of interest in the company's business
6. Inability to sell or express yourself
7. Unrealistic salary demands
8. Poor appearance
9. Lack of maturity, no leadership potential
10. Lack of extracurricular activities
11. Lack of preparation for the interview, no knowledge about company
12. Objecting to travel
13. Excessive interest in security and benefits
14. Inappropriate background

Department of Labor studies have proven that smart, "prepared" job hunters can increase their beginning salary while getting a job in *half* the time it normally takes. (4½ months is the average national length of a job search.) Here, from PREP, are some questions that can prepare you to find a job faster.

Are you in the "right" frame of mind?

It seems unfair that we have to look for a job just when we're lowest in morale. Don't worry *too* much if you're nervous before interviews. You're supposed to be a little nervous, especially if the job means a lot to you. But the best way to kill unnecessary fears about job hunting is through 1) making sure you have a great resume and 2) preparing yourself for the interview. Here are three main areas you need to think about before each interview.

Do you know what the company does?
Don't walk into an interview giving the impression that, "If this is Tuesday, this must be General Motors."

Research the company before you go to interviews.

Find out before the interview what the company's main product or service is. Where is the company heading? Is it in a "growth" or declining industry? (Answers to these questions may influence whether or not you want to work there!)

Information about what the company does is in annual reports, in newspaper and magazine articles, and on the Internet. If you're not yet skilled at Internet research, just visit your nearest library and ask the reference librarian to guide you to printed materials on the company.

Do you know what you want to do for the company?
Before the interview, try to decide how you see yourself fitting into the company. Remember, "lack of exact background" the company wants is usually the last reason people are not offered jobs.

Understand before you go to each interview that the burden will be on you to "sell" the interviewer on why you're the best person for the job and the company.

How will you answer the critical interview questions?
Anticipate the questions you will be asked at the interview, and prepare your responses in advance.

Put yourself in the interviewer's position and think about the questions you're most likely to be asked. Here are some of the most commonly asked interview questions:

Q: "What are your greatest strengths?"
A: Don't say you've never thought about it! Go into an interview knowing the three main impressions you want to leave about yourself, such as "I'm hard-working, loyal, and an imaginative cost-cutter."

Q: "What are your greatest weaknesses?"
A: Don't confess that you're lazy or have trouble meeting deadlines! Confessing that you tend to be a "workaholic" or "tend to be a perfectionist and sometimes get frustrated when others don't share my high standards" will make your prospective employer see a "weakness" that he likes. Name a weakness that your interviewer will perceive as a strength.

Q: "What are your long-range goals?"
A: If you're interviewing with Microsoft, don't say you want to work for IBM in five years! Say your long-range goal is to be *with* the company, contributing to its goals and success.

Q: "What motivates you to do your best work?"
A: Don't get dollar signs in your eyes here! "A challenge" is not a bad answer, but it's a little cliched. Saying something like "troubleshooting" or "solving a tough problem" is more interesting and specific. Give an example if you can.

Q: "What do you know about this organization?"

A: Don't say you never heard of it until they asked you to the interview! Name an interesting, positive thing you learned about the company recently from your research. Remember, company executives can sometimes feel rather "maternal" about the company they serve. Don't get onto a negative area of the company if you can think of positive facts you can bring up. Of course, if you learned in your research that the company's sales seem to be taking a nose-dive, or that the company president is being prosecuted for taking bribes, you might politely ask your interviewer to tell you something that could help you better understand what you've been reading. Those are the kinds of company facts that can help you determine whether or not you want to work there.

Q: "Why should I hire you?"

A: "I'm unemployed and available" is the wrong answer here! Get back to your strengths and say that you believe the organization could benefit by a loyal, hard-working cost-cutter like yourself.

In conclusion, you should decide in advance, before you go to the interview, how you will answer each of these commonly asked questions. Have some practice interviews with a friend to role-play and build your confidence.

Go to an interview prepared to tell the company why it should hire you.

STEP FOUR: Handling the Interview and Negotiating Salary

Now you're ready for Step Four: actually handling the interview successfully and effectively. Remember, the purpose of an interview is to get a job offer.

Eight "do's" for the interview

According to leading U.S. companies, there are eight key areas in interviewing success. You can fail at an interview if you mishandle just one area.

A smile at an interview makes the employer perceive of you as intelligent!

1. **Do wear appropriate clothes.**
    You can never go wrong by wearing a suit to an interview.

2. **Do be well groomed.**
    Don't overlook the obvious things like having clean hair, clothes, and fingernails for the interview.

3. **Do give a firm handshake.**
    You'll have to shake hands twice in most interviews: first, before you sit down, and second, when you leave the interview. Limp handshakes turn most people off.

4. **Do smile and show a sense of humor.**
    Interviewers are looking for people who would be nice to work with, so don't be so somber that you don't smile. In fact, research shows that people who smile at interviews are perceived as more intelligent. So, smile!

5. **Do be enthusiastic.**
    Employers say they are "turned off" by lifeless, unenthusiastic job hunters who show no special interest in that company. The best way to show some enthusiasm for the employer's operation is to find out about the business beforehand.

6. Do show you are flexible and adaptable.

An employer is looking for someone who can contribute to his organization in a flexible, adaptable way. No matter what skills and training you have, employers know every new employee must go through initiation and training on the company's turf. Certainly show pride in your past accomplishments in a specific, factual way ("I saved my last employer $50.00 a week by a new cost-cutting measure I developed"). But don't come across as though there's nothing about the job you couldn't easily handle.

7. Do ask intelligent questions about the employer's business.

An employer is hiring someone because of certain business needs. Show interest in those needs. Asking questions to get a better idea of the employer's needs will help you "stand out" from other candidates interviewing for the job.

8. Do "take charge" when the interviewer "falls down" on the job.

Go into every interview knowing the three or four points about yourself you want the interviewer to remember. And be prepared to take an active part in leading the discussion if the interviewer's "canned approach" does not permit you to display your "strong suit." You can't always depend on the interviewer's asking you the "right" questions so you can stress your strengths and accomplishments.

Employers are seeking people with good attitudes whom they can train and coach to do things their way.

An important "don't": Don't ask questions about salary or benefits at the first interview.
Employers don't take warmly to people who look at their organization as just a place to satisfy salary and benefit needs. Don't risk making a negative impression by appearing greedy or self-serving. The place to discuss salary and benefits is normally at the second interview, and the employer will bring it up. Then you can ask questions without appearing excessively interested in what the organization can do for you.

Now...negotiating your salary
Even if an ad requests that you communicate your "salary requirement" or "salary history," you should avoid providing those numbers in your initial cover letter. You can usually say something like this: "I would be delighted to discuss the private details of my salary history with you in person."

Once you're at the interview, you must avoid even appearing *interested* in salary before you are offered the job. Make sure you've "sold" yourself before talking salary. First show you're the "best fit" for the employer and then you'll be in a stronger position from which to negotiate salary. **Never** bring up the subject of salary yourself. Employers say there's no way you can avoid looking greedy if you bring up the issue of salary and benefits before the company has identified you as its "best fit."

Don't appear excessively interested in salary and benefits at the interview.

Interviewers sometimes throw out a salary figure at the first interview to see if you'll accept it. You may not want to commit yourself if you think you will be able to negotiate a better deal later on. Get back to finding out more about the job. This lets the interviewer know you're interested primarily in the job and not the salary.

When the organization brings up salary, it may say something like this: "Well, Mary, we think you'd make a good candidate for this job. What kind of salary are we talking about?" You may not want to name a number here, either. Give the ball back to the interviewer. Act as though you hadn't given the subject of salary much thought and respond something like this: "Ah, Mr. Jones, I wonder if you'd be kind enough to tell me what salary you had in mind when you advertised the job?" Or ... "What is the range you have in mind?"

Don't worry, if the interviewer names a figure that you think is too low, you can say so without turning down the job or locking yourself into a rigid position. The point here is to negotiate for yourself as well as you can. You might reply to a number named by the interviewer that you think is low by saying something like this: "Well, Mr. Lee, the job interests me very much, and I think I'd certainly enjoy working with you. But, frankly, I was thinking of something a little higher than that." That leaves the ball in your interviewer's court again, and you haven't turned down the job either, in case it turns out that the interviewer can't increase the offer and you still want the job.

Salary negotiation can be tricky.

Last, send a follow-up letter.

Mail, e-mail, or fax a letter right after the interview telling your interviewer you enjoyed the meeting and are certain (if you are) that you are the "best fit" for the job. The people interviewing you will probably have an attitude described as either "professionally loyal" to their companies, or "maternal and proprietary" if the interviewer also owns the company. In either case, they are looking for people who want to work for *that* company in particular. The follow-up letter you send might be just the deciding factor in your favor if the employer is trying to choose between you and someone else. You will see an example of a follow-up letter on page 16.

A follow-up letter can help the employer choose between you and another qualified candidate.

A cover letter is an essential part of a job hunt or career change.

Many people are aware of the importance of having a great resume, but most people in a job hunt don't realize just how important a cover letter can be. The purpose of the cover letter, sometimes called a **"letter of interest,"** is to introduce your resume to prospective employers. The cover letter is often the critical ingredient in a job hunt because the cover letter allows you to say a lot of things that just don't "fit" on the resume. For example, you can emphasize your commitment to a new field and stress your related talents. The cover letter also gives you a chance to stress outstanding character and personal values. On the next two pages you will see examples of very effective cover letters.

A cover letter is an essential part of a career change.

Please do not attempt to implement a career change without a cover letter. A cover letter is the first impression of you, and you can influence the way an employer views you by the language and style of your letter.

Special help for those in career change

We want to emphasize again that, especially in a career change, the cover letter is very important and can help you "build a bridge" to a new career. A creative and appealing cover letter can begin the process of encouraging the potential employer to imagine you in an industry other than the one in which you have worked.

As a special help to those in career change, there are resumes and cover letters included in this book which show valuable techniques and tips you should use when changing fields or industries. The resumes and cover letters of career changers are identified in the table of contents as "Career Change" and you will see the "Career Change" label on cover letters in Part Two where the individuals are changing careers.

Date

**Addressing the Cover
Letter:** Get the exact
name of the person to
whom you are writing. This
makes your approach
personal.

Exact Name of Person
Title or Position
Name of Company
Address
City, state, zip

Dear Exact Name of Person (or Sir or Madam if answering a blind ad):

I would appreciate an opportunity to talk with you soon about how I could contribute to your organization through my background in firefighting, emergency response, and hazardous material response and education.

Second Paragraph: You
have a chance to talk
about whatever you feel is
your most distinguishing
feature.

As you will see from my resume, I have completed training leading to certification by the State of South Carolina in the following career specialties: Emergency Medical Technician-B, Fire Driver/Operator, Confined Space Rescue Instructor, Fire Fighter III, Instructor — Level II, and Hazardous Materials Specialist — Level III. I also attended courses at the National Fire Academy in Emmittsburg, MD, in HazMat Site Operating Practices, Chemistry of Hazardous Materials, and Incident Command as well as Radiological Response.

Third Paragraph: You
bring up your next most
distinguishing qualities and
try to
sell yourself.

Through my simultaneous jobs as a Fire Fighter with the City of Macon and as a volunteer with the Mercer Fire Department in Mercer, GA, I have become adept at handling multiple simultaneous tasks and projects, coordinating activities between various agencies, and dealing extensively with the public. Respected as an instructor, I am frequently requested by name to teach members of civic organizations, firefighting professionals, and local businesses in HazMat, firefighting, and emergency response.

Fourth Paragraph: Here
you have another
opportunity to reveal
qualities or achievements
which will impress your
future employer.

Throughout my career I have become familiar with other aspects of administration and operations including writing policy statements, developing standard operating procedures, and using automated systems to maintain records and information and to perform budgeting and purchasing.

Final Paragraph: He asks
the employer to contact
him. Make sure your
reader knows what the
"next step" is.

If you are in need of an energetic, enthusiastic quick learner with excellent problem-solving skills, I hope you will welcome my call soon to arrange a brief meeting to discuss your current and future needs and how I might serve them. Thank you in advance for your time.

Sincerely,

**Alternate Final
Paragraph:** It's more
aggressive (but not too
aggressive) to let the
employer know that you
will be calling him or her.
Don't be afraid to be
persistent. Employers are
looking for people who
know what they want to
do.

Leland Ray Camembert

Alternate last paragraph:
I hope you will call or write me soon to suggest a time convenient for us to meet and discuss your current and future needs and how I might serve them. Thank you in advance for your time.

Date

Exact Name of Person
Exact Title
Exact Name of Company
Address
City, State, Zip

Dear Exact Name of Person (or Dear Sir or Madam if answering a blind ad):

With the enclosed resume, I would like to make you aware of my interest in exploring employment opportunities with your organization. My wife and I are in the process of permanently relocating back to the Midwest, where we grew up and where our extended families still live.

As you will see from my resume, I recently completed six years of distinguished service to my country while serving in the U.S. Army. While excelling in full-time jobs in the supply management field, I pursued training through a respected community college in order to obtain my firefighting certification. In addition to receiving my Firefighter Certification in Georgia, I worked as a Volunteer Firefighter for the Red Springs Emergency Service. I am interested in pursuing professional employment opportunities which can utilize my background related to firefighting and law enforcement.

As a military professional, I gained extensive knowledge related to law enforcement. After completing professional driver's training sponsored by the U.S. Army, I received my Driver Badge. Entrusted with a Secret security clearance, I was specially selected to attend Primary Leadership Development Course, the Army's course designed to refine the management skills and leadership ability of middle managers. My law enforcement training also included Airborne School, Unit Armorer School, Alcohol and Drug Abuse Prevention training, as well as extensive training in supply management. I was promoted ahead of my peers to supervisory positions and became known for my strong personal initiative and problem-solving skills. In my most recent position, I trained and managed six individuals while controlling $2 million in equipment and supplies.

I hope you will contact me to suggest a time when we could meet in person to discuss your needs. I can provide excellent personal and professional references. Thank you.

Yours sincerely,

Andy Frank

This individual is in career transition, and his job hunt is geographically oriented. He knows where he and his family want to live, and this letter is designed so that he can send his resume and cover letter to a broad range of employers in the area. He can use this cover letter, sometimes called a letter of introduction or letter of interest, to approach employers in the law enforcement community or the firefighting field.

Date

Exact Name of Person
Title or Position
Name of Company
Address (number and street)
Address (city, state, and zip)

Follow-up Letter

A great follow-up letter
can motivate the
employer
to make the job offer,
and the salary offer may
be influenced by the
style and tone of your
follow-up
letter, too!

Dear Exact Name:

I am writing to express my appreciation for the time you spent with me on December 9, and I want to let you know that I am sincerely interested in the position of Director of Firefighting Services which we discussed. I am confident that I could contribute to your organization through my 30 years of experience in fire services.

As you know, I possess national certification in the following areas: Fire Officer I, Training Officer I, Inspector I, and Firefighter III. During my years of service I have developed a working knowledge of all federal and military regulations pertaining to the fire protection career field as well as the 40 series which pertains to civilians.

Currently the Lead Firefighter and Station Chief with the 23rd Civil Engineers in Los Angeles, I also am the Training Chief for my reserve unit, the 915th CES. I am licensed as an Electrical Contractor and apply this knowledge as part of the Los Angeles Arson Squad.

Although I was aggressively recruited to remain in military service, I decided to leave the military and establish my firefighting career in the civilian world. I am confident that I could quickly learn your organization's style and procedures, and I would welcome being trained to do things your way.

Yours sincerely,

Jacob Evangelisto

In this section, you will find resumes and cover letters of firefighting or related professionals— and of people who want to work in the firefighting or related field. How do firefighters and related firefighting professionals differ from other job hunters? Why should there be a book dedicated to people seeking jobs in the firefighting field? Based on more than 20 years of experience in working with job hunters, this editor is convinced that resumes and cover letters which "speak the lingo" of the field you wish to enter will communicate more effectively than language which is not industry-specific. This book is designed to help people (1) who are seeking to prepare their own resumes and (2) who wish to use as models "real" resumes of individuals who have successfully launched careers in the firefighting or related industry or advanced in the field. You will see a wide range of experience levels reflected in the resumes in this book. Some of the resumes and cover letters were used by individuals seeking to enter the field; others were used successfully by senior professionals to advance in the field.

Newcomers to an industry sometimes have advantages over more experienced professionals. In a job hunt, junior professionals can have an advantage over their more experienced counterparts. Prospective employers often view the less experienced workers as "more trainable" and "more coachable" than their seniors. This means that the mature professional who has already excelled in a first career can, with credibility, "change careers" and transfer skills to other industries.

Newcomers to the field may have disadvantages compared to their seniors. Almost by definition, the inexperienced firefighting professional—the young person who has recently entered the job market, or the individual who has recently received certifications respected by the industry—is less tested and less experienced than senior managers, so the resume and cover letter of the inexperienced professional may often have to "sell" his or her potential to do something he or she has never done before. Lack of experience in the field she wants to enter can be a stumbling block to the junior manager, but remember that many employers believe that someone who has excelled in anything—academics, for example—can excel in many other fields.

Some advice to inexperienced professionals...
If senior professionals could give junior professionals a piece of advice about careers, here's what they would say: Manage your career and don't stumble from job to job in an incoherent pattern. Try to find work that interests you, and then identify prosperous industries which need work performed of the type you want to do. Learn early in your working life that a great resume and cover letter can blow doors open for you and help you maximize your salary.

Special help for career changers...
For those changing careers—either out of firefighting or into firefighting—you will find useful the resumes and cover letters marked "Career Change" on the following pages. Consult the Table of Contents for page numbers showing career changers.

CAREER CHANGE

Date

Exact Name of Person
Title or Position
Exact Name of Company
Address (no., street)
City, state, zip

AEROSPACE PROPULSION SPECIALIST & FIREFIGHTER

This military professional with firefighting credentials is leaving the Air Force and hopes to become associated with a firefighting organization in California or obtain a federal job with the Park Rangers.

Dear Exact Name of Person (or Dear Sir or Madam if answering a blind ad.):

With the enclosed resume, I would like to make you aware of my interest in exploring employment opportunities with your organization.

As you will see from my resume, I served my country in the U.S. Air Force and excelled in the aerospace field while gaining a variety of skills and certifications. While acquiring expertise in performing maintenance and inspections on jet engines and related systems, I was trained as a professional firefighter. On numerous occasions, I utilized my firefighting skills while responding to flightline emergencies. I discovered that I possess an ability to remain calm during emergencies, and I also realized that I wished to join the firefighting profession after military service.

Although the Air Force strongly encouraged me to remain in military service, I decided to leave the military and establish my career as a civilian firefighter. I grew up in California, and I have watched for years as California firefighters have battled the forest fires that frequently rage through the state, and I want to become a part of the "fighting force" that protects the public against such disasters.

In addition to my technical knowledge and certifications, I offer outstanding leadership experience gained through military service. As a Crew Chief, I routinely managed up to 12 individuals as we all worked in environments in which there was "no room for error." I take pride that I have trained numerous individuals who earned honors including "employee of the quarter" and "employee of the year."

I hope you will call or write me to suggest a time convenient for us to meet and discuss your current and future needs and how I might serve them. Thank you in advance for your time.

Sincerely yours,

Geoffrey Curtis

GEOFFREY CURTIS

1110½ Hay Street, Fayetteville, NC 28305   •   preppub@aol.com   •   (910) 483-6611

OBJECTIVE   To benefit an organization that can use an experienced aircraft mechanic who offers specialized skills in jet engine maintenance/repair as well as training and experience in firefighting.

CERTIFICATIONS Jet Engine Specialist
Emergency Medical Technician
Certified Firefighter; completed Fire Department Orientation/Safety I & II, Dover Community College.

CERTIFICATION Completed Personal Protective Equipment Course, Dover Community College and Delaware Fire/Rescue College, 2002. Courses taken include:

Portable Extinguishers	Fire Hose, Appl. And Streams	Ladders I & II
Emergency Medical Care	Salvage — Level I & II	Fire Prevention
Sprinklers	Rescue — Level I & II	Fire Alarms
Fire Control	Hazardous Materials	Structural Burn
Ropes	Building Construction I & II	Fire Behavior
Safety	Forcible Entry I & II	Water Supplies
Wildland Fire Suppression	Incident Command Systems	

EXPERIENCE   **AEROSPACE PROPULSION SPECIALIST & FIREFIGHTING SPECIALIST**. U.S. Air Force, Dover AFB, DE (2000-present). Earned a reputation as a talented technician while performing flightline maintenance and inspections on jet engines and related systems; diagnose, troubleshoot, and repair malfunctions.
- Because of my technical skills, was selected for numerous worldwide training projects; maintained hundreds of aircraft operating in extreme weather conditions.
- During the field testing of new aircraft, directed the firefighting crew that responded to fire emergencies and disasters.
- Achieved a 100% reliability rate for all aircraft; receive excellent scores on inspections.
- Played a key role in receiving an "Outstanding Unit Award" for my team; troubleshoot problems and maintain tight flying schedules.
- Earned three distinguished awards for technical skills.
- Was recognized as the top Jaguar specialist in Dover AFB, 2001.

EQUIPMENT EXPERTISE   Am skilled in maintaining TF-34 engines and related systems on A-10A aircraft.
- Qualified crew chief, perform all inspections on aircraft and engines.
- Level 5 approved pneudraulics mechanic.
- Knowledgeable of the maintenance and repair of sophisticated weapon systems and equipment including Maverick, missile pods, and ECM pods.
- Operate a wide range of testing and repair equipment.

TRAINING   Excelled in 375 hours of college-level training related to jet engine maintenance and inspections; received diplomas from these courses conducted by Andrews AFB, MD:
Jet Engine Mechanic (A-10A), TF-34, Turbo Fan, August 2002
TF-34 Engine Flight Line Maintenance, 2002
Qualified as a Crew Chief, 2002
A-10A Turbine Engine Monitor System (TEMS), Jet Engine I/0 Maintenance, 2001
TF-34 Engine General Maintenance, 2001

PERSONAL   Highly motivated worker who excels in meeting any challenge! Held Secret security clearance.

Date

Exact Name of Person
Position or Title
Exact Name of Company
Address (no., street)
City, state, zip

**AIR CARGO
SUPERVISOR
&
AIRPORT
FIREFIGHTER**

This individual offers
specialized
credentials and
experience related
to airport
firefighting.

Dear Exact Name of Person (or Dear Sir or Madam if answering a blind ad.):

I would appreciate an opportunity to talk with you soon about how I could contribute to your organization through my expertise related to airport firefighting operations, air freight management, and hazardous cargo handling.

Expertise in air cargo handling and hazardous materials handling

As you will see from my resume, I have established an excellent work record because I thrive on hard work and try to excel in everything I do. I was a Distinguished Graduate of the Load Planning/Aircraft Loading Course and scored **100%** on the final exam. As an Air Cargo Supervisor, I have been promoted to supervise the processing of passengers and cargo from air terminals. With an outstanding safety record, I am licensed to operate most vehicles and equipment related to the air freight business. I have **never** had an accident with any vehicle and have driven in conditions ranging from the Arctic to the African deserts.

Qualifications and experience related to firefighting

As security concerns at airports have intensified, I have become increasingly involved in fighting airport fires and directing a team of "first response" professionals who are highly trained firefighters. I have been entrusted with one of the nation's highest security clearances. I am a Certified Airport Firefighter.

I hope you will welcome my call soon to arrange a brief meeting at your convenience to discuss your current and future needs and how I might serve them. Thank you in advance for your time.

Sincerely yours,

George Riorden

Alternate last paragraph:
I hope you will call or write me to suggest a time convenient for us to meet and discuss your current and future needs and how I might serve them. Thank you in advance for your time.

GEORGE RIORDEN

1110½ Hay Street, Fayetteville, NC 28305 • preppub@aol.com • (910) 483-6611

OBJECTIVE To contribute to an organization that can use an enthusiastic hard worker with expertise related to cargo handling and air freight, along with expert skills as an airport firefighter.

VEHICLE & EQUIPMENT EXPERTISE Have excellent driving record and am licensed to operate vehicles/equipment including:

1/4-ton truck	10,000-lb. forklift	4,000-lb. tug
1 1/2-ton truck	25,000-lb. forklift	1/4-ton jeep
4,000-lb. loader	C-5 mobile staircase	Baggage conveyor
Latrine service truck	Wide-body mobile staircase	

CERTIFICATIONS Certified Airport Firefighter, International Fire Service Accreditation Congress, University of Alaska Fairbanks (2002).

Certified Firefighter II, International Fire Service Accreditation Congress, University of Alaska Fairbanks (2002).

Supervisor On-The-Job Training Course, 12 hours, Training Certificate awarded by the United States Air Force (1999).

National Fire Academy (Certificate of Training) "Pesticide Challenge," 16 hours (1998).

National Fire Academy (Certificate of Training) "Recognition and Identification of Hazardous Materials," 6 hours (1998).

National Fire Academy (Certificate of Training) "Hazardous Materials Incident Analysis," 6 hours (1998).

Munitions/Hazardous Materials Firefighting, 56 hours, Training Certificate awarded by the United States Air Force (1997).

Fire Protection Specialist Course, 262 hours, Received Certificate of Training from the United States Air Force (1996).

EXPERIENCE **AIR CARGO SUPERVISOR & AIRPORT FIREFIGHTER.** U.S. Air Force, Elmendorf AFB, AK (2001-04). Have been promoted to supervise six specialists involved in processing passengers and cargo from mobile air terminals. Inspect cargo for proper packing, markings, and documentation. Process hazardous materials supporting NATO and Joint Chiefs of Staff training projects.
- Was selected as **Firefighter Instructor** to train other airmen.
- As a **Team Chief** during a special project, played a key role in moving 2,000 tons of cargo and 1,500 passengers on 173 aircraft with no delay.
- As an Airport Firefighter, responded to numerous airport emergencies.
- Was praised in writing as an "intelligent manager who is quick to grasp details."

AIRCRAFT RAMP SERVICES SPECIALIST and **FIRE PROTECTION SPECIALIST.** U.S. Air Force, Brooks AFB, TX (1996-01). While driving aircraft loading vehicles and operating the Cochran Loader for loading civilian aircraft, did not have an accident in over two years. Played a significant part in handling 5,000 tons of cargo and 1,500 aircraft monthly.

EDUCATION & TRAINING Excelled in extensive training related to these and other areas:

Air cargo	Airdrop techniques	Customs
Traffic safety	Aerial delivery rigging	HAZMAT Airlift

- **Distinguished Graduate of the Load Planning/Aircraft Loading Course**; scored 100% on the final exam. Certified **Material Handling Equipment (MHE) Operator**.
- Have been hazardous cargo trained for four years; am qualified until 2005.

PERSONAL Get along well with supervisors and co-workers. Work well under stress.

Date

Exact Name of Person
Title of Person
Exact Name of Company
Address
City, State zip

Dear Exact Name (or Dear Sir or Madam if answering a blind ad):

I would appreciate an opportunity to talk with you soon about how I could contribute to your organization through my background related to safety management. I am responding to your advertisement for an Airport Operations Manager with extensive experience in managing firefighting activities.

As you will see from my resume, I have developed successful safety and accident prevention programs which have been hailed as "models" and which produced perfect safety records. I have also taken over the management of busy, accident-prone operations in harsh environments and transformed them into top-notch activities. For the past eight years, I have managed teams of firefighters in responding to aviation accidents and airport emergencies.

In one job I established safety programs for a school/training center while managing those safety programs in an experimental and testing environment which included special electronic aircraft. I have played a key role as a member of accident investigation boards, and I have excelled in training and developing other safety professionals.

You would certainly find me to be a congenial professional with very strong abilities related to finance and budgeting as well as personnel supervision. I have held a Top Secret security clearance with SBI, and I am skilled in using Word and PowerPoint software.

I hope you will write or call me soon to suggest a time when we might meet to discuss your current and future needs and how I might meet them. Thank you in advance for your time.

Yours sincerely,

Andrea S. Rooney

Alternate last paragraph:
I hope you will welcome my call soon when I try to arrange a brief meeting with you to discuss your current and future needs and how I might serve them. Thank you in advance for your time.

ANDREA S. ROONEY

1110½ Hay Street, Fayetteville, NC 28305   •   preppub@aol.com   •   (910) 483-6611

OBJECTIVE

To contribute to an organization that can use a versatile manager who offers extensive experience in the occupational safety field along with exceptionally strong skills related to budgeting, personnel supervision, as well as safety management and inspection.

EDUCATION & TECHNICAL TRAINING

Completing **Master of Aeronautical Science (M.A.S.) degree**, Embry Riddle Aeronautical University; degree to be awarded in 2004.

Earned **Bachelor of Science (B.S.) degree in Professional Aeronautics**, Embry Riddle Aeronautical University, Daytona Beach, 1993.

As a Chief Warrant Officer, completed extensive technical training related to accident investigation, safety management, OSHA, as well as occupational and aeronautical safety.

EXPERIENCE

AIRPORT OPERATIONS MANAGER. New Haven Airport, New Haven, CT (2002-present). Developed and implemented a safety and accident prevention program that is hailed as a "model"; supervised a staff of 27 personnel working in an air traffic control (ATC) facility.
- Maintained a perfect safety record of "no accidents/no incidents." Directed a team of firefighting professionals in responding to three major catastrophes.

AIRPORT OPERATIONS MANAGER. Raytheon, Inc., Nome, AK (2000-01). In the harsh arctic environment of Alaska, was assigned management of an airfield which had suffered safety mishaps; completely revised operational procedures for the ATC facility and flight dispatch operations; led this busy, accident-prone airfield to achieve a perfect safety record.

SAFETY MANAGER. Boeing Aircraft, Los Angeles, CA (1998-99). Formulated safety policies and procedures for this major aviation organization and participated in two major aircraft accident investigations while excelling as safety manager.
- Was commended on my excellent training and development of other safety personnel.

FIRST-LINE SUPERVISOR. Allen Aircraft, Fairfield, CT (1996-97). In an essentially entrepreneurial role, directed the "start up" of a new aviation organization; routinely briefed visiting executives and VIP's on the organization's strategies and tactics.
- Controlled $36 million in aircraft/assets; motivated people toward a common goal.

SAFETY OFFICER. Flight Training Center & School, San Diego, CA (1992-95). Established safety programs for a school/training center which had 15 special electronic aircraft; learned to manage safety in an experimental and testing environment.
- Conducted safety surveys; coordinated monthly safety meetings and semiannual safety audits/inspections.
- Wrote the school's first aviation accident prevention plan.
- Trained 36 pilots on EH-60 electronics systems.

PERSONNEL ADMINISTRATOR. Boeing Aircraft, Los Angeles, CA (1988-91). Gained skills in personnel administration while directing hiring of personnel to staff the safety department; participated in safety investigations.

Other experience: Earned a reputation as an outstanding writer, manager, problem-solver, and strategic thinker in earlier "building block" jobs.

PERSONAL

Top Secret security clearance with SBI. Extensive OSHA knowledge. Hold Commercial FAA Rotary Wing Multi-Engine Instrument pilot license. Emergency Medical Technician (EMT).

Date

Exact Name of Person
Title or Position
Exact Name of Company
Address (no., street)
City, state, zip

ARSON INVESTIGATOR

Not all firefighters work out of fire stations. This particular "firefighter" works for an insurance company as an arson claims specialist.

Dear Exact Name of Person (or Dear Sir or Madam if answering a blind ad.):

With the enclosed resume, I would like to make you aware of my interest in exploring employment opportunities with your organization. I am responding to your recent advertisement in *The Wall Street Journal* for an arson investigator and claims specialist.

As you will see from my resume, I have completed extensive training related to firefighting operations and arson investigation through Nationwide Insurance. After beginning as a medical malpractice claims agent, I quickly transitioned into the department which specializes in investigating fires and claims of arson. In order to perform my job, I have established close working relationships with firefighting organizations and firefighting professionals all over the U.S., and I also work closely with law enforcement agencies and federal investigators as I investigate suspected arson activities.

Although I am held in the highest regard by my current employer and can provide outstanding references at the appropriate time, I would appreciate your holding my interest in your company in confidence at this time. Although I am grateful to Nationwide for helping me become established in the arson investigation field, Nationwide is a "small player" in the field compared to Lloyds of London. I am confident that my excellent analytical and investigative skills would be of great value to Lloyds of London.

I hope you will welcome my call soon to arrange a brief meeting at your convenience to discuss your current and future needs and how I might serve them. Thank you in advance for your time.

Sincerely yours,

Jeanie Cregar

Alternate last paragraph:
I hope you will call or write me to suggest a time convenient for us to meet and discuss your current and future needs and how I might serve them. Thank you in advance for your time.

JEANIE CREGAR

1110½ Hay Street, Fayetteville, NC 28305   •   preppub@aol.com   •   (910) 483-6611

OBJECTIVE   To obtain a claims representative position with a professional liability insurance carrier.

EDUCATION   **B.A. in Psychology**, Wichita State University, Wichita, KS, 2001.
A.A., Creighton University, Omaha, NE, 1994.
Completed numerous training programs sponsored by Nationwide Insurance and federal agencies related to firefighting, arson, criminal investigations, and claims analysis.

EXPERIENCE   **ARSON INVESTIGATOR & CLAIMS REPRESENTATIVE.** Nationwide Insurance, Tulsa, OK (2001-present). Was recruited by Nationwide after college graduation. Investigate, evaluate, and determine the status of arson claims. Determine coverage, liability, and source of indemnification.
- Make reserve recommendations, assign defense counsel, and monitor defense handling and involvement. Determine settlement value in claims to be settled and conduct negotiations.
- On average, monitor 145 arson claims with indemnity reserves totalling $70 million.
- Routinely work with fire station chiefs and firefighting professionals throughout the U.S. in analyzing the complex issues of arson cases. Also work with federal and state law enforcement officials in charge of apprehending suspects involved in arson.
- Utilize my communication skills to interview involved parties and write reports providing detailed analyses and recommendations.

MENTAL HEALTH COUNSELOR. Kansas Memorial Hospital, Wichita, KS (2000-01). Implemented individual treatment plans for adolescent patients.
- Counselled patients on a daily basis. Supervised group therapy and activities.
- Documented patient's mental and physical status.

TEACHER'S AIDE. Wichita School System, Wichita, KS (1998-99). Supervised high school as well as elementary level students in a classroom environment.
- Created and implemented daily lesson plans and exams.
- Evaluated and updated student's progress.

ASSISTANT HEAD CASHIER. Wal-Mart, Wichita, KS (1996-98). Maintained and updated monthly inventory records.
- Assisted in balancing daily receipts.
- Trained new employees in all facets of register operations.
- Supervised monthly staff meetings.

CO-MANAGER. Internet Cafe, Wichita, KS (1995-96). Controlled cash flow and capital expenditures.
- Ordered supplies and maintained inventory control and upkeep of equipment.
- Created and implemented weekly advertising.
- Handled all personnel matters including hiring and firing.

ASSISTANT DIRECTOR. YMCA, Omaha, NE (1994). Planned and implemented daycare and recreational programs for children ages 6-18.
- Supervised staff.
- Maintained financial records and inventory.

PERSONAL   Offer outstanding personal and professional references. Will cheerfully travel and relocate according to the needs of my employer.

Exact Name of Person
Title or Position
Exact Name of Company
Address (no., street)
City, state, zip

**ARSON
INVESTIGATOR &
SPECIAL
AGENT**

Dear Exact Name of Person (or Dear Sir or Madam if answering a blind ad.):

With the enclosed resume, I would like to make you aware of my interest in exploring employment opportunities with your organization.

You will see from my resume that I have earned a reputation as a highly motivated individual with unlimited personal initiative. After joining the U.S. Army as a military policeman, I used my spare time to earn my bachelor's degree and master's degree. I discovered that the military police field was well suited to my strong analytical skills, and I was recommended for Officer's Candidate School. After completing OCS, I was commissioned as a second lieutenant and transitioned into the criminal investigation field. I have been very successful in apprehending arson suspects and conducting arson investigations.

While gaining expertise related to arson investigations, I have worked with firefighters and firefighting organizations throughout the U.S.

I hope you will welcome my call soon to arrange a brief meeting at your convenience to discuss your current and future needs and how I might serve them. Thank you in advance for your time.

Sincerely yours,

Jonathan Davenport

Alternate last paragraph:
I hope you will call or write me to suggest a time convenient for us to meet and discuss your current and future needs and how I might serve them. Thank you in advance for your time.

JONATHAN DAVENPORT

1110½ Hay Street, Fayetteville, NC 28305 • preppub@aol.com • (910) 483-6611

OBJECTIVE

I am seeking a security-related and investigative position in a company that seeks an individual with extensive experience in arson and criminal investigations.

CLEARANCE

Defense Department Security Clearance: Top Secret valid to 2005.

EDUCATION

Master of Criminal Justice Administration, Columbus College, Columbus, GA, 2002.
Bachelor of Science degree in Health, Physical Education, Recreation, & Safety, Columbus College, Columbus, GA, 1998.
Associate of Science degree in Physical Education with emphasis on Secondary Education, Columbus College, Columbus, GA, 1996.
Completed the U.S. Army **Criminal Investigation Division Course**, Fort Bragg, NC, 1996.
Completed the U.S. Army **Military Police School**, Fort Bragg, NC, 1996.

EXPERIENCE

ARSON INVESTIGATOR & SPECIAL AGENT. Criminal Investigation Command (CID), U.S. Army, Ft. Benning, GA (2003-present). Accredited federal criminal investigator performing felony investigations in the fields of arson, general, and drug-related crimes. Examine government contracts and supporting documents for fraud indicators.
* Implement apprehensions, searches, and seizures. Conduct fraud awareness briefings.
* Conduct physical security by using procedures and physical measures designed to safeguard and protect personnel, property, and operations including espionage, terrorism, sabotage, damage, misuse, and theft.
* Interview/interrogate subjects, victims, and witnesses. Photograph, sketch, evaluate, and preserve evidence.
* Testify before courts and boards.
* Participate in crime prevention surveys.
* Provide protective service operations for visiting dignitaries.
* Develop sources and collect criminal information.
* Conduct surveillance and covert operations.
* Coordinate with other federal agencies.
* Draft reports of investigations documenting results.
* Train subordinates and new personnel.

STUDENT, OFFICERS CANDIDATE SCHOOL. U.S. Army, Ft. Leonard Wood, MO (2002-03). Completed professional training required to be commissioned as an officer. Upon graduation, was commissioned as a second lieutenant.

MILITARY POLICEMAN. U.S. Army, Ft. Benning, GA (1996-02). Performed duties of law enforcement and traffic violations within the military community. Was promoted ahead of my peers and was recommended for Officers Candidate School.
* Became known for my high level of motivation and discipline as I utilized my spare time to earn a bachelor's degree and a master's degree.

EQUIPMENT EXPERTISE
* Utilize personal computers.
* Expert marksman. Carry concealed firearms.
* Proficient in technical listening equipment, video, and still photography.
* Installation of security alarm/intrusion detection systems.

PERSONAL

Excellent references. Willing to relocate.

Date

Exact Name of Person
Title or Position
Exact Name of Company
Address (no., street)
City, state, zip

CHEMICAL OPERATOR & PLANT FIRE CHIEF

This manufacturing professional has rather quietly "changed careers" over the past several years. He has worked in manufacturing for most of his life, and in his spare time he intelligently pursued opportunities for training and education which allowed him to become a "technical expert" on firefighting within the manufacturing field. (Here's a tip: you don't always have to change your industry to change careers. Sometimes you can find a new niche within your industry.)

Dear Exact Name of Person (or Dear Sir or Madam if answering a blind ad.):

With the enclosed resume, I would like to make you aware of my interest in exploring employment opportunities with your organization. I am responding to your advertisement for a Plant Safety Manager.

As you will see from my resume, I have excelled in a track record of promotion with a Fortune 500 company. Known for my high level of initiative, I have aggressively pursued opportunities for additional education and training in my spare time. For example, I earned a B.S. degree in Occupational Safety Management, and I was specially selected by my employer to complete training which allowed me to become certified as a Plant Fire Chief. I am one of only 200 Plant Fire Chiefs in the country and, within that group, I am considered a leading safety expert.

Since becoming the first Plant Fire Chief at the 3,000-person plant where I work, I have become the "go-to" individual for any safety problems and chemical spill issues. I provided leadership in developing the plant's first safety procedures related to firefighting issues, and we have been successful in reducing injuries and accidents in the current fiscal year compared to the previous year.

My interest in specializing in safety and fire protection was sparked by my work as a volunteer firefighter during the past 15 years. I have found it very gratifying to bring that body of knowledge into the plant where I work, and it is now my desire to benefit another manufacturing environment with my vast knowledge base.

I hope you will call or write me to suggest a time convenient for us to meet and discuss your current and future needs and how I might serve them. Thank you in advance for your time.

Sincerely yours,

James Davies

JAMES DAVIES

1110½ Hay Street, Fayetteville, NC 28305   •   preppub@aol.com   •   (910) 483-6611

OBJECTIVE   I want to benefit an organization that can use a versatile manager with experience in industrial maintenance and plant safety, along with certifications in fire safety.

EDUCATION   Completed **B.S. in Occupational Safety Management,** University of Pittsburgh, Pittsburgh, PA, 2003. Pursued this degree while excelling in my full-time position.

CERTIFICATIONS   Am certified by the State of Pennsylvania as a **Journeyman Mechanic**
Certified **Emergency Medical Technician (EMT)**
- Earned **Intermediate EMT** certification which is valid until 2008.
- Was certified as a **Hazardous Materials Responder Level I** (the Operations Level) by the State of Pennsylvania Fire and Rescue Commission.
- Was certified as a **Level II Firefighter** by the Pennsylvania Fire and Rescue Commission.
- Completed certifications as a **Plant Safety Officer** by the Pennsylvania Fire and Rescue Commission.

EXPERIENCE   **Excelled in the following track record of promotion with a Fortune 500 Company, Napoli & Turner Products, Inc:**
2002-present: CHEMICAL OPERATOR and **PLANT FIRE CHIEF.** For this Fortune 500 company, monitor and control the Lysol disinfectant manufacturing process through constant observation of controls and equipment while ensuring normal operating conditions and safety precautions. Serve as the Fire Chief within this 3,000-person plant, and direct a team of firefighters in responding to chemical spills and fire problems.
- Have acquired knowledge of inventory control procedures by performing periodic checks on raw material and product storage levels.
- Refined my communication and coordinating abilities working with the personnel in the laboratory and other areas of the plant to plan joint activities such as maintenance or sample analysis.
- As this plant's first Plant Fire Chief, contribute to the safety of employees and protection of facilities by working closely with fire and emergency personnel. Developed new fire protection procedures which reduced hazardous spills and improved employee knowledge of fire protection. Routinely hold firefighting safety briefings for employees.

2001-02: MAINTENANCE SUPERVISOR. Performed troubleshooting, repair, and maintenance on industrial equipment and electrical systems for this plant, the world's largest tire producer. Learned to work with electrical test equipment repairing wiring and electrical connections related to the manufacturing equipment. Supervised 11 employees.

1991-01: MAINTENANCE MECHANIC. Was promoted to this job maintaining, troubleshooting, and repairing various types of industrial equipment throughout the plant.
- Completed company-sponsored technical training related to pump repair, and welding.

Other experience:
- As **Chemical Operator,** prepared chemicals for a manufacturing process.
- As a **Troubleshooter,** supervised 15 people maintaining and repairing a variety of equipment; modified machinery for increased production.
- As an **Instructor,** trained operators for a technician manufacturing process.

PERSONAL   Am a hardworker with a background in a variety of industrial maintenance areas as well a volunteer firefighter. Offer an ability to train and motivate employees.

Date

Exact Name of Person
Title or Position
Exact Name of Company
Address (no., street)
City, state, zip

CLAIMS ADJUSTER & FIRE INCIDENT SPECIALIST

In this resume, you see an individual who has decided to specialize in a field where he can accumulate "expert knowledge." His job hunt is very selective. He is sending out resumes to the leading insurers in the arson investigation field, and he is addressing the letter to the individual in the company who manages fire incident investigations.

Dear Exact Name of Person (or Dear Sir or Madam if answering a blind ad.):

With the enclosed resume, I would like to make you aware of my interest in exploring employment opportunities with your organization. I offer credentials and certifications related to arson investigation and fire incidents which could benefit your company.

As you will see from my resume, I went to work full-time after high school and earned my undergraduate degree in my spare time. A member of the National Guard during college, I served on active duty in the U.S. Army when my unit was called into active duty to support the War on Terrorism. As a member of a unit which specialized in nuclear, biological, and chemical activities, I gained extensive experience in handling fire emergencies in combat environments including Iraq and Afghanistan.

When my active duty service in the U.S. Army ended, I decided that I wished to pursue a career in the insurance industry. I have utilized my NBC training and fire incident experience as a Claims Adjuster and Fire Incident Specialist, and I have earned a reputation for outstanding investigative and analytical skills.

Although I am excelling in my current position, I am selectively exploring opportunities in other insurance companies. I am aware that your organization is well known for its expertise in arson investigations, and I am interested in discussing the possibility of becoming a part of your highly respected team.

I hope you will welcome my call soon to arrange a brief meeting at your convenience to discuss your current and future needs and how I might serve them. Although I can provide outstanding references at the appropriate time, I would appreciate your keeping my expression of interest in confidence at this time. Thank you in advance for your time.

Sincerely yours,

Norman Stewart

Alternate last paragraph:
I hope you will call or write me to suggest a time convenient for us to meet and discuss your current and future needs and how I might serve them. Thank you in advance for your time.

NORMAN STEWART

1110½ Hay Street, Fayetteville, NC 28305   •   preppub@aol.com   •   (910) 483-6611

OBJECTIVE

To benefit an organization that can use a dedicated professional who offers outstanding management and administration skills along with specialized knowledge of firefighting procedures, arson investigation, and insurance claims.

LICENSES

Authorized **Insurance Adjuster** in Rhode Island.

EDUCATION & TRAINING

B.S. degree in Social Sciences, Rhode Island College, Providence, RI, 2000.
• Partially financed my college education through participation in the National Guard.
High School: As a high school student, was an all-state athlete in football, basketball, and track.
Military training: Excelled in college-level U.S. Army training related to administrative management as well as nuclear, biological, and chemical (NBC) matters.
Insurance training: Completed an eight-week course for insurance adjusters on claims procedures.
Firefighting training: Completed numerous training programs sponsored by OSHA, the National Firefighters Association, the U.S. Army, and Providence Insurance related to firefighting, arson investigation, and other areas. Certified Arson Investigator.

EXPERIENCE

CLAIMS ADJUSTER and **FIRE INCIDENT SPECIALIST.** Providence Insurance, Providence, RI (2004-present). Investigate personal, casualty, and property loss/damages claims and negotiate out-of-court settlements; interview claimants and witnesses and consult with authorities to determine the company's liability.
• Completed training in the specialized field of arson investigation. Travel throughout the U.S. in order to investigate suspected arson in commercial and industrial facilities.
• Prepare detailed reports of findings. Recommend legal actions.
• Determine property damages and estimating repair costs; make decisions based on costs of replacement compared to the market value.
• Coordinate with local, state, and federal law enforcement agencies in investigating suspected arson incidents.

ADMINISTRATIVE SPECIALIST. U.S. Army, Fort Wainwright, AK (2000-04). As a proud member of the U.S. National Guard, was a member of a unit called into active duty during the War on Terrorism. Excelled in performing a wide range of duties in a fast-paced organization; refined my leadership skills while supervising up to five personnel.
• Earned three respected medals recognizing me as a firefighting specialist.
• As a specialist in the Nuclear, Biological, and Chemical (NBC) area, gained practical experience in responding to fire emergencies and chemical spills.

MACHINE OPERATOR. American Machinery, Co., Providence, RI (summers 1996-00). While earning my college degree in my spare time, was promoted to supervise three workers while operating state-of-the-art manufacturing machinery.

Other experience: As a high school student, became known for my energy and reliability as a construction worker, truck driver, and cashier.

PERSONAL

Excellent communication and negotiation skills. Excel in maximizing the use of my time. Continue to refine my leadership skills as a noncommissioned officer in the National Guard. Will provide outstanding personal and professional references at the appropriate time.

CAREER CHANGE

Date

Exact Name of Person
Title or Position
Exact Name of Company
Address (no., street)
City, state, zip

DEMOLITIONS SUPERVISOR & FIREFIGHTER

It is important to find work that is meaningful, and this individual has decided that he wishes to be involved in the heroic work of firefighting.

Dear Exact Name of Person (or Dear Sir or Madam if answering a blind ad.):

With the enclosed resume, I would like to make you aware of my interest in exploring employment opportunities with your organization.

As you will see from my resume, I recently excelled as a Demolitions Supervisor in the U.S. Army, and I gained extensive experience in firefighting in both the U.S. and the Middle East. Although I was strongly encouraged to remain in military service and assured of continued rapid advancement, I decided to leave the U.S. Army and embark upon a career as a civilian firefighter. It is now my desire to utilize my demolitions and firefighting knowledge to benefit the City of New York. I admired the heroic achievements of the New York firefighters in the aftermath of the 9/11 tragedy, and it is my desire to join this premier firefighting force.

During my service in the U.S. Army, I managed a team of emergency operations specialists who responded to hundreds of incidents that involved chemical emergencies as well as fires in residential and commercial buildings. I am known for my ability to remain calm during crises.

Prior to joining the U.S. Army, I worked in a nuclear plant and then in manufacturing plants as a Field Engineer and Quality Inspector.

I hope you will call or write me to suggest a time convenient for us to meet and discuss your current and future needs and how I might serve them. Thank you in advance for your time.

Sincerely yours,

Edward Smith

EDWARD SMITH

1110½ Hay Street, Fayetteville, NC 28305   •   preppub@aol.com   •   (910) 483-6611

OBJECTIVE

To contribute to an organization that can use an outstanding planner, communicator, and manager who offers extensive knowledge of the engineering, quality control, and scheduling functions in construction.

COMPUTERS

Use Microsoft Word, Excel, Access and other software programs.

EXPERIENCE

DEMOLITIONS SUPERVISOR. U.S. Army, Fort Jackson, SC (2001-present). Have excelled in training and supervising teams of employees involved in:

demolitions	patrolling	firefighting
reconnaissance/ambushes	airborne operations	chemical emergencies

- Earned a reputation as a resourceful manager with top-notch motivational skills.
- Received respected medals for outstanding technical skills and leadership ability.

QUALITY INSPECTOR. Carolina Materials, Columbia, SC (2001). Was involved in every aspect of the origination of wall and column products; directed the set-up, pouring, and inspection of products including "T" & "I" beams and pre-stressed/prefabricated wall panels.

- Performed slump tests; regulated ordering and quality of concrete.
- Verified placement of penetrations, blockouts, and embedded plates.
- Provided quality for concrete pours in excess of 500 yards daily.

SENIOR FIELD ENGINEER. Atlantic Engineering, Co., Miami, FL (1998-00). At the $2 billion Stone Creek Nuclear Generating Station, established databases used in tracking rework control forms for structural, mechanical, piping, HVAC, and electrical disciplines.

- Reviewed nonconformance/deficiency reports and specifications/drawings.
- Reported to construction manager; prepared weekly status reports.
- Developed system documentation packages for engineers and quality control.
- Resolved problems among contractors, client, and all craftsmen.

FIELD ENGINEER. Cowan Construction Co., Miami, FL (1996-98). Directed fabrication of supports on site, ordered supports from vendors, and supervised installation of supports at the Clarence Nuclear Generating Station; established quality control.

- Resolved installation problems; initiated field change requests, deficiency reports, and nonconformance reports involving installation.
- Interfaced directly with craftsmen, subcontractors, job shoppers, architects/engineers, and the client.
- Performed liaison related to piping supports in the control and diesel generator buildings and the feed water pump house.
- Provided quality criteria for thermal/stress load tolerances.

Other experience: In a nuclear plant, solved overall plant problems as well as material shortages, welding abnormalities, ASME-identified site problems, and managed the interchanging of vendor-supplied parts.

EDUCATION

A.S. in Architectural Engineering, University of South Carolina, Columbia, SC, 1995. Completed Special Forces Qualification Course and extensive NBC training.

PERSONAL

Held a Secret security clearance. Member, ASTM, ASME, ANSI, and American Welding Society. Certified Emergency Medical Technician and Firefighter.

CAREER CHANGE

Date

Exact Name of Person
Exact Title
Exact Name of Company
Address
City, State, Zip

Dear Exact Name of Person (or Dear Sir or Madam if answering a blind ad):

With the enclosed resume, I would like to make you aware of my interest in exploring employment opportunities with your organization.

As you will see from my resume, I have worked with the public all my life and I feel good about the contributions I have made to the physical and mental health of others through my positive attitude and outgoing personality. I believe that a positive attitude is a key to good mental and physical health, and I excel in communicating with others in a way that they find uplifting, motivating, and encouraging. I have obtained numerous certifications and credentials which include being certified as an Emergency Medical Technician, becoming trained as an Alcohol and Drug Abuse Counselor, and becoming certified as a Mental Health Specialist and Paramedic. I was motivated to earn all those certifications because I thought they would enable me to reach out to others in a positive and helpful manner. My greatest satisfaction seems to come from helping others, and I have a proven ability to work effectively with others in a team situation. My most satisfying work, however, has been as a Volunteer Firefighter and I wish to embark upon a full-time career as a Firefighter.

You will notice that most of my paid professional work has been in the medical field as an Emergency Medical Technician. I am confident that my background in emergency medical services could be of great value to a firefighting organization.

I am in the process of relocating to New York where extended family lives, and I am seeking employment with an organization that can make use of a versatile individual with a true desire to contribute to an organization and to others. I can provide strong personal and professional references, and I hope you will contact me to suggest a time when we might meet to discuss your needs.

Yours sincerely,

Vincent C. Ivey

VINCENT C. IVEY

1110½ Hay Street, Fayetteville, NC 28305   •   preppub@aol.com   •   (910) 483-6611

OBJECTIVE

I want to contribute to an organization that can use a versatile and outgoing professional who offers an outstanding personal and professional reputation along with a strong desire to contribute to an organization which provides quality services aimed at helping others.

MEDICAL & FIREFIGHTING SKILLS

Certified **Emergency Medical Technician (EMT)** (certificate # 654321); certified in **CPR**. Certified **Paramedic** (certificate # 1234).
Completed Alcohol & Drug Abuse Training, Paul S. Hutton Veterans Hospital, Newark, DE. Accreditation in Occupational Hearing Conservation. Certified Mental Health Specialist II. Certified as a **Hazardous Materials Responder Level I** (the Operations Level) by the State of Delaware Fire and Rescue Commission.
Certified as a **Level II Firefighter** by the Delaware Fire and Rescue Commission.

EXPERIENCE

EMERGENCY MEDICAL TECHNICIAN. Department of Health and Human Services, Wilmington, DE (2003-present). Supervise four junior health technicians at this in-processing station which processed up to 280 people weekly undergoing physical examinations for entrance into this government agency. Complete paperwork reviewed by other government officials.
• In my spare time, am a **Volunteer Firefighter** for Wilmington's Station 9352.

HEALTH TECHNICIAN. Paul S. Hutton Veterans Hospital, Newark, DE (2000-03). Provided aid to the injured, sick, and shut-in. Screened and triaged patients as appropriate. Utilized proper aseptic techniques and infection control procedures.
• Performed a wide variety of tasks under the supervision of a physician's assistant or medical doctor which included minor surgical, medical, or nursing treatment; applied and removed sutures; treated burns, blisters, and insect bites.
• Obtained lab readings; rendered tine tests; reported and documented positive reactions.
• Set up and operated specialized equipment such as resuscitation equipment, EKG monitors, and other equipment.

NURSING ASSISTANT. Wilmington Health Care Systems, Newark, DE (1998-00). Performed post-operative care which included irrigating indwelling catheters, performing gastric tube irrigations, and applying simple sterile dressings.
• Operated medical equipment; collected specimens; monitored patient's vital signs.

Highlights of U.S. Army experience: EMERGENCY MEDICAL TECHNICIAN. Worked under the supervision of a flight surgeon and assisted in rigorous flight physicals.

COMMUNICATION SKILLS

Completed Customer Relations Training, Department of Health and Human Services.
Musical talents: Am a concert singer of gospel music. Songwriter, singer, composer.
• In college at University of Delaware and at Wilmington College, was a tenor soloist under the direction of Dr. Michael Hollingsworth and Dr. Andrew Merritt. Continued as a soloist with a church vocal group as the group performed throughout the U.S.
Publications: Published a CD entitled *The Storm Is Over No*w and other songs. Authored publications including *Yet I'll Rise, What I Have Found,* and *What a Wonder.*

EDUCATION

Associate of Arts degree in Safety Management, Wilmington College, Wilmington, DE, 2003.

PERSONAL

Have a compassionate, empathetic personality with a strong desire to help others.

Exact Name of Person
Exact Title
Exact Name of Company
Address
City, State, Zip

EMERGENCY MEDICAL TECHNICIAN, INSTRUCTOR & FIREFIGHTER

Dear Exact Name of Person: (or Dear Sir or Madam if answering a blind ad)

I would appreciate an opportunity to talk with you soon about how I could contribute to your organization through my experience, education, and training in the medical field and knowledge of firefighting procedures. I am interested in joining your team of professional firefighters.

As you will see from my enclosed resume, I have built a reputation as a skilled and talented young professional who has excelled in the medical profession and firefighting field. While serving my country in the U.S. Army, I received extensive training as a medical specialist with an emphasis on orthopedic surgery and care. I received several medals and awards for my professionalism and for effectiveness while working in jobs three skill levels above my assigned level. My adaptability and versatility have been displayed while providing patient care in a medical clinic and on frequent exercises and projects as a firefighter with a combat engineering unit with worldwide missions.

I am on the national registry of Emergency Medical Technicians and a Certified Nursing Assistant as well as being certified in Firefighting, Combat Lifesaving, First Aid, and CPR. I am also pursuing an Associate in Science degree at Tiffin Technical Community College.

If you can use an experienced firefighter and medical technician who is willing to work hard to achieve success, I hope you will contact me to suggest a time when we might meet to discuss your needs. I can assure you in advance that I could rapidly become an asset to your organization.

Sincerely,

Scott Cleaves

SCOTT CLEAVES

1110½ Hay Street, Fayetteville, NC 28305 • preppub@aol.com • (910) 483-6611

___

OBJECTIVE   To contribute through my medical skills and knowledge of medical procedures to an organization that can use a self-motivated young professional who is recognized as a dedicated and exceptionally skilled individual.

EDUCATION   Pursuing an **Associate in Science** degree in Occupational Safety and Health, Tiffin Technical Community College, Tiffin, OH.

Attended the U.S. Army's General Medical Orientation, Medical Specialist, Orthopedic Specialist Phase I, and Orthopedic Specialist Phase II Courses.

Completed numerous correspondence courses through the U.S. Army Academy of Health Sciences, Ft. Sam Houston, TX, including: Operating Room Specialist Sustainment, Practical Nurse Preparatory, and Practical Nurse Sustainment Courses.

TRAINING &   Attended training programs leading to certification in these areas:
CERTIFICATIONS **Emergency Medical Technician** — am on the National EMT Registry

              Certified Nursing Assistant I

              Combat Lifesaving

              CPR and First Aid

Completed nonmedical training programs including airborne, bus driver training, hazardous materials handling and certification, combat engineering courses, and leadership courses.

Certified as a **Level II Firefighter** by the Fire and Rescue Commission.

EXPERIENCE   *Have built a reputation as a talented young medical specialist, U.S. Army:*
INSTRUCTOR & FIREFIGHTER. Fort Bragg, NC (2000-present). In a medical clinic setting, provide assistance for all phases of inpatient and outpatient care as well as simultaneously acting as a firefighter at the nation's second largest military base.

- Handle direct patient care which included conducting medical examinations, collecting and preparing specimens for lab analysis, and administering immunizations.
- Maintain accurate and up-to-date medical records on each patient.
- As an Instructor for personnel in an engineering organization, teach classes in subjects ranging from first aid and CPR; to inventory control including ordering supplies, equipment, and medications; to the proper procedures for supervising clinical and field medical facilities.
- Received the Army Commendation Medal for "meritorious achievements" while directing team of firefighters during a large-scale airport emergency. Received a respected medal praising my achievements in rescuing 10 individuals from burning buildings.
- Recognized with an Army Achievement Medal for efforts during an exercise in Georgia with an engineering unit, identified and treated two people for the early signs of heat injuries and saved them from potentially life-threatening conditions.
- Received an Achievement Medal for sustained performance during activities which included independent leadership of a cleanup crew following Hurricane Fran in North Carolina, establishment of two base camps in Haiti which are still in use, leading a construction team in Puerto Rico, and accident-free driving records in numerous projects.

ORTHOPEDIC TECHNICIAN. Lancaster, PA (1996-00). Worked in a field hospital environment where my responsibilities included assisting doctors during minor orthopedic surgical procedures and with patient care.

PERSONAL   Offer a reputation as a hard worker who can be counted on to work well with others.

CAREER CHANGE

Date

Exact Name of Person
Exact Title
Exact Name of Company
Address
City, State, Zip

EMERGENCY MEDICAL TECHNICIAN & CERTIFIED FIREFIGHTER

This individual is leaving military service and embarking on a civilian career. He is applying with the city of San Antonio for jobs in law enforcement or firefighting. (Here's a tip: job hunts are often either geographically focused or industry-focused. In this job hunter's case, he and his family have made the decision that they wish to live in San Antonio so he is pursuing employment with the city as well as with civilian companies.)

Dear Exact Name of Person (or Dear Sir or Madam if answering a blind ad):

With the enclosed resume, I would like to make you aware of my experience, skills, and knowledge as well as of my strong interest in contributing to the effectiveness of law enforcement and firefighting activities.

As you will see from my enclosed resume, I am pursuing an A.S. degree in Law Enforcement and have completed the San Antonio Firefighters Academy program from which I received a certificate in Firefighting. Other training has led to placement on the National Register of Emergency Medical Technicians. Qualified as an Expert Marksman with the M-16 rifle, I received extensive military training in subject matter ranging from leadership and training management techniques, to defensive driving and threat recognition, to rifle and bayonet fighting, to combat lifesaving.

While serving in the U.S. Army, I was awarded U.S. Army Commendation and Achievement Medals in recognition of my accomplishments as a supervisor, instructor, and maintenance mechanic. In each case I was evaluated for "exceptionally meritorious service" and described as a dedicated professional who was willing to accept responsibility and meet challenges head on.

If you can use a mature professional with experience, education, and training related to security, law enforcement, and firefighting operations, I hope you will contact me to suggest a time when we might talk about your needs. I can provide outstanding references at the appropriate time.

Sincerely,

Thomas C. Gartner

Alternate last paragraph:
If you can use a mature professional with experience, education, and training related to security and law enforcement operations, I hope you will welcome my call soon to discuss how I could contribute to your organization. I can provide outstanding references at the appropriate time.

THOMAS C. GARTNER

1110½ Hay Street, Fayetteville, NC 28305　　•　　preppub@aol.com　　•　　(910) 483-6611

OBJECTIVE

To offer a strong interest in law enforcement to an organization that can use a hardworking and dedicated young professional with a background in providing security for personnel and material assets while also applying my skills and certifications in firefighting.

EDUCATION & TRAINING

Pursuing **A.S. in Criminal Justice**; have completed the San Antonio Firefighting Academy and received a certificate in Firefighting, San Antonio College, TX, 2002.

Completed military training programs emphasizing hazardous material handling, risk management, combat lifesaving, and power generation equipment repair as well as courses in such areas as:

signal communications	marksmanship	training management
NBC operations	defense and first aid	rifle and bayonet fighting
defensive driving	threat recognition	land navigation

SPECIAL SKILLS & KNOWLEDGE

Am on the **National Register of Emergency Medical Technicians** as an EMT-Basic.
Weapons: am qualified as an Expert Marksman with the M-16 and M-4.
Physical conditioning and training: consistently score above 290 on a 300-point test.

FIREFIGHTING EXPERTISE & SKILLS

Pursuing certification as a National Firefighter.
Knowledgeable of a wide range of firefighting activities including:

scene evaluation	hazardous material control	building inspection
equipment inspection	nozzle design	advanced rescue

Offer expertise in using/maintaining firefighting equipment including:

hoses	advanced breathing apparatus	ladders
hydrants	salvage/overhaul equipment	

- A highly skilled mechanic, maintain, troubleshoot, and repair a wide range of automobiles and trucks; operate and repair power generators.

EXPERIENCE

Received several medals for my professionalism while serving in the U.S. Army:
TEAM LEADER & FIREFIGHTING TEAM MANAGER. Fort Sam Houston, TX (2002-present). Refined supervisory and training skills as the leader teams of personnel while controlling $500,000 in equipment used in support of Special Operations teams worldwide.

INTELLIGENCE TEAM LEADER. Korea (1998-01). Displayed the ability to build cooperation and accomplish results as supervisor of four subordinate personnel while also working closely with Korean national personnel.

TECHNICAL INSTRUCTOR and **SECTION SUPERVISOR.** Fort Sam Houston, TX (1994-98). Oversaw the day-to-day operation of a power generation section which provided support for training activities at the U.S. Medical Center and School.

- Applied technical expertise related to the operation of power generation equipment as an instructor for a program which trained an average of 55,000 students annually.
- Was awarded a U.S. Army Commendation Medal for "exceptionally meritorious service."

ASSISTANT SECTION SUPERVISOR. Germany (1992-94). Assisted in the day-to-day running of a power generation equipment repair section for an ammunition depot.

- Received a U.S. Army Achievement Medal which cited "willingness to assume responsibilities and accept challenging missions" and for my impact on unit success.

PERSONAL

Have basic working knowledge of German. Am a mentally and physically tough professional.

CAREER CHANGE

Exact Name of Person
Exact Title
Exact Name of Company
Address
City, State, Zip

**EMERGENCY MEDICAL
TECHNICIAN
&
FIRE DIRECTOR**

Dear Exact Name of Person (or Dear Sir or Madam if answering a blind ad):

I would appreciate an opportunity to talk with you soon about how I could contribute to your organization through my experience gained while serving in the U.S. Army where I have advanced ahead of my peers and excelled in roles usually reserved for more experienced personnel.

Having completed more than 4,200 hours of training related to fire safety and medical services, I was the recipient of honors including the Meritorious Service, two Army Commendations, and five Army Achievement Medals for my contributions as a Fire Director.

An accomplishment of which I am proud was being recognized as "NCO of the Year" from among 1,320 candidates at the Frankfurt Regional Medical Center in Germany. I also am proud of the leadership I provided to a team which developed a prototype fire safety program which reduced fire incidents at U.S. military bases throughout the world.

My ability to communicate with others, my decisiveness, and my coolness under the pressure of rapidly changing priorities are qualities which will allow me to contribute in any environment.

I hope you will contact me soon to suggest a time when we might meet to discuss your needs. I can assure you in advance that I could rapidly become an asset to your organization. Thank you in advance for your time.

Sincerely,

Nigel Steven Johnson

Alternate last paragraph:
I hope you will welcome my call soon to suggest a time for us to meet and discuss your current and future needs and how I might serve them. Thank you in advance for your time.

NIGEL STEVEN JOHNSON

1110½ Hay Street, Fayetteville, NC 28305   •   preppub@aol.com   •   (910) 483-6611

OBJECTIVE

To offer my reputation as a quick learner who handles pressure and change with authority and sound judgment, along with my military experience with an emphasis on medical services and firefighting, to an organization in need of a skilled leader and manager.

EDUCATION & TRAINING

Received certification as an **Emergency Medical Technician**, City Colleges of Kansas, 1993. Honor graduate of several courses while completing in excess of 4,200 hours of training including Ranger School, the military's "stress test" of mental and physical condition; an instructor training program; and numerous firefighting training programs.
Certified Firefighter; completed Fire Department Orientation/Safety I & II.

SKILLS

Possess knowledge in areas including **personnel protection, military medical operations, communications equipment, computers, security, urban combat, reconnaissance, surveillance,** and **close quarters combat.**
Weapons skills: M16A2, 9 mm, M60 machine gun, up to 50 caliber machine guns, and M203 grenade launcher; am familiar with small arms repair
Computer knowledge: MS Word, Excel, and PowerPoint; Windows 3.0 and Windows 95

EXPERIENCE

Consistently selected for roles usually reserved for more experienced, higher-ranking personnel, excelled in this track record of accomplishments, U.S. Army:
FIRE DIRECTOR & MEDICAL OPERATIONS MANAGER. Fort Hood, TX (2001-present). Supervise 28 people providing firefighting support and emergency medical care for a 1,500-person task force based at the nation's largest military post worldwide.
- Developed plans which reduced training costs as well as authoring the Standard Operating Procedures for community firefighting operations and patient evacuation.
- Control a $2.3 million inventory of vehicles and firefighting equipment.

FIREFIGHTING TRAINING & OPERATIONS SUPERVISOR. Fort Winooski, WI (2000-01). Cited for "self-confidence, authority, and enthusiasm," ensured the smooth operation of the U.S. Army's Firefighting School including scheduling of 350 students annually.
- Earned several awards in recognition of my leadership during the creation of a prototype fire safety program; was one of two team members who acted as presenters to members of Congress in December 2000. That fire safety program incorporates numerous antiterrorist features and was adopted for use at all U.S. military bases.

MEDICAL CLINIC SUPERVISOR. Germany (1996-00). Supervised 13 employees in a medical clinic which served a 2,000-person community while acting as the advisor to senior administrators on daily clinic operations and maintaining a $230,000 annual budget.
- Oversaw areas including personnel, finance, physical security, training, counseling, and evaluation preparation in a job usually reserved for more experienced supervisor.
- Cited as creator of a "flawless" facility closure plan, oversaw the project to completion.
- Earned a Meritorious Service Medal and was chosen from 1,320 people as "NCO of the Year" for the Frankfurt Regional Medical Center.

PATIENT CARE SPECIALIST. Fort Flynn, OR, and Saudi Arabia (1995-96). Acted as administrator of a 29-bed unit in a 241-bed medical center and was frequently called on to be Acting Ward Master in his absence. Earned numerous medals and awards.

PERSONAL

Work well in supervisory jobs which require decisiveness and natural leadership skills as well as while contributing to team efforts toward reaching common goals. Secret clearance.

CAREER CHANGE

Date

Exact Name of Person
Exact Title
Exact Name of Company
Address
City, State, Zip

Dear Exact Name of Person (or Dear Sir or Madam if answering a blind ad)

I would appreciate an opportunity to talk with you soon about how I could contribute to your organization through my experience related to firefighting and the medical field. I am interested in pursuing a career with the National Park Service.

With an associate's degree with a concentration in EMS Management, I am a licensed EMT with a strong background in logistics management and firefighting. During my career in the U.S. Army as a medical supervisor and firefighter, I earned numerous medals in recognition of my initiative, leadership, and professionalism and was handpicked for vital roles requiring expertise in emergency operations management. I have managed property accounts worth in excess of $20 million and supervised up to 50 people while earning a reputation as an individual who can be counted on to get the job done, no matter how challenging or difficult. In one job, I received a letter of commendation from the Governor of Kentucky for the leadership I provided to a firefighting team that fought a fire that paralyzed the western half of Kentucky for three weeks.

After leaving the U.S. Army, I applied my sales and communication abilities as a Sales Representative. While selling an average of four manufactured homes a month, I dealt with a wide range of people including customers, real estate agents, land owners, and contractors. Although I have excelled in that position, I have decided that I wish to pursue full-time employment in the firefighting field.

I am confident I could become a valuable asset to your organization through my proven firefighting expertise and extensive management background. I hope you will contact me to suggest a time when we might meet to discuss your needs.

Sincerely yours,

Jonathon DeCarlo

JONATHAN DeCARLO

1110½ Hay Street, Fayetteville, NC 28305 • preppub@aol.com • (910) 483-6611

OBJECTIVE

To contribute an extensive logistics management background, firefighting expertise, and medical operations to an organization that can use a mature and dedicated hard worker who offers outstanding communication and motivational skills.

EDUCATION, TRAINING, & LICENSES

Associate's degree with concentration in EMS Management, Sanderson Technical Community College, Sanderson, NC, 1998.
Excelled in training including Operating Room, Medical Laboratory, and Medical Supply Specialist Courses as well as programs for medical logistics supervisors, a Primary Leadership Development Program, and hazardous material handling.
Licensed **Emergency Medical Technician**; current CPR certification expires April, 2008.
Licensed in Hazardous Material Handling; operation of forklifts (up to 10,000 lbs.) and buses (up to 90-passenger); Manufactured Housing Sales; and am a Registered Housing Specialist.
Certified **Firefighter II**, International Fire Service Accreditation Congress, 2002.

EXPERIENCE

SALES REPRESENTATIVE. Paradise Housing, Sanderson, NC (2001-present). Apply communication, sales, and organizational skills while selling an average of four manufactured homes a month to include assisting customers in making selections, figuring payments, inventorying stock on hand, and scheduling employees.
• Work closely with people ranging from customers, to real estate agents, to land owners.

Excelled in the following track record of advancement as a skilled and knowledgeable professional, U.S. Army:
MEDICAL SUPERVISOR & FIREFIGHTER. Fort Campbell, KY (2000-01). Received "commendable" ratings during major inspections as supervisor of 50 people involved in responding to imminent hazards, including forest fires and fires caused by chemical spills.
• Received a letter of commendation from the Governor of Kentucky for my leadership in responding to a forest fire which paralyzed the western part of the state for three weeks.

FIREFIGHTING TEAM CHIEF & MEDICAL LOGISTICS SECTION SUPERVISOR. Fort Campbell, KY (1999). Cited as a professional who could be counted on to get the job done, supervised 12 people while directing a team of firefighters who responded to fire emergencies in 12 states.
• Provided instruction which produced skilled automated system users.

SUPERVISOR, PROPERTY MANAGEMENT SECTION. Fort Ord, CA (1998). Handpicked to supervise eight people, advise a senior official on supply and personnel issues and act as assistant systems administrator for a task force accounting for property and equipment during base closures and unit functional reorganization projects.
• Designed and implemented a database used to track equipment transfers and turn-ins.

MATERIAL BRANCH SUPERVISOR. Fort Ord, CA (1996-98). Credited with reducing medical excesses 75% while accounting for $49,000 worth of property and equipment, supervised 22 people operating automated systems; conducted training.

PROPERTY MANAGEMENT BRANCH SUPERVISOR. Germany (1993-96). Managed assets of $20.7 million for a 150-bed hospital, eight dental clinics, and seven clinics.

PERSONAL

Earned numerous honors including three Meritorious Service, one Army Commendation, and four Army Achievement Medals in recognition of my initiative and leadership.

CAREER CHANGE

Date

Exact Name of Person
Title or Position
Name of Company
Address (no., street)
Address (city, state, zip)

EMERGENCY MEDICAL TECHNICIAN

This jobhunter has enjoyed his life as a Professional Ski Patroller, but he has become increasingly interested in obtaining certifications that will enable him to protect the environment. Firefighting interests him, and he is approaching organizations including the U.S. Fish and Wildlife Service, National Park Service, U.S. Department of Agriculture Forest Service, and other organizations with an "outdoors" orientation.

Dear Exact Name of Person: (or Dear Sir or Madam if answering a blind ad):

With the enclosed resume, I would like to make you aware of my interest in exploring employment opportunities with your organization.

As you will see from my resume, I am a licensed Professional Ski Patroller by the National Ski Patrol. As a Professional Ski Patroller, I perform a wide variety of tasks related to keeping mountains skiable at this fast-growing resort near Anchorage. While working in this winter paradise, I have become knowledgeable of environmental issues regarding wildlife endangerment, air pollution, overpopulation, diminishing scarce resources, and the disposal of hazardous wastes and toxic substances.

I extensively trained in the Search and Rescue with the National Association of Search and Rescue. Therefore, I participate in avalanche patrols and work with explosives as required. I have refined my decision-making skills handling numerous emergencies, including organizing the medical rescue of a skier who broke his femur.

In my spare time, I have also acquired numerous certifications related to the firefighting field, and I am interested in joining an organization which can utilize my certifications related to protection of the environment.

I hope you will call or write me soon to suggest a time convenient for us to meet to discuss your current and future needs. Thank you in advance for you time.

Sincerely yours,

Terry Samson

TERRY SAMSON

1110½ Hay Street, Fayetteville, NC 28305 • preppub@aol.com • (910) 483-6611

OBJECTIVE To contribute my strong communication, management, and public relations skills to an organization that can use a versatile and energetic professional.

EDUCATION **Bachelor of Arts (B.A.) degree, Political Science and Political Philosophy**, The Colorado College, Denver, CO, 2003.
- Was awarded a $1,000 scholarship; worked every summer to finance my education.
- As a senior, took a graduate course in International Law.
- Was elected Senator, Student Government Association, freshman year.

Graduated from Rocky Senior High School, Denver, CO, 2000.
- Was inducted into the Key Club, a service organization.
- Member, German Club.

LANGUAGE Speak and read German with moderate ease

LICENSES
- National Registry of Emergency Medical Technicians (EMT)
- Winter Emergency Care Technician
- Completed the Tahoe Outdoor School, Mountaineering Course
- Professional Ski Patroller, licensed by National Ski Patrol, 2004
- Extensively trained in the Search and Rescue, National Association of Search and Rescue.

CERTIFICATION Completed Personal Protective Equipment Course, Girdwood Community College, 2002. Courses taken included training related to these and other areas:

Portable Extinguishers	Fire Hose, Appl. And Streams	Ladders I & II
Emergency Medical Care	Salvage — Level I & II	Fire Prevention
Sprinklers	Rescue — Level I & II	Fire Alarms
Fire Control	Hazardous Materials	Structural Burn
Ropes	Building Construction I & II	Fire Behavior
Safety	Forcible Entry I & II	Water Supplies

EXPERIENCE **PROFESSIONAL SKI PATROLLER**. Alyeska Ski Resort, Girdwood, AK (2003-present). Am one of 28 ski patrollers who perform a wide variety of tasks related to keeping mountains skiable at this fast-growing resort near Anchorage.
- Participate in avalanche patrols and work with explosives as required.
- Have refined my decision-making skills handling numerous emergencies, including organizing the medical rescue of a skier who broke his femur.
- While working in this winter paradise, have become knowledgeable of environmental issues regarding wildlife endangerment, air pollution, overpopulation, diminishing scarce resources, and the disposal of hazardous wastes and toxic substances.

CARPENTER. Frontier Construction, Co., Denver, CO (Summers 2000-03). In summer jobs during college, worked in construction companies performing trim work, constructing concrete form, and setting reinforcing steel and wire.

LANDSCAPE TECHNICIAN/NURSING HOME WORKER. Rocky Mountain House Nursing Home, Denver, CO (Summers 1994-98). Worked on the grounds crew and in plant maintenance for a large medical facility with 7 1/2 acres of lawns.

PERSONAL Congenial personality and desire to help others. Traveled extensively in Europe and Asia.

Date

Exact Name of Person
Exact Title
Exact Name of Company
Address
City, State, Zip

Dear Exact Name of Person (or Dear Sir or Madam if answering a blind ad):

With the enclosed resume, I would like to make you aware of my interest in exploring employment opportunities with your organization.

In addition to completing a B.S. degree in Health Care Management, I have earned other certifications including Emergency Medical Technician and certification as a Firefighter. In my most recent position in Boston, I worked as an Emergency Medical Technician and excelled in all aspects of patient assessment and customer relations while transporting elderly patients to and from fires and other emergencies.

While earning my college degree, I was active in programs that benefited the community. I raised more than $2,000 for the cure and prevention programs of the Arthritis Foundation, and I enjoyed the challenge of recruiting volunteers and motivating them to achieve ambitious goals. I also served on the Executive Board of Health and Human Performance at Boston University. In the process of completing my internship in Health Care Management, I demonstrated my strong personal initiative as I developed a plan to provide fire prevention training at public schools in Boston. The plan was approved by the School Board and is being readied for implementation through a pilot program.

I believe strongly in maintaining a high level of personal fitness, and prior to obtaining my college degree I worked in jobs as an Aerobic Instructor and as a Trainer at Patriot Health Club. Those early work experiences significantly refined my ability to work with the public and I learned how to interview people about personal and sensitive subjects.

You will see from my resume that I have chosen not to work outside the home for the past year, since relocating with my husband to Ft. Richardson. I am now eager to return to work, and I would welcome the opportunity to discuss full-time or part-time positions with your organization. I am a very versatile individual who enjoys working with the public, and I believe I am especially well suited for jobs which involve helping people. I can provide excellent personal and professional references.

Yours sincerely,

Rosalie Moses

ROSALIE MOSES

1110½ Hay Street, Fayetteville, NC 28305 • preppub@aol.com • (910) 483-6611

OBJECTIVE
I want to contribute to an organization that can use a caring and compassionate individual who offers excellent organizational and administrative skills along with a proven ability to motivate and communicate effectively with others while establishing strong personal relationships.

EDUCATION
Earned **Bachelor of Science degree (B.S.) in Health Care Management**, Boston University Boston, MA, 2001.

COMMUNITY SERVICE
Raised more than $2,000 for the Arthritis Foundation's cure and prevention programs. Served on the Executive Board of Health and Human Performance, Boston University.

CERTIFICATIONS
Emergency Medical Technician (EMT - Basic), Massachusetts Department of Health, 2003.
American Heart Association for the BLS for Healthcare Providers Program, CPR/AED, 2003.
Aerobic and Fitness Association of America (AFAA), 2001.
Certified Nurse Aide, Massachusetts Department of Health, 1996.
Completed approximately 1,200 hours of continuing education credit hours which led to the **National Fire Protection Association Firefighter Professional Qualifications for Firefighter I and II**, Boston Technical Community College, MA.

EXPERIENCE
EMERGENCY MEDICAL TECHNICIAN (EMT). Medic Care, Co., Boston, MA (2003-04). Drove an emergency vehicle while transporting victims of fires and other emergencies to the hospital. Was commended for my common sense as well as my excellent customer service skills. Resigned from this position when I relocated with my husband to Ft. Richardson.
- Refined my ability to determine patient conditions while assessing the environment as well as the patient's complaint and appearance. Determined patient responsiveness and level of consciousness. Assessed airway and breathing; initiated appropriate oxygen therapy and assured adequate ventilation. Assessed circulation; took steps to control bleeding and assessed pulse. Assessed skin color, temperature, and condition.

Internship: FIRE PREVENTION INTERN. Boston Firefighting Station #237, Boston, MA (2001). Gained insight into firefighting operations and emergency vehicle dispatching while excelling in an internship which was part of my bachelor's degree requirements. Was praised for my strong personal initiative as I accomplished multiple goals.
- Initiated a plan to initiate fire prevention training at public schools in Boston. Arranged a fundraiser to increase revenue for the development of the program. Researched and developed solutions for staffing and administrative problems. Computed and verified financial reports. Evaluated quality control and safety compliance. Assisted the administrator in daily functions. Communicated with students and public officials.

AEROBICS INSTRUCTOR. Boston University, Boston, MA (1999-01). Developed and implemented a complete physical fitness program which stresses cardiovascular efficiency and endurance, muscular strength and endurance, flexibility, and optimal body composition. Monitored students for body alignment or performance errors to help prevent musculoskeletal injuries.

COMPUTERS
Familiar with Word and other software programs; proficient with Windows.

PERSONAL
Am respected for my ability to work independently or as part of a team. Can provide excellent personal and professional references. Am committed to fitness and have run marathons.

Date

Exact Name of Person
Title or Position
Name of Company
Address (no., street)
Address (city, state, zip)

EMERGENCY OPERATIONS CHIEF

Dear Exact Name of Person (or Dear Sir or Madam if answering a blind ad):

I would appreciate an opportunity to talk with you soon about how I could benefit your organization through my extensive management experience as well as my special background related to disaster response and air evacuation.

In my current position with an air ambulance company, I manage the scheduling of aircraft and air crews who are responding to emergencies worldwide. Since the organization works under contract with numerous government agencies, I have worked with organizations including the National Park Service, Drug Enforcement Administration, and the Bureau of Land Management in providing medical evacuation during forest fires and drug sweeps. I am an FAA-licensed Commercial Pilot with 7,130 hours of flight time.

In previous experience in the U.S. Army as a chief warrant officer, I advanced in a "track record" of exceptional performance which has been recognized with medals including two Bronze Stars, a Silver Star, and the Distinguished Flying Cross as well as more than 40 achievement and commendation medals.

Widely recognized as a decisive leader who can be counted on to make difficult decisions under pressure, I have controlled multimillion-dollar budgets, planned large-scale international projects, and gained the respect of my peers and superiors for my leadership skills.

I hope you will welcome my call soon to arrange a brief meeting at your convenience to discuss your current and future needs and how I might serve them. Thank you in advance for your time.

Sincerely yours,

Gideon McCarthy

Alternate last paragraph:
I hope you will call or write soon to suggest a time convenient for us to meet and discuss your current and future needs and how I might serve them. Thank you in advance for your time.

GIDEON McCARTHY

1110½ Hay Street, Fayetteville, NC 28305   •   preppub@aol.com   •   (910) 483-6611

OBJECTIVE   To contribute through my highly-refined problem-solving, communication, and leadership abilities which have been thoroughly tested in a distinguished career as a military officer.

LICENSE   FAA-licensed Commercial Pilot with 7,130 hours of flight time.
Offer strong understanding of FAA, OSHA, and ICAO (international aviation) regulations.

CERTIFICATIONS   Firefighter Level I & II
Hazardous Materials Level I Responder
Wildland Fire Suppression
Emergency Medical Technician (Defibrillation)-BLS

EDUCATION   **B.S. and A.S degrees in Safety Management**, Embry-Riddle, 1989 and 1988. Excelled in more than 18 months of advanced training for military executives.

EXPERIENCE   **EMERGENCY OPERATIONS CHIEF.** Air Ambulance, Inc., Dalton, GA (1998-present). "Juggle" the demands of multiple critical roles by scheduling aircraft/air crews, training and evaluating instructor pilots, ensuring safety standards, and piloting a $9.5 million helicopter in a 24-hour-a-day, seven-day-a-week air ambulance company with 44 aircraft in four states.
- Wrote standard operating procedures (SOP's) on training and standardization which received "commendable" ratings and are currently used worldwide.
- Consistently brought flight hours program in under budget while maintaining "the highest standards" in a unit which flew 20,000 hours in seven years with no accidents.
- Was handpicked to provide the DEA (Drug Enforcement Administration) with medical support/evacuation during a drug interdiction "sweep" in Santa Fe, NM.
- Coordinated with law enforcement, fire, and medical personnel while providing the only air ambulance coverage in the first 15 days after a fire ravaged Miami, FL.

EMERGENCY OPERATIONS MANAGER. Arrow Air, Inc., Savannah, GA (1992-97). Traveled to Savannah to establish this company's operation "from scratch"; managed operations as the company grew from 2 to 16 aircraft in a 90-day period.
- Developed the standard operating procedures used by 10 organizations.
- Trained 12 instructor pilots who in turn refreshed pilot training and accomplished all assigned missions with no losses while working under contract for organizations which required emergency evacuation of people from major forest fires and other situations.
- Designed a 27-acre heliport which was completed nearly a month ahead of schedule.

FLIGHT EXAMINER and **STANDARDIZATION MANAGER.** On-Time Air Services, Frankfort, KY (1990-91). "Turned around" an aircraft company with the worst safety record in Kentucky. Updated operating procedures to bring them in line with government standards.

After previously excelling as a pilot, instructor pilot, operations manager, and airfield manager, U.S. Army locations worldwide, advanced in leadership roles at Ft. Dix, NJ:
Served as **DIRECTOR OF FLIGHT STANDARDS** (1987-89) and as a **PILOT** (1984-86).

COMPUTERS   Am familiar with IBM computer operations and various software programs.

PERSONAL   Have been awarded the Silver Star, Distinguished Flying Cross, and two Bronze Star medals for heroism/exceptional service in combat in Vietnam and Saudi Arabia. Will relocate.

Date

Exact Name of Person
Exact Title
Exact Name of Company
Address
City, State, Zip

**EMERGENCY
OPERATIONS
COORDINATOR
&
FIREFIGHTING
CHIEF**
Some of the best
firefighters come out
of a military
background. This
Navy-trained
firefighter offers
expertise which he
hopes will be of
interest to a
municipality,
government agency,
or firefighting
organization.

Dear Exact Name of Person (or Dear Sir or Madam if answering a blind ad):

With the enclosed resume, I would like to make you aware of my reputation as an enthusiastic leader with an extensive background in emergency operations management and firefighting.

As you will see from my resume, while serving in the U.S. Navy I was promoted ahead of my peers to managerial roles and given the opportunity to succeed in planning and overseeing large-scale projects. Although I was being groomed for higher levels of responsibility in a competitive environment, I made the decision to leave the military service and pursue civilian opportunities.

My accomplishments in the Navy included bringing a multimillion-dollar ship overhaul project in ahead of schedule and under budget. On one occasion, I developed a model doctrine accepted for widespread use in fighting major fires in engineering spaces. I also developed the first comprehensive guidelines for fighting fires onboard ships.

With a broad range of knowledge related to managing personnel in such operational areas as firefighting and damage control, mine hunting and clearing, physical security, HAZMAT transportation and defense, and nuclear power plant reactor operations, I have become a well-rounded professional who can adapt to any environment quickly.

If you can use an articulate and intelligent management professional known for high levels of initiative, I hope you will welcome my call soon when I try to arrange a brief meeting to discuss your goals and how my background might serve your needs. I can provide outstanding references at the appropriate time.

Sincerely,

Casey Baldwin

Alternate last paragraph:
I hope you will write or call me soon to suggest a time when we might meet to discuss your needs and goals and how my background might serve them. I can provide outstanding references at the appropriate time.

CASEY BALDWIN

1110½ Hay Street, Fayetteville, NC 28305   •   preppub@aol.com   •   (910) 483-6611

OBJECTIVE

To offer proven skills in project coordination, communication, and management to an organization that can benefit from my versatile background and ability to rapidly learn and apply new technology as well as from specialized experience gained in firefighting.

EDUCATION & TRAINING

B.S., Political Science, Golden West College, Huntington Beach, CA, 1998.
Completed U.S. Navy management training including a legal officer program as well as numerous technical courses in surface warfare, firefighting and damage control, diesel engineering, and naval nuclear power (electronics, nuclear reactors, and steam plants).

EXPERIENCE

Was widely recognized as a talented, intelligent, and self-motivated leader with a knack for quickly mastering new technology while serving in the U.S. Navy:
DAMAGE CONTROL DEPARTMENT MANAGER & FIREFIGHTING CHIEF.
Jacksonville, FL (2003-present). Supervised a four-person staff of firefighting and damage control specialists while overseeing internal shipwide training programs in the areas of firefighting, hazardous material response, nuclear/biological/chemical warfare defense, and gas free engineering.

- Developed doctrine for fighting major fires in engineering spaces which was passed on to other ships as a model to follow while revamping their operations.
- Was honored for my success in revitalizing the damage control training program and for leading the way to exceptional results during a large no-notice inspection.
- Completed a training program which led to qualification as a supervisor for field operations (both offshore and onshore) of cement treatments for oil wells.
- Received a Class A license for operating tractor trailers to transport hazardous material.

ADMINISTRATIVE AND NAVIGATION MANAGER. Huntington Beach, CA (2000-03). Selected for a position usually reserved for a more experienced manager, directed 13 people in six different job specialties while ensuring the safe operation of a multimillion-dollar warship. Managed a successful comprehensive shipwide repair project.

- Singled out to develop and implement firefighting training.

TECHNICAL OPERATIONS DEPARTMENT MANAGER. Jacksonville, FL (1998-00). Officially evaluated as a "well-rounded qualified engineer," managed a 20-person department handling highly technical mine hunting and clearance, navigation, and visual warning operations.

- Was honored with a Navy-Marine Corps Achievement Medal for my success in bringing a multimillion-dollar ship overhaul project in under budget and ahead of schedule.
- Cited for my organizational skills and ability to handle multiple simultaneous tasks, during one six-month period completed an advanced NATO mine-hunting operation, a major inspection, two major overhauls, a public relations trip to provide support for the Mardi Gras, and the transfer of all personnel and equipment to a new ship.
- Developed the ship's first-ever comprehensive shipboard firefighting program.

TECHNICAL EXPERTISE

Offer a broad range of technical knowledge which includes:
Nuclear power plant reactor operator
Firefighting systems, equipment, training, and leadership
Oil field cementing equipment (cement and acid pump and twin cement pump units)
HAZMAT spill response

PERSONAL

Was entrusted with a Secret security clearance. Am especially skilled in team building.

Date

Exact Name of Person
Title or Position
Exact Name of Company
Address
City, state, zip

FIRE DISPATCH
OPERATOR
&
TELECOMMUNICATIONS
SUPERVISOR

In the third job on her
resume,
her skills are shown with a
functional emphasis. Even
though her previous jobs
were not related to
emergency operations
management, she shows
her work experience
without gaps. Don't leave
off experience which you
feel is unrelated. The
employer is curious about
all of your work experience.
(The general rule
is that you should go back
at least ten years.)

Dear Exact Name of Person (or Dear Sir or Madam if answering a blind ad.):

I would appreciate an opportunity to talk with you soon about how I could contribute to your organization through my experience related to fire dispatch operations and emergency operations management.

As you will see from my resume, I have excelled in a field dominated by fire and rescue professionals. I started out as a Fire Dispatch Operator for the City of Raleigh and was promoted to Telecommunications Supervisor of Wake County's Emergency Operation Center based on strong work performance and professional recommendations.

A hard-working and highly motivated individual, I am always seeking to refine my skills and knowledge. I am certified as an Emergency Medical Technician and trained to provide CPR and other medical support.

My husband and I have recently relocated to your area, and I am seeking employment in your areas. I hope you will call or write me soon to suggest a time convenient for us to meet and discuss your current and future needs and how I might best serve them. Thank you in advance for your time.

Sincerely yours,

Katie Eubanks

KATIE EUBANKS

1110½ Hay Street, Fayetteville, NC 28305   •   preppub@aol.com   •   (910) 483-6611

OBJECTIVE	To contribute to an organization that can use a well-organized young professional who offers extensive experience in fire dispatch operations and emergency telecommunications.
EXPERIENCE	**TELECOMMUNICATIONS SUPERVISOR III.** Wake County Emergency Operation Center, Raleigh, NC (2002-present). Was promoted to this job because of my excellent performance in the job below; was commended for remaining calm in emergencies and for my ability to soothe people in stressful situations while supervising the Emergency Operation Center.

- At a time when the emergency dispatch field was dominated by fire and rescue professionals, became a respected supervisor because of my significant contributions to the city/county when they were enhancing their 911 system.
- Monitored electronic telecommunications equipment; maintained detailed dispatch records for response to fires and other emergencies.

FIRE DISPATCH OPERATOR. City of Raleigh Fire Department, Raleigh, NC (1998-01). Learned to operate complex communications equipment while monitoring multichannel fire and rescue dispatch equipment.

- Made decisions about appropriate equipment to dispatch to emergencies.
- Received a Letter of Congratulation from the Chief of Police and was promoted.

MEDICAL ACCOUNTS MANAGER. U.S. Health Services, Raleigh, NC (1992-98). While balancing accounts totaling $190,000 monthly, mastered new computerized accounting procedures as the company expanded to a new automated accounting and billing system; continuously increased my efficiency as patient volume increased by 20%.

- *Accounts receivable:* Receive and post payments to patients' accounts.
- *Accounts payable:* Prepare a wide range of bills for companies and individuals.
- *Billing/collections:* Bill more than 150 patients monthly; follow up on past due accounts.
- *Insurance billing:* Prepare paperwork for Medicare, Medicaid, and commercial companies for insurance billing purposes.
- *Data entry:* Perform data entry for hundreds of accounts which require numerous entries weekly.
- *Customer service/public relations:* Have earned a reputation as a hard-working professional with a cheerful disposition and a helpful attitude toward the public.

INSURANCE CLERK. Mainline Insurance Company, Dallas, TX (1988-92). While operating a wide range of office equipment and learning internal operations of an insurance company, determined correct charges for patients' premiums, and distributed correct insurance policies to both companies and individuals.

EDUCATION	Studied Computer Programming, Wake Technical College, Raleigh, NC, 1998-99. Completed Supervisory School, Wake Technical College, Raleigh, NC, 1986. Certified Emergency Medical Technician; completed Basic Life Support studies, 1990.
SKILLS	*Medical equipment:* Skilled in oxygen setup and knowledgeable of equipment used to record vital signs; operate traction equipment. *Medical skills:* Can provide basic life support, CPR, airway management, splinting, bandaging, hemorrhage control, and shock management.
CERTIFICATIONS	Certified as an EMT and in CPR, State of North Carolina, since 1990.
PERSONAL	Am a highly motivated person who strives to make a contribution in my job.

Exact Name of Person
Title or Position
Exact Name of Company
Address (no., street)
City, state, zip

FIRE SUPPORT MANAGER & CERTIFIED FIREFIGHTER

Dear Exact Name of Person (or Dear Sir or Madam if answering a blind ad.):

With the enclosed resume, I would like to make you aware of my interest in exploring employment opportunities with your organization.

As you will see from my resume, I have proudly served my country in the U.S. Army and have acquired expertise in the firefighting field. Even in my spare time, I always found time to volunteer as a firefighter and emergency medical technician. I have played a key role in rescuing people from house fires and forest fires, and I am currently pursuing advanced certifications in the firefighting field.

While in military service, I had an opportunity to refine my administrative skills. As a Training Officer (Volunteer) with the Ft. Drum Volunteer Fire Department, I was responsible for recordkeeping related to formal training and continuing education hours for all firefighting personnel, and it was my privilege to serve some of our nation's best firefighters in that capacity.

The recipient of numerous medals and honors for outstanding performance in the U.S. Army, I was strongly encouraged to remain in military service and assured of continued advancement ahead of my peers. I have decided, however, that I wish to pursue full-time employment in the firefighting field.

I hope you will welcome my call soon to arrange a brief meeting at your convenience to discuss your current and future needs and how I might serve them. Thank you in advance for your time.

Sincerely yours,

Aaron Anderson

Alternate last paragraph:
I hope you will call or write me to suggest a time convenient for us to meet and discuss your current and future needs and how I might serve them. Thank you in advance for your time.

AARON ANDERSON

1110½ Hay Street, Fayetteville, NC 28305 • preppub@aol.com • (910) 483-6611

OBJECTIVE	To offer my leadership and communication skills as well as my expertise in firefighting and emergency operations management.
CIVILIAN EDUCATION	High School Diploma, K.C. Alman High School, Pelican Rapids, MN, 2000. **Emergency Medical Technician Course** (licensed), Jefferson Community College, Watertown, NY, 2004.
FIREFIGHTING & MILITARY TRAINING	**Certified Firefighter;** completed Fire Department Orientation/Safety I & II, New York Community College. Naval Gunfire School; Combat Lifesaver Course; Specter Gunship Training Course
EXPERIENCE	**FIREFIGHTING SPECIALIST.** U.S. Army, Fort Drum, NY (2004-present). Refined my skills in firefighting, land navigation, target location, and fire support planning; jumped into Iraq as a member of the fighting force in the War on Terrorism. Participated in numerous search-and-rescue missions during which I proudly played a role in rescuing military professionals from fires and other emergencies.

FIRE SUPPORT NCO. U.S. Army, Fort Drum, NY (2000-04). While supporting 10th Mountain Division, provided fire support planning for platoon and company maneuvers and supervised three forward observer teams; managed vehicle and equipment maintenance.
- Prior to promotion, as a fire support specialist, I assisted the 10th Mountain Division support officer; planning indirect fire for flight plans and air assault missions.

Volunteer experience as a Firefighter and EMT at Ft. Drum, NY:
TRAINING OFFICER (Volunteer) & FIREFIGHTER. Fort Drum Volunteer Fire Department, Fort Drum, NY. Responsible for recordkeeping of all training and continuing education hours for firefighting personnel. Scheduled and instructed classes pertaining to state certifications.

VOLUNTEER EMERGENCY MEDICAL TECHNICIAN-DEFIBRILLATION. Ft. Drum Emergency Medical Services, Ft. Drum, NY. Functioned as primary caregiver in basic and advanced life support. Responsible for defibrillating and intubating patients in an attempt to sustain life.
Extensive medical knowledge: Became knowledgeable of subjects including trauma and wound care. Take steps to prevent further head, neck, and c-spine injuries.

VOLUNTEER RESCUER. Ft. Drum, NY. Assisted with all BLS/ALS medical calls. Assisted with all heavy and technical rescue operations.
- **Advanced lifesaving skills:** Became skilled in advanced lifesaving techniques.

SPECIAL SKILLS	• Am skilled in map reading. • Operate Ground Vehicular Laser Locator Designator (GVLLD), Laser Range Finder, and Hand-held Laser Designator.
CLEARANCE	Hold Secret security clearance.
PERSONAL	Excellent supervisor skills. Take pride in "going the extra mile" to do the best job possible.

Exact Name of Person
Title or Position
Name of Company
Address
City, state, zip

FIREFIGHTER Dear Exact Name of Person (or Sir or Madam if answering a blind ad):

I would appreciate an opportunity to talk with you soon about how I could contribute to your organization through my background in firefighting, emergency response, and hazardous material response and education.

As you will see from my resume, I have completed training leading to certification by the State of Georgia in the following career specialties: Emergency Medical Technician-B, Fire Driver/Operator, Confined Space Rescue Instructor, Firefighter III, Instructor — Level II, and Hazardous Materials Specialist — Level III. I also attended courses at the National Fire Academy in Emmittsburg, MD, in HazMat Site Operating Practices, Chemistry of Hazardous Materials, and Incident Command as well as Radiological Response.

Through my simultaneous jobs as a Firefighter with the City of Macon and as a volunteer with the Mercer Fire Department in Mercer, GA, I have become adept at handling multiple simultaneous tasks and projects, coordinating activities between various agencies, and dealing extensively with the public. Respected as an instructor, I am frequently requested by name to teach members of civic organizations, firefighting professionals, and local businesses in HazMat, firefighting, and emergency response.

Throughout my career I have become familiar with other aspects of administration and operations including writing policy statements, developing standard operating procedures, and using automated systems to maintain records and information as well as with budgeting and purchasing.

If you are in need of an energetic, enthusiastic quick learner with excellent problem-solving skills, I hope you will welcome my call soon to arrange a brief meeting to discuss your current and future needs and how I might serve them. Thank you in advance for your time.

Sincerely,

Leland Ray Camembert

Alternate last paragraph:
I hope you will call or write me soon to suggest a time convenient for us to meet and discuss your current and future needs and how I might serve them. Thank you in advance for your time.

LELAND RAY CAMEMBERT

1110½ Hay Street, Fayetteville, NC 28305 • preppub@aol.com • (910) 483-6611

OBJECTIVE

To contribute my extensive experience as a firefighter and recognized subject matter expert in the specialized area of emergency management and hazardous material handling to an organization that can benefit from my planning, human relations, and communication skills.

CERTIFICATIONS

Excelled in training programs which led to certification by the State of Georgia.

Emergency Medical Technician-B	Firefighter III
Fire Department Driver/Operator	Instructor — Level II
Confined Space Rescue Instructor	Hazardous Material Specialist — Level III

EXPERIENCE

Have become adept at handling multiple simultaneous tasks and projects, coordinating activities between various agencies, and dealing with co-workers and the public:

FIREFIGHTER. Macon Fire Department, Macon, GA (2000-present). Have become widely recognized as thoroughly knowledgeable in the highly sensitive area of hazardous material emergency response, equipment maintenance, planning, and follow-up report writing procedures and am often called on to provide education and instruction.

- Represented the department to the public while responding to fire, rescue, and hazardous material incidents and became known as an informative teacher with a clear, concise manner of providing instruction to civic groups, professionals, or the public.
- Frequently requested as an instructor by agencies throughout the state, have taught HazMat for organizations including the Department of Insurance, Fire & Rescue Division as well as for area companies such as Monsanto, ICI, and DuPont.
- Applied my analytical skills and technical knowledge while preparing risk assessments.
- Provided assistance in establishing specifications and purchasing new equipment.
- Gained understanding of EPA, OSHA, and local policies for toxic release reporting.
- Assisted in establishing operating procedures for several related areas of activities as well as maintaining detailed, accurate records and providing regular reports.
- Wrote policy statements on subjects including EMS response, carbon monoxide detector alarm response, and air monitoring equipment calibration and maintenance.
- Achieved familiarity with computer equipment used to input, review, and access information and records; used industry-specific software including TOMES and Cameo.
- Served on the Hazardous Materials Regional Response Team #3 which covers 16 surrounding counties.
- Expanded my knowledge of environmental and occupational compliance.

OPERATIONS CAPTAIN and **VOLUNTEER FIREFIGHTER.** The Mercer Fire Department, Mercer, GA (1990-2000). Selected in 1994 for this supervisory role after several years as a part-time employee, oversee daily operations, participate in routine report writing, budgeting, purchasing, and personnel supervision as well as emergency planning.

- Played an important role in developing a fire prevention program that was accepted for use throughout the county.
- Served as chairman of a committee which helped develop uniform promotion standards.

EDUCATION & TRAINING

Studied Criminal Justice at Macon Technical Community College, GA.

Attended National Fire Academy (Emmittsburg, MD) courses in Hazardous Material Site Operating Practices, Chemistry of Hazardous Materials, and Incident Command as well as in Radiological Response.

PERSONAL

Am an enthusiastic, energetic, and self-motivated individual. Have excellent problem-solving skills and the ability to learn new concepts and equipment quickly.

Exact Name of Person
Title or Position
Exact Name of Company
Address (no., street)
City, State, Zip

FIREFIGHTER Dear Exact Name of Person (or Dear Sir or Madam if answering a blind ad):

I look forward to having the opportunity to talk with you soon about how I could contribute to the City of Wilmington as an experienced firefighter who offers outstanding technical, motivational, and communication skills.

In my current position with the City of Myrtle Beach Fire Department in South Carolina, I have demonstrated expert firefighting techniques. I am particularly proud that I was named Firefighter of the Year in 2004 because that was an honor bestowed upon me by the community.

With strong public relations skills, I have been specially selected to organize and implement activities related to educating the public about fire safety in the community. I work with schools in order to educate the public about fire safety and to perform demonstrations by firefighters, and I personally give speeches to youth groups about fire prevention and fire safety.

I take great pride in being a part of such a noble profession as the firefighters, and I hope you will give me an opportunity to discuss opportunities available with the city of Wilmington. My husband has just been relocated to the Wilmington community, and I would like to become a professional firefighter in that fine city.

I hope you will contact me to suggest a time when we might meet to discuss your current and future needs and how I might serve them. Thank you in advance for your time.

Sincerely yours,

Patricia Knowles

PATRICIA KNOWLES

1110½ Hay Street, Fayetteville, NC 28305   •   preppub@aol.com   •   (910) 483-6611

OBJECTIVE   I want to contribute to an organization that can use a professional firefighter with outstanding technical knowledge along with a gracious style of dealing with the public.

HONOR   Named **FIREFIGHTER OF THE YEAR, 2004**, Myrtle Beach, SC.

EXPERIENCE   **FIREFIGHTER & EMERGENCY MEDICAL TECHNICIAN (EMT)**. Myrtle Beach Fire Station, Myrtle Beach, SC (2001-present). Serve as a member of a firefighting crew engaged in the protection of life and property. Respond to major emergencies, and respond to alarms. Respond to and combat fires in wooded areas and on structures which potentially contain ammunitions, fuels, gases, and volatile chemicals. Combat fires while performing the full performance of firefighting tasks involving structures, equipment, facilities, as well as fuel and chemical fires. When combating structural fires, wear self-contained breathing apparatus and move through dark interior corridors and stairways to locate the origin of the fire. Control and extinguish fires while performing rescues.

- **Hazardous Material Incident Management**. Utilize my training in incident response management while performing the above responsibilities. Have been trained to utilize advanced control containment and/or confinement procedures, cleanup, decontamination, and related operations.
- **Safety, First Aid, and Rescue Operations:** Evacuate and rescue occupants. Administer first aid and protect fellow firemen during firefighting.
- **Detection, Reduction, and Elimination of Potential Fire Hazards:** Perform fire protection inspections. Check fire alarms and sprinkler systems in buildings to ensure operability. Prepare detailed assessments and reports of potential fire problems in commercial buildings. Brief building owners and others on potential problems and suggest remedies. Prepare reports of fire inspections.
- **Public Relations:** Organize and implement activities related to ensuring the public safety and educating the public about fire safety in the community. Work with schools in order to educate the public about fire safety and to perform demonstrations by firefighters. Personally give speeches to youth groups about fire prevention and fire safety.
- **Operation of fire communications equipment:** Operate communication alarm center and monitor sprinklered buildings and alarm systems. Operate computerized telecommunications equipment. Receive administrative and emergency telephone calls. Serve as an emergency driver of a pumper and tanker fire truck.
- **Crosstraining:** On as-needed basis, am skilled in performing the duties of hoseman, ladderman, hydrantman, rescueman, nozzleman, salvageman, and hand lineman. Am skilled at technical duties including unreeling connects, laying and operating hose lines, placing and raising ladders, and operating portable and stationary firefighting apparatus.

FIREFIGHTER & EMERGENCY MEDICAL TECHNICIAN (EMT)-DEFIBRILLATION. City of Conway, SC (1998-01). Worked on a shift with nine different firefighters. Worked on the pumper for the first year at this station. During my second year at this station, was a member of the two-person Rescue Squad and operated the station's rescue vehicle. Provided rescue services while responding to EMS calls. Gained extensive experience in responding to emergencies which included stabbings, gun shootings, and car wrecks. Drove emergency response vehicle while handling varied responsibilities. Responded to medical and trauma emergencies. Functioned as primary care giver in basic and advanced life support.

CERTIFICATIONS Certified EMT; NFPA Certified Firefighter I, II, and III.

Date

Exact Name of Person
Title or Position
Exact Name of Company
Address (no., street)
City, State, Zip

FIREFIGHTER   Dear Exact Name of Person (or Dear Sir or Madam if answering a blind ad):

I look forward to having the opportunity to talk with you soon about how I could contribute to the City of Charlotte as an experienced firefighter who offers outstanding technical, motivational, and communication skills.

In my current position with the National Park Service, I have demonstrated expert firefighting techniques while responding to emergencies in one of the country's fastest growing communities. I hold the I, II, and III Level firefighting certifications, and I offer expert skills in using equipment, rescue and firefighting techniques, and fire safety. I hold the National Firefighter certification.

A proven leader, I earned rapid promotion to "middle management" while supervising a team of ten mechanics in the U.S. Army. While expertly diagnosing and repairing automobiles and trucks, I was chosen for supervisory roles ahead of my peers and earned numerous commendations for my technical and leadership skills.

You would find me to be a dedicated and energetic professional with the ability to lead in life-or-death situations. Known for giving unselfishly of my time, I volunteer my time working for the Special Olympics.

I hope you will contact me to suggest a time when we might meet to discuss your current and future needs and how I might serve them. Thank you in advance for your time.

Sincerely yours,

Elmer Bernstein

ELMER BERNSTEIN

1110½ Hay Street, Fayetteville, NC 28305   •   preppub@aol.com   •   (910) 483-6611

OBJECTIVE
To benefit an organization that can use a dedicated professional who offers outstanding technical ability, proven motivational and management skills, as well as specialized firefighting expertise.

CERTIFICATION
NFPA certified Level I, II, and II firefighter in North Carolina.

FIREFIGHTING EXPERTISE & SKILLS
Certified National Firefighter.
Knowledgeable of a wide range of firefighting activities including:

scene evaluation	hazardous material control	building inspection
equipment inspection	nozzle design	advanced rescue

Offer expertise in using/maintaining firefighting equipment including:

hoses	advanced breathing apparatus
hydrants	salvage/overhaul equipment

- Operate computers with various software.
- A highly skilled mechanic, maintain, troubleshoot, and repair a wide range of automobiles and trucks; operate and repair power generators.

EXPERIENCE
FIREFIGHTER. National Park Service, Charlotte, NC (2002-present). In one of the country's fastest growing communities which is surrounded by numerous parks and protected wilderness areas, fight forest fires while continuously testing and operating firefighting equipment; educate the public on fire safety and continuously "fine tune" my skills in weekly training.

- Play a key role in responding to hundreds of calls yearly for this department serving a community of 200,000 people.
- Because of my ability to provide leadership in stressful situations, was unanimously elected by the station to serve as Training Coordinator.

SHOP SUPERVISOR. U.S. Army, Fort Bragg, NC (1996-02). Earned rapid promotion to "middle management" while supervising ten mechanics performing routine and unscheduled maintenance on over 160 vehicles; diagnose problems and make repairs on systems including:

braking systems	engines	body work
exhaust systems	steering components	electrical systems

- Earned numerous respected commendations for technical and leadership skills; was promoted to a supervisory role ahead of ten other mechanics.
- Was praised for my "attention to detail" while performing quality control checks and technical inspections.
- Became known as a skilled instructor and motivator.

EDUCATION & TRAINING
Completed courses in Level I, II, and III Firefighting, Community College of Charlotte, NC.
Completed course work in Industrial Engineering, Community College of Charlotte, NC.
Excelled in college-level Army training related to personnel management and leadership, automotive repair, and parachute operations.

- Was named Distinguished Honor Graduate, Basic Training and Advanced Automotive Training.

PERSONAL
Member, North Carolina Firefighter Association. Known for my energy and dedication, have the ability to lead in life-or-death situations. Hold Secret security clearance. Volunteer my time working with Special Olympics.

Date

Exact Name of Person
Exact Title
Exact Name of Company
Address
City, State, Zip

FIREFIGHTER   Dear Exact Name of Person (or Dear Sir or Madam if answering a blind ad):

With the enclosed resume, I would like to make you aware of my interest in exploring employment opportunities with your organization. My wife and I are in the process of permanently relocating back to the Midwest, where we grew up and where our extended families still live.

As you will see from my resume, I recently completed six years of distinguished service to my country while serving in the U.S. Army. While excelling in full-time jobs in the supply management field, I pursued training through a respected community college in order to obtain my firefighting certification. In addition to receiving my Firefighter Certification in Georgia, I worked as a Volunteer Firefighter for the Red Springs Emergency Service. I am interested in pursuing professional employment opportunities which can utilize my background related to firefighting and law enforcement.

As a military professional, I gained extensive knowledge related to law enforcement. After completing professional driver's training sponsored by the U.S. Army, I received my Driver Badge. Entrusted with a Secret security clearance, I was specially selected to attend Primary Leadership Development Course, the Army's course designed to refine the management skills and leadership ability of middle managers. My law enforcement training also included Airborne School, Unit Armorer School, Alcohol and Drug Abuse Prevention training, as well as extensive training in supply management. I was promoted ahead of my peers to supervisory positions and became known for my strong personal initiative and problem-solving skills. In my most recent position, I trained and managed six individuals while controlling $2 million in equipment and supplies.

I hope you will contact me to suggest a time when we could meet in person to discuss your needs. I can provide excellent personal and professional references. Thank you.

Yours sincerely,

Andy Frank

ANDY FRANK

1110½ Hay Street, Fayetteville, NC 28305   •   preppub@aol.com   •   (910) 483-6611

OBJECTIVE

To contribute to an organization that can use an accomplished young professional who offers strong computer operations skills along with a versatile background related to firefighting and law enforcement as well as supply system management and inventory control.

EDUCATION

College: Completed more than one year of college courses, Presidio Technical Community College, Presidio, GA.
Supply Management: Graduated from the Army's Supply Management Course, Quartermaster School, Ft. Lee, VA, 1999; Supply Specialist Courses, Army Institute for Professional Development, Ft. Eustis, VA, 2002; Sanitation Course, Ft. Campbell, KY, 2003.
Leadership Development and Executive Training: Completed the Army's Primary Development Course for mid-level managers, Noncommissioned Officer Academy, 2002.
Technical Training: Graduated from Airborne School, Unit Armorer Course, Serbo/Croatian Language Training, and the Alcohol and Drug Abuse Prevention Course.
Driver's Training: Gained professional driving certifications; completed Bus Driver Training, 2000; awarded my Driver Badge.

FIREFIGHTING

Certified Firefighter; completed Fire Department Orientation/Safety I & II, Cape Fear Community College.

CERTIFICATIONS

Completed Personal Protective Equipment Course, Foxhall Community College and Southeast Fire/Rescue College, 2002. Courses taken include:

Portable Extinguishers	Fire Hose, Appl. And Streams	Ladders I & II
Emergency Medical Care	Salvage — Level I & II	Fire Prevention
Sprinklers	Rescue — Level I & II	Fire Alarms
Fire Control	Hazardous Materials	Structural Burn
Ropes	Building Construction I & II	Fire Behavior
Safety	Forcible Entry I & II	Water Supplies
Wildland Fire Suppression	Incident Command Systems	

COMPUTERS

Completed formal training in Excel, Windows NT, Access, Windows, Word; have used automated systems for supply management.

EXPERIENCE

FIREFIGHTER. Red Springs Emergency Service, Cameron, GA (2002-present). While earning my state Firefighter Certification, performed all the duties of a firefighter as a volunteer.

SUPPLY MANAGER. U.S. Army, Fort Stewart, GA (2000-present). At one of the nation's U.S. military bases, was promoted to train and manage six supply technicians while tracking and maintaining more than $2 million in equipment and supplies; was authorized to utilize a military credit card for supply purchases; held a Secret security clearance.
• Led employees to earn "excellent" rating during a major inspection of supply operations.

PROPERTY CONTROL CUSTODIAN & SUPPLY TECHNICIAN. U.S. Army, Fort Campbell, KY (1998-00). Excelled in a succession of assignments and received nearly 10 medals, including the Joint Service Commendation Medal; was recognized as a highly motivated young professional and recommended for rapid promotion ahead of my peers.

PERSONAL

Highly motivated individual who constantly seeks to improve skills and increase knowledge.

Date

Exact Name of Person
Title or Position
Name of Company
Address (no, street)
City, state, zip

FIREFIGHTER   Dear Exact Name of Person (or Dear Sir or Madam if answering a blind ad):

Please accept the enclosed resume as my formal indication of interest in pursuing a position within your organization.

As you will see from my resume, I am an experienced firefighter currently serving as Station Captain in Goldsboro, NC. In prior experience as a Search and Rescue Team member, I played a key role in land searches and high angle rescues on statewide response areas, and I was instrumental in planning and implementing all aspects of rescue training for S.A.R. team members. Prior to that, as a Volunteer Firefighter and Captain in Conway, SC, I supervised recordkeeping and operations for a small fire station.

My wife and I are relocating to your area, and I am seeking a position in the firefighting field. I can provide outstanding references which will attest to my reputation for personal initiative and strong leadership.

I hope that you will contact me soon to suggest a time convenient for us to meet and discuss your current and future needs and how I might serve them.

Sincerely yours,

Caison Stanfield

CAISON STANFIELD

1110½ Hay Street, Fayetteville, NC 28305   •   preppub@aol.com   •   (910) 483-6611

OBJECTIVE

To benefit an organization through my skills as a professional firefighter.

EXPERIENCE

CAPTAIN & FIREFIGHTER. Fire Station 603, Goldsboro, NC (2003-present). Began as a Firefighter in 2003 and was promoted in 2004 to Shift Captain. Serve as a member of a firefighting crew engaged in the protection of life and property. Respond to major emergencies, and respond to alarms. Combat fires while performing the full performance of firefighting tasks involving structures, equipment, facilities, as well as fuel and chemical fires. When combating structural fires, wear self-contained breathing apparatus and move through dark interior corridors and stairways to locate the origin of the fire. Control and extinguish fires while performing rescues.

- Supervise up to 30 personnel on small and large-scale emergency situations.
- As Shift Captain, handle supervisory responsibilities related to medical emergencies, fire suppression related emergencies, and Hazmat incidents. Play a key role in determining and implementing response plan and termination of the incident.
- Evacuate and rescue occupants. Administer first aid and protect fellow firemen during firefighting.
- Perform fire protection inspections. Check fire alarms and sprinkler systems in buildings to ensure operability. Prepare reports of fire inspections.
- Operate computerized telecommunications equipment. Operate communication alarm center and monitor sprinklered buildings and alarm systems. Receive administrative and emergency telephone calls.

SEARCH AND RESCUE (S.A.R.) TEAM MEMBER. Fire Station 65, Chapel Hill, NC (1999-02). Member of a highly skilled search and rescue team. Assisted with all tactical search and rescue operations. Provided swiftwater and dive rescue operations. Played a key role in land searches and high angle rescues on statewide response areas. Was instrumental in planning and implementing all aspects of rescue training for S.A.R. team members.

- Worked with more than 45 instructors at Glendale Community College to coordinate training in fire protection, counterterrorism, Hazmat, and public fire education.

CAPTAIN & TRAINING OFFICER (Volunteer). Fire Station 12, Conway, SC (1997-98). As the Officer in Charge in the absence of the chief and deputy chief, was responsible for recordkeeping of all training and continuing education hours for firefighting personnel.

EMERGENCY MEDICAL TECHNICIAN (DEFIBRILLATION). Midland Station, Midland, SC (1996-97). Function as primary care giver in basic and advanced life support. Responsible for defibrillating and intubating patients in an attempt to sustain life. Take steps to prevent further head, neck, and c-spine injuries.

- Became knowledgeable of subjects including trauma and wound care.

VOLUNTEER RESCUER. Raleigh, NC (1993-95). Assisted with all BLS/ALS medical calls. Assisted with all heavy and technical rescue operations.

- Became skilled in advanced lifesaving techniques.

CERTIFICATIONS

Fire Officer Level I, 180 hours
Public Fire Educator, 80 hours
Firefighter Level II, 260 hours
Hazardous Materials Level I, 40 hours

Exact Name of Person
Title or Position
Name of Company
Address (no, street)
City, state, zip

FIREFIGHTER Dear Exact Name of Person (or Dear Sir or Madam if answering a blind ad):

Please accept the enclosed resume as my formal indication of interest in pursuing a position within your organization. I have visited your website and I understanding that you are recruiting professional firefighters for positions in Afghanistan and Iraq. I am single and will cheerfully travel and relocate as your needs require.

As you will see from my resume, I am an experienced firefighter currently serving as a firefighter with the Eielson Air Force Base Fire Department in Fairbanks, AK. I am proud to be a part of a professional team which protects the environment while rescuing individuals in emergency situations.

I have held a Secret security clearance in the U.S. Army and can provide outstanding personal and professional references at the appropriate time.

Thank you in advance for your time and consideration. I hope that you will be contacting me soon to suggest a time convenient for us to meet and discuss your current and future needs and how I might serve them.

Sincerely yours,

Ryan Livingston

RYAN LIVINGSTON

1110½ Hay Street, Fayetteville, NC 28305 • preppub@aol.com • (910) 483-6611

OBJECTIVE

I would like to contribute to an organization that can use a highly skilled firefighter who is known for personal integrity and unlimited initiative.

EDUCATION

National Registry of Emergency Medical Technicians, 264 hours, Fairbanks, AK (2004).
Alaska Career Academy, Confined Space Rescue, 24 hours, Fairbanks, AK (2004).
National Fire Academy (Certificate of Achievement) "Chemistry of Hazardous Materials" (off-site) 96 hours (2004).
Alaska Career Academy, **First Responder Course,** 40 hours, Fairbanks, AK (2003).
University of Alaska Fairbanks, **Hazardous Material Technician Course,** 80 hours, Fairbanks, AK (2003).
University of Alaska Fairbanks, **Hazardous Materials Operations Course,** 30 hours, Fairbanks, AK (2003).
University of Alaska Fairbanks, **Hazardous Material Awareness Course,** 6 hours, Fairbanks, AK (2003).
Certified Apparatus Driver/Operator-Pumper, International Fire Service Accreditation Congress, University of Alaska Fairbanks (2002).
Certified Apparatus Driver/Operator-ARFF, International Fire Service Accreditation Congress, University of Alaska Fairbanks, (2002).
Certified Airport Firefighter, International Fire Service Accreditation Congress, University of Alaska Fairbanks (2002).
Certified Firefighter II, International Fire Service Accreditation Congress, University of Alaska Fairbanks (2002).
Environmental Medicine Specialist Course, 480 hours, Received Diploma from United States Air Force School of Aerospace Medicine (2000).
Supervisor On-The-Job Training Course, 12 hours, Training Certificate awarded by the United States Air Force (1999).
National Fire Academy (Certificate of Training) "Pesticide Challenge," 16 hours (1998).
National Fire Academy (Certificate of Training) "Recognition and Identification of Hazardous Materials," 6 hours (1998).
National Fire Academy (Certificate of Training) "Hazardous Materials Incident Analysis," 6 hours (1998).
Munitions/Hazardous Materials Firefighting, 56 hours, Training Certificate awarded by the United States Air Force (1997).
Fire Protection Specialist Course, 262 hours, Received Certificate of Training from the United States Air Force (1994).

EXPERIENCE

FIREFIGHTER. Department of Defense, Eielson Air Force Base (2002-present). Assigned as a Driver Operator and Crew Chief. Drive and operate structural and crash firefighting equipment. Certified EMT and Hazardous Materials Technician.

MILITARY PUBLIC HEALTH TECHNICIAN. United States Army, Ft. Bragg, NC (1999-01). Served as Noncommissioned Officer in charge of military public health, Communicable Disease Counselor, Food Inspector, and Occupational Health Representative.

FIRE PROTECTION SPECIALIST. United States Army, Ft. Benning, GA (1995-01). Duties included firefighting, crash firefighting and rescue, hazardous material team firefighting, and dispatching of equipment during fire alarms.

PERSONAL

Outstanding references upon request.

MARCELLA JACOBS

1110½ Hay Street, Fayetteville, NC 28305 • preppub@aol.com • (910) 483-6611

OBJECTIVE

To contribute to an organization that can use my extensive background related to management and staff development and my specialized background in training firefighters.

EDUCATION

Completed three years of college toward a **Bachelor of Arts in Hospital Administration**, University of Utah, Salt Lake City, UT.

Earned **Associate of Arts (A.A.) in General Education**, Salt Lake Community College, UT, 2001; 3.8 GPA.

Earned **A.A. in Recreation Management**, College of Charleston, SC, 1997; 3.6 GPA.

Extensive training and certifications including **UT Fire Rescue Commission Firefighter Level II**.

CERTIFICATIONS

Hold a Utah Emergency Medical Technician-Defibrillator (EMT-D) Certification.

Certified Lifestyle Counselor (CLC), American Association of Lifestyle Counselors.

Certified as a Health Fitness Instructor by the Institute of Aerobic Research, Salt Lake City, UT.

EXPERIENCE

FIREFIGHTER INSTRUCTOR. Town of Ogden, UT (2004-present). Direct the physical fitness training for 150 firefighters and lead the physical fitness work team. Handle a variety of administrative responsibilities that include maintaining individual and program data. Recommend budget items for the fitness program to the Chief.

- Administer first aid in accordance with basic emergency medical protocols while operating and maintaining equipment ranging from basic hand tools to hydraulic equipment.

OUTDOOR RECREATION DIRECTOR. U.S. Air Force, Hill AFB, UT (2001-04). Prepared a $200,000 operating budget while planning, managing, and promoting all athletic and outdoor recreational activities for a large military community; received **Outstanding Performance Award, 2002.**

- Supervised 10-12 employees, including lifeguards and recreation department staff; recruited, trained, and directed a staff of 40-45 volunteers.
- Programmed year-round land and water-based activities; managed budgetary requirements and accounted for all funds involved in the programs.
- Planned and directed programs including camping, canoeing, fishing, hiking, whitewater rafting, riding, sailing, scuba diving, skydiving, hang gliding, skiing, and wilderness medicine.
- Managed swimming pool operations, Red Cross swimming lessons, water survival classes, and special recreational swimming activities; supervised all lifeguards.
- Marketed program throughout the community; distributed publicity materials.

- Interviewed, hired, and trained all personnel; ensured that all certifications were current.

FITNESS DIRECTOR. U.S. Air Force, Hill AFB, UT (1992-01). Began as a Recreation Specialist and was promoted to Fitness Director; managed and developed an operating budget of more than $700,000 while organizing sports and fitness programs for military professionals and their families; was named **Recreation Technician of the Year,** 1997 & 1999.
- Played a key role in operating a major Fitness Center; directed front desk operations; controlled sports and uniform supplies and equipment for all activities.
- Coordinated the fitness program for the entire installation and served as advisor to the Health Promotions Committee; administered group exercise program schedules and contracts.
- Developed new program ideas and implementation procedures for incorporation into the annual calendar; scheduled employees; evaluated personnel.
- Developed a unique weight management program for overweight personnel; educated all types of customers on equipment utilization; prescribed training programs.
- Trained staff on scheduling leagues/tournaments; organized coaches' and officials' meetings; served as tournament director for various championships.

CHIEF OF MORALE AND RECREATION DIVISION. U.S. Air Force, Charleston AFB, SC (1999-01). Directed all recreational activities at a remote classified location during the war in the Middle East; developed "from scratch" a broad-based recreational program, supervised the staff, and created a monthly newsletter to communicate and promote activities.
- Served as liaison to the Chief Executive on matters related to recreation/fitness programs.

YOUTH CENTER DIRECTOR. U.S. Air Force, Charleston AFB, SC (1996-98). Supervised a staff of eight while directing all youth programs—social, recreational, and sports; promoted all events.
- Was one of only four individuals from 5,000 personnel recognized for outstanding performance during an installation-level inspection.

AFFILIATIONS & MEDALS

National Strength and Conditioning Association; Fellowship of Christian Firefighters; Co-Chair of State Senior Games Facilities Committee. Have received numerous medals for outstanding performance, leadership, and initiative.

COMPUTERS

Proficient in operating and maintaining computers; utilize Word, Excel, Power Point; Quick Books Pro.

Date

Exact Name of Person
Title or Position
Name of Company
Address (no., street)
Address (city, state, zip)

**FIREFIGHTER &
EMERGENCY
MEDICAL TECHNICIAN**

Dear Exact Name of Person (or Dear Sir or Madam if answering a blind ad):

I would appreciate an opportunity to talk with you soon about how I could contribute to your organization through my background as a Firefighter and Emergency Medical Technician.

You will see from my resume that I am currently serving the city of Charlotte as a Firefighter and EMT. I am excelling in all aspects of my job and can provide outstanding references at the appropriate time.

My wife has just completed a master's degree program in Gerontology and we are in the process of relocating to Syracuse, NY, where she has accepted a management position with a private practice. Naturally I am seeking to relocate along with her, and I feel confident that I could benefit a fire department through my extensive experience and attractive personal qualities which include initiative and integrity.

I hope you will welcome my call soon to arrange a brief meeting at your convenience to discuss your current and future needs and how I might serve them. Thank you in advance for your time.

Sincerely yours,

Lloyd Byrd

LLOYD BYRD

1110½ Hay Street, Fayetteville, NC 28305   •   preppub@aol.com   •   (910) 483-6611

OBJECTIVE To offer my strong working knowledge of emergency services to an organization that can benefit from my abilities related to administration and supervision of emergency services operations through my well-developed communication skills.

CERTIFICATIONS Completed training programs leading to certification in the following areas:

NC Firefighter Level I	NC Firefighter Level II
NC Level II Fire Service Instructor	NC Firefighter Level III
NC Emergency Medical Technician (EMT)	Basic Vehicle Extraction
NC Hazardous Materials Operation Level I	Basic Trauma Life Support

EDUCATION Attend continuing education courses in **Fire/Emergency Services,** Charlotte Technical Community College (CTCC), Charlotte, NC.

Am knowledgeable of a wide range of firefighting activities including:

hazardous material control	scene evaluation	building inspection
advanced rescue techniques	incident command system	equipment inspection

EXPERIENCE *Have developed the ability to manage my time for maximum productivity while holding multiple jobs and volunteer roles simultaneously:*

FIREFIGHTER and **EMERGENCY MEDICAL TECHNICIAN.** Charlotte Fire Department, Charlotte, NC (2001-present). Have developed a working knowledge of PROBE Chief and Microsoft Word software and how to use these computer programs for record keeping and preparing reports.

INSTRUCTOR. Charlotte Community College, Charlotte, NC (2003-present). Serve as the Lead Instructor for the Fire Academy portion of the school's curriculum.

VOLUNTEER FIREFIGHTER. Matthews Fire Department, Matthews, NC (2003-present).

FIREFIGHTER. Charlotte Fire Department, Charlotte, NC (2002-03). Made important contributions to this station's operations including doing extensive public relations work and was promoted to hold a captain's slot.
- Developed and implemented a HAZ-COM policy in accordance with NC General Statutes 95-173-95-218 of the Hazardous Chemicals Right-to-Know Act — also included information from OSHA and SARHA regulations.
- Implemented a fire prevention program after developing information geared to hold the interest of elementary school children.
- Presented fire prevention programs to nursing homes serviced by this station.

VOLUNTEER FIREFIGHTER. Charlotte Fire Department, Charlotte, NC (1997-02).

SQUAD SERGEANT. Charlotte County Rescue Squad, Charlotte, NC (1996-97). Supervised a six-person squad at substation #60, Cedar Creek Road.

AFFILIATIONS Hold membership in the following professional organizations:
NC Firefighters Association

PERSONAL Outstanding references on request. Physically robust individual known for common sense.

Date

Exact Name of Person
Title or Position
Name of Company
Address (no., street)
Address (city, state, zip)

**FIREFIGHTER &
EMERGENCY MEDICAL
TECHNICIAN**

Dear Exact Name of Person (or Dear Sir or Madam if answering a blind ad):

I would appreciate an opportunity to talk with you soon about how I could contribute to your organization through my background as a Firefighter and Emergency Medical Technician.

I offer strong credentials as an EMT and Firefighter. I was placed on the National Registry of Emergency Medical Technicians in 2000 as a Basic EMT and I subsequently earned Intermediate EMT certification which is valid until 2008. I also became certified as a Hazardous Materials Responder Level I (the Operations Level) .

In my current position as an Emergency Medical Technician with the Columbus County Emergency Medical Service, I work on a part-time basis while still serving on active duty with the U.S. Army. I have completed the county protocol and megacode tests, and I only need to respond to 12 calls with a preceptor to observe to be fully certified by Columbus County. It is my desire to become employed with Columbus County full time when I leave military service.

I hope you will welcome my call soon to arrange a brief meeting at your convenience to discuss your current and future needs and how I might serve them. Thank you in advance for your time.

Sincerely yours,

Oliver G. Lorgnette

OLIVER C. LORGNETTE

1110½ Hay Street, Fayetteville, NC 28305 • preppub@aol.com • (910) 483-6611

OBJECTIVE

To offer my experience and strong interest in emergency services to an organization that can use a certified firefighter and emergency medical technician who is known for possessing a high level of self motivation and a pleasant and concerned personality.

TRAINING & CERTIFICATION

Have completed approximately 1,200 hours of continuing education credit hours which led to **National Fire Protection Association Firefighter Professional Qualifications for Firefighter I and II**, Columbus Technical Community College, GA. Specific courses included:

sprinklers	overhaul	ropes
foam fire streams	ventilation	safety
portable extinguishers	fire control	rescue
emergency medical care	water supplies	ladders
CPR instructor training	forcible entry	salvage
fire department organization	fire behavior	streams
fire alarms and communication	building construction	trench rescue
fire hose appliances and streams	personal protective equipment	
fire prevention education and cause determination		

- Was placed on the **National Registry of Emergency Medical Technicians**, December 15, 2000, as a Basic EMT.
- Earned **Intermediate EMT** certification which is valid until October 31, 2008
- Was certified as a **Hazardous Materials Responder Level I** (the Operations Level) by the State of Georgia Fire and Rescue Commission.
- Was certified as a **Level II Firefighter** by the Georgia Fire and Rescue Commission.

EXPERIENCE

Am expanding my knowledge base and gaining skills with fire and rescue squads in the Columbus, GA, area:

EMERGENCY MEDICAL TECHNICIAN. Columbus County Emergency Medical Service, Columbus, GA (August 2000-present). Hired on a part-time basis while still serving on active duty with the U.S. Army, am called on to work an average of 25 hours a week.

- Completed the county protocol and megacode tests; only need to respond to 12 calls with a preceptor to observe to be fully certified by Columbus County.

VOLUNTEER FIREFIGHTER. Landsome Fire Department, Landsome, GA (July 1996-present). Assist in responding to approximately 15 or 20 calls a month in a small rural volunteer fire department.

VOLUNTEER FIREFIGHTER. Manchester VFD, Columbus, GA (February to July 1997). Assisted in responding to as many as 30 to 45 calls a month in this rural area department.

Other experience: **ADMINISTRATIVE SPECIALIST.** U.S. Army, Ft. Benning, GA (1990-present). Earned numerous awards and certificates for my accomplishments and service in office management and stock control after earlier gaining experience as a vehicle mechanic.

- Based on my skills and abilities, was selected to attend training which resulted in qualifications in the specialized field of chemical equipment repair: learned to troubleshoot, repair, and maintain a wide range of equipment.

PERSONAL

Am a soft-spoken and pleasant person who gets along well with others. Work effectively and productively either independently or as a contributor to team efforts.

Date

Exact Name of Person
Title or Position
Exact Name of Company
Address
City, state, zip

**FIREFIGHTING
DISPATCHER
&
EMERGENCY
VEHICLE
DISPATCH
OPERATOR**

Dear Exact Name of Person (or Dear Sir or Madam if answering a blind ad.):

With the enclosed resume, I would like to express my interest in exploring employment opportunities with your organization.

As you will see from my resume, I am a highly motivated self-starter who offers a proven ability to excel in any job I take on. After graduating from high school in Williamsburg, VA, I worked briefly for a temporary agency and then became employed as a Nanny for a professional couple with two adopted children. After marrying and having two children of my own, I established a day care facility in my own home, and I provided full day care to children ranging from toddlers to older preschool children.

Always seeking to improve myself and refine my knowledge, I have excelled in training programs including Certified Nursing Assistant, Emergency Medical Technician, as well as firefighting and rescue training. As a professional C.N.A. and Home Health Nurse, I have provided therapy and rehabilitation to victims of strokes and heart disease, and I have been told by many patients that my cheerful and enthusiastic personality was instrumental in their recovery. I was voted C.N.A. of the Month.

In my current position, I play a key role in safeguarding the lives of others as I direct emergency vehicles and emergency response professionals to the scene of crimes, fires, and other emergencies. I have recently relocated to the San Diego area and wish to continue this type of work in San Diego. I can provide outstanding references, and I would appreciate your contacting me to suggest a time when we might meet to discuss your needs.

Sincerely yours,

Grace Everett

GRACE EVERETT

1110½ Hay Street, Fayetteville, NC 28305 • preppub@aol.com • (910) 483-6611

OBJECTIVE

I offer my proven abilities related to emergency operations management and medical services.

EDUCATION

College and Professional education and training:
Certified Nurses Assistant (C.N.A.), College of William and Mary, Williamsburg, VA, 1996.
Completed 168 hours of training as an **Emergency Medical Technician**, College of William and Mary, Williamsburg, VA, 1998.
High School: Graduated from Williamsburg High School, Williamsburg, VA.

FIREFIGHTING TRAINING

Completed more than 200 hours of training related to **firefighting and rescue operations,** College of William and Mary, Williamsburg, VA, 1997.
CPR Certified; **HAZMAT** Certified.

HONOR

Named "C.N.A. of the Month" in August 2001 because of my outstanding skills in establishing relationships with patients and their families.

EXPERIENCE

EMERGENCY VEHICLE DISPATCH OPERATOR. TriCare Alternatives, Radford, VA (2003-present). Operate a busy switchboard while working 12-hour shifts to direct emergency vehicle support to crime scenes, fires, and other emergency needs.

HOME HEALTH NURSE. TriCare Alternatives, Radford, VA and self-employed, Radford, VA (1999-2003). Provided therapy and rehabilitation to victims of stroke and heart disease.
- Provided wound care therapy, ordered supplies, administered catheters, and helped patients gain a new zest for life and an appreciation of their capabilities and limitations.
- Was told by many patients that my outgoing and enthusiastic personality was a motivating influence in their recovery.

CERTIFIED NURSE'S ASSISTANT. Highmount Hospital, Radford, VA (1997-98). Provided skilled nursing care in this major hospital environment; expertly handled charting, and became known for my gracious style of dealing with patients.

PATIENT CARE ASSISTANT & CERTIFIED NURSE'S ASSISTANT. Rest Haven Nursing, Radford, VA (1996-97). In this long-term care environment, provided skilled nursing care to the elderly; fed and bathed patients; took vital signs; performed charting.
- Assisted senior nursing professionals and physicians as needed.

ASSISTANT MANAGER. Shear Dimensions, Williamsburg, VA (1995-96). Became the trusted "right arm" of the owner of this popular hair and tanning salon with multiple stylists.
- On my own initiative, extended the salon's hours in order to increase profitability.
- Prepared payroll; handled bank deposits; purchased supplies; opened/closed salon daily.

OWNER & MANAGER, DAY CARE FACILITY. Self-employed, Williamsburg, VA (1992-95). Established a day care center in my own home, and became knowledgeable of the local, state, and federal guidelines regarding such businesses.
- Provided care ten hours a day for five children from toddlers to older preschool children.
- Designed play activities suitable for different age groups, and created an environment in which children were stimulated to explore, learn, and discover their creative abilities.

PERSONAL

Enjoy helping others, especially children and the elderly. Have excellent people skills.

CAREER CHANGE

Date

Exact Name of Person
Title or Position
Exact Name of Company
Address
City, state, zip

FIREFIGHTING COORDINATOR

Sometimes even experienced professionals find themselves lacking in the kind of experience they need for specific jobs. Here you see a warehouse professional trying to become a firefighter.

Dear Exact Name of Person (or Dear Sir or Madam if answering a blind ad.):

With the enclosed resume, I would like to formally initiate the process of becoming considered for a job as a Firefighter within your organization.

As you will see when you read my resume, I have excelled in every job I have ever taken on. Currently I am a member of the management team for one of the area's largest and oldest furniture stores, and I have become skilled at problem solving and decision making. I began with the company in a part-time job, was hired full-time after one week, and have been promoted to increasing responsibilities because of my proven ability to make sound decisions under pressure.

While serving my country in the U.S. Army, I was promoted ahead of my peers to a job as Telecommunications Center Operator and earned numerous commendations for my management ability and technical skills. I was praised on numerous occasions for my ability to "think on my feet" and to remain calm and make prudent decisions under stressful circumstances. I was entrusted with a Secret NAC security clearance.

Throughout my life, I have been known as a highly motivated self starter with a strong drive to excel in all I do. Even in high school, I was on the All-Star baseball team and was elected Captain of the football team in my senior year.

I am sending you my resume because it is my strong desire to make a career in the firefighting field, and I am willing to start in an entry-level position and prove myself. I am always seeking new ways in which to improve my skills and increase my knowledge; for example, I am learning Spanish in my spare time because I feel Spanish language skills will be an asset in any field with our growing Hispanic population. I can assure you that I would bring that same level of self motivation to firefighting as a career field, and I hope you will give me an opportunity to show you in person that I am a dependable young individual who could become a valuable part of your organization.

I hope you will contact me to suggest a time when we might meet to discuss your needs and how I might serve them. I can provide outstanding personal and professional references. Thank you in advance for whatever consideration and time you can give me in my goal of becoming a professional firefighter.

Sincerely,

Jorge Perez

JORGE PEREZ

1110½ Hay Street, Fayetteville, NC 28305   •   preppub@aol.com   •   (910) 483-6611

OBJECTIVE   To contribute to an organization that can use a hard-working young professional in excellent physical condition who offers a proven ability to make prudent decisions under stressful conditions and within tight deadlines.

LANGUAGES   Working knowledge of Spanish and German; am highly motivated to better myself and master new skills, and am learning Spanish in my spare time.

EDUCATION   **College:** Completed two years of college course work concentrated in History and Liberal Arts, University of Maryland.
Military: Excelled in more than a year of college-level training sponsored by the U.S. Army related to electronics and telecommunications, safety and quality control, and management.
High School: Graduated from Jamestown High School, Jamestown, RI, 1996.
- Was an **All-Star** Baseball player, **Captain** of the Football team in my senior year and a starter on the football team all three years of high school.
First Aid: Obtained First Aid and CPR Certification through ROTC training.

EXPERIENCE   **WAREHOUSE MANAGER.** Fancy Furniture, Chesterfield, VT (2003-present). Began in a part-time position and was offered full-time employment after one week; worked in the warehouse and learned the "nuts and bolts" of warehouse operations while working my way up from warehouse worker to driver's helper; was selected as Warehouse Manager after eight months.
- Supervise, train, and evaluate seven warehouse employees while also filling in for absent employees as needed; operate 24-foot truck and forklift.
- Oversee security of a furniture inventory worth half a million dollars.
- Have become skilled in problem solving and decision making while handling public relations and solving customer complaints; am now entrusted with the authority to make numerous management decisions independently.
- Have refined my planning and organizational skills while earning a reputation as a prudent decision maker who thinks well on my feet and who excels in maximizing efficiency and productivity.

INDEPENDENT CONTRACT REPAIRMAN. Bath and Kitchen Fixtures, Chesterfield, VT (2001-02). Increased new business accounts by 30% through my outstanding sales and customer service skills.
- Traveled from store to store that sold bath and kitchen fixtures and provided personal demonstrations and testimonials of my repair work; accounts skyrocketed through my personal selling skills.

TELECOMMUNICATIONS CENTER OPERATOR. U.S. Army, Fort Bliss, TX (1996-00). Learned valuable work habits and acquired a disciplined approach to work while becoming promoted ahead of my peers to Telecommunications Center Operator; earned numerous commendations for my excellent coordinating and management skills.
- Held a Secret NAC security clearance.

PERSONAL   Outstanding personal and professional references. Strong work ethic.

Date

Exact Name of Person
Title or Position
Exact Name of Company
Address (no., street)
City, state, zip

FIREFIGHTING
ENGINEER
&
AIRCRAFT
MAINTENANCE
ENGINEER

This individual has
been trained in the
aviation
maintenance field,
and he is now
seeking to become
a part of the
firefighting effort
at an airport.

Dear Exact Name of Person (or Dear Sir or Madam if answering a blind ad.):

With the enclosed resume, I would like to make you aware of my interest in exploring employment opportunities with your organization.

After excelling in extensive training in the aircraft maintenance field, I pursued training in the firefighting field in my spare time. I have become a Certified Apparatus Driver/Operator-Pumper as well as a Certified Airport Firefighter. On several occasions, I have applied my skills in airport firefighting with outstanding results. In the recent bombing of an airport in Italy, I was specially requested to act as a consultant to the Italian government. I am a graduate of the National Fire Academy, and I completed the U.S. Air Force's Fire Protection Specialist Course.

Although I was strongly encouraged to remain in military service and assured of continued rapid promotion ahead of my peers, I decided to leave military service and enter the civilian work force. I am confident that I can be a valuable asset to an airport which requires a steadfast individual known for excellent problem-solving skills and unquestioned integrity.

I hope you will welcome my call soon to arrange a brief meeting at your convenience to discuss your current and future needs and how I might serve them. Thank you in advance for your time.

Sincerely yours,

Sharon Fueller

Alternate last paragraph:
I hope you will call or write me to suggest a time convenient for us to meet and discuss your current and future needs and how I might serve them. Thank you in advance for your time.

SHARON FUELLER

1110½ Hay Street, Fayetteville, NC 28305   •   preppub@aol.com   •   (910) 483-6611

OBJECTIVE

I want to offer my state-of-the-art expertise in aircraft maintenance to an organization that can use a safety-conscious professional with proven time management and decision-making skills and a keen eye for "attention to detail."

EXPERIENCE

FIREFIGHTING ENGINEER & AIRCRAFT MAINTENANCE ENGINEER. United Airlines, Chicago, IL (2000-present). Worked on various sections in the main maintenance and quality assurance departments and also served as an aircraft inspector.
- Became proficient in several areas, including line maintenance and airframe maintenance.
- Utilized my troubleshooting and repairing expertise to ensure safety and efficient performance.
- Assured optimum airworthiness in the meeting of safety requirements.
- Gained valuable experience working with aircraft such as:

B747-400	B747	DC-10	A-300	F-28
B707	B727	MD-11	MD-80	F-27

ELECTRICAL MAINTENANCE ENGINEER. Fox Shipyard, Chicago, IL (1995-99). Maintained and repaired Goliath cranes and electrical systems in the company.

AIRCRAFT MECHANIC. U.S. Air Force, Altus AFB, OK (1990-94). Serviced the F-86F and F-4D Phantom fighter jets until expiration of military service.

TRAINING

Completed numerous training courses including the following:
Aircraft Maintenance Technical Training. Completed 150 hours of instruction for repairing F-4D Phantom fighter jets.
Aircraft Power Plant General Maintenance Technical Training. Excelled in multiple intensive on-month training courses for the following aircraft:

B707	B747-200/300	A-300
DC-10	B747-400	MD11

Electrical Department Maintenance Technical Training. Fulfilled the requirements for a one-year in-depth training program at the Fox Shipyard.
Mechanical Department Training. Illinois Institute of Technology, Chicago, IL
Certified Apparatus Driver/Operator-Pumper, International Fire Service Accreditation Congress
Certified Apparatus Driver/Operator-ARFF, International Fire Service Accreditation Congress
Certified Airport Firefighter, International Fire Service Accreditation Congress
Certified Firefighter II, International Fire Service Accreditation Congress
Environmental Medicine Specialist Course, 480 hours, Received Diploma from United States Air Force School of Aerospace Medicine
National Fire Academy
Munitions/Hazardous Materials Firefighting, 56 hours, Training Certificate awarded by the United States Air Force
Fire Protection Specialist Course, 262 hours, Received Certificate of Training from the United States Air Force

LICENSES

Licensed as an Aircraft Maintenance Engineer (Certificate # 1110) for the following aircraft:

A-300	B747-400	DC-10	B747-200/300	B707

Exact Name of Person
Title or Position
Exact Name of Company
Address (no., street)
City, state, zip

FIREFIGHTING SPECIALIST

Dear Exact Name of Person (or Dear Sir or Madam if answering a blind ad.):

With the enclosed resume, I would like to make you aware of my interest in exploring employment opportunities with your organization.

As you will see from my resume, I have acquired numerous firefighting credentials while serving my country in the U.S. Air Force. In the current environment where all airport personnel must remain constantly vigilant of potential terrorist activity, I have acquired expertise in supervising air cargo specialists while also directing teams of firefighters in responding to aviation mishaps and airport fires. I hold the designation of Certified Airport Firefighter through training provided by the International Fire Service Accreditation Congress.

With a Secret security clearance, I am known for integrity. I can provide outstanding personal and professional references at the appropriate time.

I hope you will welcome my call soon to arrange a brief meeting at your convenience to discuss your current and future needs and how I might serve them. Thank you in advance for your time.

Sincerely yours,

Clifford Charles

Alternate last paragraph:
I hope you will call or write me to suggest a time convenient for us to meet and discuss your current and future needs and how I might serve them. Thank you in advance for your time.

CLIFFORD CHARLES

1110½ Hay Street, Fayetteville, NC 28305   •   preppub@aol.com   •   (910) 483-6611

OBJECTIVE

To benefit an organization that can use a conscientious young professional with a reputation for adaptability and technical expertise related to airport firefighting, aircraft loading, and hazardous materials handling.

SPECIAL SKILLS

- Offer extensive experience in loading/unloading palletized cargo, wheeled vehicles, passengers, and airdropped cargo using 463L materials handling equipment manufactured by American Aircraft Corporation.
- Am familiar with aircraft including the following:

C-130	C141-B	C-5A	KC-10	DC-10

LICENSES

Am licensed to operate loading equipment and vehicles such as:

25,000 lb. loaders   40,000 lb. loaders   10,000 lb. gas and diesel forklift
M1009 and M1008 4x4 diesel cargo pickup trucks

Hazardous Cargo Certifier/Handler and **Quality Control Inspector.**
Certified Airport Firefighter, International Fire Service Accreditation Congress.
Certified Firefighter II, International Fire Service Accreditation Congress.

EXPERIENCE

Earned early promotion on the basis of technical expertise, adaptability, and leadership skills. U.S. Air Force, Cannon AFB, NM (2001-present).

FIREFIGHTING SPECIALIST & SUPERVISING AIR CARGO SPECIALIST. (2003-present). Oversaw up to 11 employees while loading and unloading aircraft at fixed military aerial ports and field operating sites during training or performance appraisals.

- Worked closely with terminal operation personnel while coordinating flightline activity.
- Was selected over 12 other nominees as the community's "2003 Employee of the Year."
- Recently earned promotion approximately six months ahead of my peers as one of nine employees selected for performance reviews.
- Learned to evaluate subordinates and prepare official annual performance appraisals.
- Gained experience in effective supervisory techniques.

AIR CARGO LOAD TEAM MEMBER & FIREFIGHTER. (2001-03). Was often cited for "outstanding performance and dedication" while participating in numerous large-scale projects and refining my knowledge of air cargo handling procedures.

- Officially evaluated as an "invaluable asset," contributing to the success of the largest project of its kind involving the loading of more than 2,200 tons of cargo and 8,000 people on 675 aircraft.
- During the presidentially-ordered emergency relief project to Iraq and Afghanistan; achieved a **100% on time** departure rate while loading 60 planes with 4,000 people and 1,080 tons of cargo.
- In other projects, loaded as much as 3,060 tons of cargo and 8,000 people with no delays or errors.
- Contributed to my unit's recognition as 2002s "Outstanding Air Terminal."

EDUCATION & TRAINING

Completed course work in Computer Aided Drafting and Architectural Drafting. Excelled in training related to handling hazardous cargo, planning aircraft loads, and supervising employees.

PERSONAL

Hold a Secret security clearance. Am known for remaining calm and in control under pressure. Offer a positive attitude and cheerful personality.

Date

Exact Name of Person
Title or Position
Name of Company
Address (number and street)
Address (city, state, and zip)

Dear Exact Name of Person: (or Sir or Madam if answering a blind ad)

With the enclosed resume, I would like to make you aware of my interest in exploring employment opportunities with your organization.

Technical maintenance know-how

You will see from my resume that I have worked for only company since college, and I have worked my way up from an entry-level position to the dual responsibilities of Fleet Maintenance Manager and Operations Manager. As Fleet Maintenance Manager, I oversee maintenance and repairs performed on special use equipment including firefighting vehicles as well as wheel vehicles, track vehicles, and industrial equipment. Although I am "second in command" of the business, all company personnel report to me, including the shop mechanics and technicians as well as office personnel handling accounts payable and receivable.

Expertise related to computer software

Throughout the past ten years, I have made significant contributions to profitability and customer satisfaction through my ability to develop and implement new computer programs. In addition to supervising office personnel in their use of QuickBooks accounting, I have developed computer programs that permit the detailed tracking of maintenance expenses by individual vehicle. Our computerized approach to preventive maintenance has helped our customers avoid major repair expenses while allowing an organized and systematic approach to scheduling and preventive maintenance.

Ability to manage people and satisfy customers

I offer a proven ability to manage personnel for optimum productivity, and I have established warm and effective relationships with all of our company's customers.

I am sending a page listing numerous individuals and companies who will provide outstanding references of my business ability and technical expertise. I would appreciate your not contacting those references until we have a chance to talk, however, because I have not made my current employer aware of my interest in exploring employment outside the company. I would enjoy an opportunity to talk with you in person about your current and future needs, and I hope you will invite me to talk with you in person about the position you advertised. Thank you in advance for your time.

Sincerely,

James Dean Geldado

JAMES DEAN GELDADO

1110½ Hay Street, Fayetteville, NC 28305   •   preppub@aol.com   •   (910) 483-6611

OBJECTIVE

To benefit an organization that can use an expert in fleet maintenance operations who is skilled in supervising the maintenance of firefighting vehicles and equipment, adept at managing multiple projects, and experienced in producing accurate and timely reports.

EXPERIENCE

FIREFIGHTING FLEET MAINTENANCE MANAGER & OPERATIONS MANAGER. Firefighting Equipment Services, Inc, Old Dunn Road, Charlotte, NC (1984-present). For a 30-year-old business, I am second-in-charge, and I manage all areas of operation for a company which performs maintenance for hundreds of municipalities and fire stations that operate equipment including:

Wheel vehicles: firefighting trucks, forklifts, backhoes, construction equipment, bucket trucks, ditch witch, cranes, and other wheel vehicles

Track vehicles: including bulldozers

Industrial equipment: such as forklifts, aerial platforms, and other equipment.

- **Preventive maintenance:** Respond to constantly changing priorities as I schedule preventive maintenance of firefighting vehicles and equipment including gasoline/diesel engines. Provide comprehensive PM service on LP and gas trucks as well as electrical trucks.
- **Safety certifications:** Offer an OSHA-approved Firefighting Vehicles Operators Safety Certification Program which trains the employees of other companies in the safe operation of firefighting trucks; graduates receive both a license and certificate.
- **Personnel supervision and training:** Hire, train, and supervise seven people who include service technicians and mechanics. Manage office personnel as well as a shop of highly skilled mechanics who perform major repairs. Have become skilled at the art of managing a small staff for maximum efficiency; maintain a low level of turnover.
- **Bidding and job costing:** Prepare job quotes; approve parts and material requisitions.
- **Computer operations:** Designed a computer program for preventive maintenance which decreased downtime and improved quality control. Designed a maintenance data base from scratch which permitted detailed cost analysis that led to reduced parts costs.
- **Customer service:** Personally service major accounts, and am the "go-to" guy when customers require emergency onsite service; dispatch mobile service vans. On a routine basis, work with customers to anticipate their future needs for maintenance and frequently act as a consultant when they plan capital expenditures and major asset purchases. Negotiate contracts for service.
- **Accounting and billing:** Supervise an office staff in handling accounts payable and accounts receivable; direct staff in handling collections.
- **Written and oral communication:** Prepare and transmit a variety of written reports, and have become respected as a skillful communicator, both orally and in writing. Prepare expense reports and preventive maintenance reports.
- **Strategic planning and organization:** Utilize spreadsheets to perform analysis of maintenance history and trends.

EDUCATION

Completed more than three years of college-level training which included one year at Vanderbilt University, Nashville, TN, 1980-81; and numerous training programs and seminars related to Safety, Quality Assurance, Preventive Maintenance, Accounting and Cost Analysis, Computer Operations, and Fleet Maintenance.

PERSONAL

Offer an outstanding personal and professional reputation. Extremely knowledgeable of OSHA and other government regulations which affect the firefighting field.

Date

Exact Name of Person
Title or Position
Exact Name of Company
Address (no., street)
City, state, zip

Dear Exact Name of Person (or Dear Sir or Madam if answering a blind ad.):

With the enclosed resume, I would like to make you aware of my interest in exploring employment opportunities with your organization.

Currently an E-4 in the United States Air Force, I hold the Air Force specialty code 28305A (Special purpose crash/rescue/structural firefighting vehicle maintenance technician). As a fire truck mechanic, I learned to quickly diagnose and repair vehicle system malfunctions during normal training and/or emergency operations. I routinely performed preventative and scheduled maintenance on several types of special purpose equipment. I also took part in designing and incorporating several modifications that have greatly improved firefighting capabilities and extended the life expectancies of Air Force firefighting vehicles. Those modifications have in turn reduced response time and improved vehicle capabilities.

As a special purpose mechanic, I have also performed maintenance on tugs, k-loaders, forklifts, cranes, refuelers, and most general purpose equipment. While performing those tasks, I discovered that I enjoy working on special purpose equipment, especially crash/rescue vehicles. Experience has taught me that preventative maintenance is the key that keeps vehicles in commission and costly major repairs to an absolute minimum.

I have had the motivation and knowledge to get the job done in all environments including Iraq during Operation Iraqi Freedom. My records reflect that I have made an outstanding contribution to the U.S. Air Force and I know I can be a very valuable asset to your organization.

I hope you will welcome my call soon to arrange a brief meeting at your convenience to discuss your current and future needs and how I might serve them. Thank you in advance for your time.

Sincerely yours,

Stewart Channing

Alternate last paragraph:
I hope you will call or write me to suggest a time convenient for us to meet and discuss your current and future needs and how I might serve them. Thank you in advance for your time.

STEWART CHANNING

1110½ Hay Street, Fayetteville, NC 28305   •   preppub@aol.com   •   (910) 483-6611

OBJECTIVE   I want to contribute to an organization that can use an experienced firefighter.

EDUCATION   Completed nearly two years of training sponsored by the U.S. Air Force related to vehicle maintenance of special purpose crash, rescue, and structural firefighting vehicles. Graduated with honors from training at Arnold AFB, TN.
Graduated from Memphis Career Center, **certified as a Diesel Truck Mechanic**, 1998.

EXPERIENCE   **FIREFIGHTING VEHICLE MAINTENANCE TECHNICIAN (Heavy Duty Equipment Maintenance Technician).** U.S. Air Force, Arnold AFB, TN (2001-present). Am a special purpose crash/rescue/structural firefighting vehicle maintenance technician.
- Inspect, troubleshoot, test and repair fire department vehicles.
- Train fire department personnel in basic techniques of maintaining firefighting vehicles.
- Have learned to quickly diagnose and repair vehicle system malfunctions during normal training and emergency operations.
- Perform preventive and unscheduled maintenance on several types of special purpose vehicles.
- Played a key role in designing and incorporating several modifications that have greatly improved firefighting capabilities and extended the life expectancies of Air Force firefighting vehicles. Those modifications reduced response time and improved vehicle capabilities.
- Maintained responsibility for a $3.2 million inventory of equipment and repair parts.
- Was specially selected to assist the 82nd Airborne Division during the War on Terrorism; traveled to Iraq to repair vital equipment, and trained Army personnel in procedures for repairing special purpose vehicles.
- Supervised firefighting teams in responding to fires and other emergencies.

AUTO MECHANIC. American Auto Parts, Memphis, TN (1998-01). Cut keys, machine brake drums, rotors and fly wheels. Took deliveries and picked up special order items.

COUNTER PERSON. Pep Boys, Memphis, TN (1996-97). Receive, inventory, and stock auto parts. Fill orders, take deliveries, and collect amount due. Fill batteries and mix paint using specifications from computers, microfiche, and service manuals.
- Received, researched, and filled orders using computers and parts manuals. Assisted machine shop personnel with machine work. Performed additional duties as directed by the store supervisor.

Highlights of other experience:
- Amusement Park: Transported amusement ride to designated locations and supervised the safe set up, operation, and take down of several children's amusement rides while overseeing the sale of tickets, computing totals, paying debts, and returning earnings to owner.
- Harold's Maintenance: Maintained general up keep including cleaning lobby, drive thru, teller, and exit and entrance areas of two banks.
- Larson's: Stocked all departments; cut, weighed, and packaged fresh produce and meats; and performed all cashier and janitorial duties.

PERSONAL   Excellent references provided upon request.

Date

Exact name of Person
Title or Position
Name of Company
Address (no., street)
Address (city, state, zip)

Dear Exact Name of Person: (or Dear Sir or Madam if answering a blind ad.)

I would appreciate an opportunity to talk with you soon about how I could contribute to your organization through my management and training skills as well as my extensive knowledge of the aviation safety field.

While serving my country in the U.S. Air Force, I have refined my staff and operations management abilities through managing numerous simultaneous projects and training hundreds of personnel. In my most recent position, I have organized and put into effect five special programs for accident prevention and organized the daily flight schedule of 200 employees.

As I was promoted ahead of my peers, I was handpicked for positions which required an individual who could protect vast resources at airports. As a Certified Airport Firefighter, I have directed teams of firefighting professionals in responding to flightline emergencies. On one occasion, I led firefighters in rescuing 12 individuals from a burning aircraft. On another occasion, I coordinated the initial investigations of two accidents which destroyed multimillion-dollar aircraft and fatally injured nine crew members. On my own initiative, I established new firefighting guidelines which integrated homeland security concerns and antiterrorism procedures; those guidelines are now being implemented at military airports worldwide.

While serving my country in the U.S. Air Force, I gained extensive experience as a special investigator for aircraft accidents and as a flight safety program developer. In my most recent position, I investigated a number of accidents involving fatalities and the destruction of multimillion-dollar equipment. I also created and put into effect five accident prevention programs and trained ten other safety officers. You would find me to be a well-organized professional with strong attention to detail. I pride myself on being a hardworking and reliable individual who performs any job to the best of my ability.

I hope you will welcome my call soon to arrange a brief meeting at your convenience to discuss your current and future needs and how I might serve them. Thank you in advance for your time.

Sincerely yours,

Jacob Riley

JACOB RILEY

1110½ Hay Street, Fayetteville, NC 28305 • preppub@aol.com • (910) 483-6611

OBJECTIVE

I want to benefit an organization through my experience in the quality assurance and safety field with particular emphasis on airport security and airport firefighting.

EXPERIENCE

FLIGHT SAFETY MANAGER & CERTIFIED AIRPORT FIREFIGHTER. U.S. Air Force (2000-present). Rapidly advanced in several management positions for this organization serving 4,000 personnel. Directed the overall flight safety program and trained ten safety officers. Chaired quarterly meetings. Coordinated the daily flight schedules of 200 personnel in five different aircrew positions. Traveled extensively in the United States, Europe, Central and South America, North Africa, and the Middle East. Specific experience included:

- Directed teams of firefighting professionals in responding to flightline emergencies. On one occasion, rescued 12 individuals from a burning aircraft.
- Coordinated the initial investigations of two accidents which destroyed multimillion-dollar aircraft and fatally injured nine crew members.
- Established new firefighting guidelines which integrated homeland security concerns and anti-terrorism procedures; those guidelines are now being implemented at airports worldwide.
- Compiled information and accurately prepared extensive reports on 17 accidents with damages totaling from $10,000 to $1,000,000.
- Developed and implemented five accident prevention programs.
- Extensively interviewed pilots, witnesses, and next-of-kin in accident investigations.

SECURITY ASSISTANT. U.S. Air Force (1996-99). Organized security operations and ground transportation for the Commander of Tactical Air Command and senior staff members. Developed and implemented security procedures and operating instructions for equipment.

SECURITY POLICEMAN. U.S. Air Force (1994-96). Held numerous positions of increasing responsibility guarding and controlling access to restricted areas. Supervised a four-person security response team during daily operations.

EDUCATION

Bachelor of Arts, Business Management, University of Kentucky, Lexington, KY, 1999.
- Graduated **cum laude**.

Associate of Arts, Industrial Security, Community College of the Air Force, 1999.
Associate of Arts, Liberal Arts, University of Kentucky, Lexington, KY, 1999.

TRAINING

Certified Airport Firefighter, International Fire Service Accreditation Congress.
Certified Firefighter II, International Fire Service Accreditation Congress.
Squadron Officer School, Seven-week course for mid-level managers on speaking and writing effectively, leadership, and human relations.
U.S. Air Force Flight Safety Officer Course, University of Alaska Anchorage six week course on organizing a safety department and training subordinates.
Security Police Academy, 12 week course in police skills and security techniques.
Successfully completed numerous schools on leadership and management.

CLEARANCE

Entrusted with a Top Secret security clearance (TS/SBI)

PERSONAL

Received more than 30 medals and other honors recognizing exceptional technical expertise and outstanding leadership ability. Can provide strong references on request.

CAREER CHANGE

Date

Exact Name of Person
Title or Position
Exact Name of Company
Address (no., street)
City, state, zip

Dear Exact Name of Person (or Dear Sir or Madam if answering a blind ad.):

With the enclosed resume, I would like to make you aware of my interest in exploring employment opportunities with your organization.

As you will see from my resume, I have excelled in environments in which there was "no room for error," and "safety first, last, and always" is my constant motto at work. In my current position at a nuclear facility, I was handpicked to serve as the plant's first Safety Chief and Plant Firefighting Director, and I have played a vital role in defining the responsibilities of that position. As the nuclear facility's Firefighting Director, I continuously train employees in firefighting procedures and safety matters.

In my previous experience, I served with distinction in the U.S. Air Force as a Fuel Systems Mechanic, and I became skilled in operating virtually all equipment used in firefighting and emergency operations.

Although I am held in high regard in my current position, I am exploring possibilities of becoming associated with an airport in some capacity in which I could utilize my firefighting knowledge and security knowledge. You will notice that I hold one of the nation's highest security clearances: Top Secret Q security clearance.

I hope you will welcome my call soon to arrange a brief meeting at your convenience to discuss your current and future needs and how I might serve them. Thank you in advance for your time.

Sincerely yours,

Silas Warner

Alternate last paragraph:
I hope you will call or write me to suggest a time convenient for us to meet and discuss your current and future needs and how I might serve them. Thank you in advance for your time.

SILAS WARNER

1110½ Hay Street, Fayetteville, NC 28305   •   preppub@aol.com   •   (910) 483-6611

OBJECTIVE

To obtain a position in aircraft maintenance where my skills and experience will be used, while providing opportunities for advancement.

EDUCATION & TRAINING

Associate's degree in **General Education and Aircraft Fuel Systems Maintenance,** Community College of the Air Force, Barksdale AFB, LA, 2001.
Graduated from Creekside High School, Plainview, TX.
Completed the three-month **Fire Academy,** Wakefield Community College, and the three-month Emergency Medical Technician (Defibrillation) Course.
Armed Guard Training, onsite at Shearon Harris Nuclear Facility.
X-ray Machine Operator Training (trained to operate an electronic scan, metal detector, and explosive detector.
Nuclear Officer Security Training, Shearon Harris Nuclear Facility.

EXPERIENCE

MASTER NUCLEAR SECURITY OFFICER. Shearon Harris Nuclear Plant, New Hill, NC (2004-present). Because of my outstanding performance, have been promoted to Master Nuclear Security Officer, and am involved in training and motivating other nuclear security personnel.

- When a new position was created for **Plant Safety Director & Firefighting Chief**, was asked to assume that responsibility in addition to my regular duties. As the first person ever to assume those responsibilities, am functioning in an essentially entrepreneurial role as I develop this vital new position within the plant.
- Developed and implemented highly effective new firefighting procedures and counterterrorism procedures at this nuclear plant.

FUEL SYSTEMS MECHANIC. U.S. Air Force, Andrews AFB, MD (2003-04). Supervised junior fuel systems mechanics, ensuring compliance with local maintenance procedures and technical publications. Troubleshot, isolated, and repaired malfunctions on aircraft fuel systems. Performed data entry by entering and verifying maintenance data in the Core Automated Maintenance Systems (CAMS) computer system. Made recommendations on improving technical orders and material deficiency reports.

- During Operation Enduring Freedom, contributed to the successful launch and recovery of the 600 missions transiting Andrews AFB.

FUEL SYSTEMS APPRENTICE/MECHANIC. U.S Air Force, Barksdale AFB, LA. (2000-2002). Excelled in troubleshooting, isolating, and repairing fuel systems to include external and hydrazine tanks. Qualified on Hydrazine (highly toxic fuel) related maintenance; responsibilities included: emergency response, decontamination, and Hydrazine servicing procedures. Became familiar with EPA requirements for containing and cleaning up petroleum and other fuel spills.

CLEARANCE & AWARDS

Top Secret Q security clearance
Air Force Good Conduct Medal, National Defense Service Medal

PERSONAL

Outstanding references available on request. Strong organizational skills; get the job done. Ability to meet or exceed goals, deadlines, and quotas. Able to read aircraft systems schematics. Versatile, fast learner; readily adapt to new procedures, concepts and ideas.

CAREER CHANGE

Date

Exact Name of Person
Title or Position
Name of Company
Address (no., street)
Address (city, state, zip)

Dear Exact Name of Person (or Dear Sir or Madam if answering a blind ad):

I would appreciate an opportunity to talk with you soon about how I could contribute to your organization through my experience in airfield operations including loading, repair parts supply support, and refueling with special emphasis on ground support equipment maintenance, repair, and inspection.

Outstanding maintenance skills

You will see from my enclosed resume that I have earned a reputation as a skilled technician and mechanic. My ability to rapidly absorb new information and pass my knowledge on to others earned me the praise of my superiors and caused them to select me for special projects. In my current position I not only accounted for a 2,300-line-item inventory of ground support equipment but also participated in training others in inspection techniques, contributed my troubleshooting and repair skills, and became the work station's safety specialist.

Expertise related to firefighting and firefighting equipment maintenance

You will also notice from my resume that I am skilled in repairing and maintaining special use equipment, particularly firefighting equipment and vehicles. Although I have enjoyed my work as an airport mechanic, it is now my desire to apply my knowledge to benefit the City of Houston in its fleet maintenance division. I am confident that I could play a key role in reducing the city's maintenance costs through my outstanding troubleshooting and problem-solving skills.

You would find me to be a congenial person who offers a high degree of self motivation and dedication to excellence. I am a natural leader who inspires others to join me in order to accomplish our group's peak levels of performance.

I hope you will welcome my call soon to arrange a brief meeting at your convenience to discuss your current and future needs and how I might serve them. Thank you in advance for your time.

Sincerely yours,

Terry A. Kinston

Alternate last paragraph:
I hope you will call or write me soon to suggest a time convenient for us to meet and discuss your current and future needs and how I might serve them. Thank you in advance for your time.

TERRY A. KINSTON

1110½ Hay Street, Fayetteville, NC 28305 • preppub@aol.com • (910) 483-6611

OBJECTIVE

To offer a background which includes a strong base of experience in aviation ground support equipment repair to an organization that can use a talented, dedicated professional with a reputation for personal qualities of dedication and reliability.

SPECIAL KNOWLEDGE & SKILLS

Through training and experience, have become skilled in repairing, maintaining, and testing aircraft ground support equipment and special use equipment including:

tow tractors: TA-75A, B, and C; JG-40 and 75; TA-35	firefighting unit: P-16
liquid oxygen carts: TMU-27 and TMU-70	oxygen cart: O2
hydraulic units: A/M27T-5, A/M27T-7, and AHT-63	forklifts: 4, 6, 20,000-lb.
mobile electric power plants: NC-8A, NC-2, NC-10 and MMG1A	
gas turbine compressors: GTC-85, NC-PP105, and AM47A-4	

Repair and adjust fuel controls, flow dividers, oil and fuel pumps, generators, motors, relays, voltage regulators, thermostats, and air valves.

Am licensed on the ground support equipment listed above as well as being qualified in the areas of Hydraulic Contamination and Tire and Wheel.

Maintained aircraft including the following:

F-18A	A-6E	EA-6B	C-2	S-3	C-141	C-5	E-2

EXPERIENCE

Built a reputation as a talented technician/mechanic with leadership and supervisory abilities while advancing as a **GROUND SUPPORT EQUIPMENT (GSE) MECHANIC**, United Airlines:

EQUIPMENT CONTROL SPECIALIST and **FIREFIGHTER.** Dulles Airport, DC (2000-present). In addition to regular responsibilities as a supervisor and mechanic, was selected to oversee a support activity in which 2,300 items of equipment for 22 customer units were properly issued, received, and accounted for.

- Developed well-trained personnel who were thoroughly knowledgeable of pre- and post-operational inspection techniques. Direct teams of firefighters in responding to flightline emergencies and airport incidents.
- Implemented a system which made scanning repair/maintenance status boards (VIDS-MAF) easier to read at a glance and streamlined maintenance tracking activities.
- Was singled out for the critical position of work center safety petty officer.
- Applied expert troubleshooting skills which allowed for flightline repairs and eliminated aircraft downtime for repair.

EQUIPMENT REPAIR SPECIALIST. LaGuardia Airport, New York, NY (1999-00). Applied my expertise to perform repairs on gas turbine compressors and preventive maintenance on all categories of ground support equipment.

- On my own initiative, spent 360 hours to create a state-of-the-art training facility which saved $40,000 by eliminating the need for outside labor.

PREVENTIVE MAINTENANCE AND REPAIR SPECIALIST. Atlanta International Airport, Atlanta, GA (1993-98). In addition to repair and maintenance on all classes of ground support equipment, gained experience in operating a 6,000-lb. forklift during a period of functional reorganization and change as activities were closed and the facility deactivated.

- Handpicked as one of two people to participate in a special project, learned the proper techniques for loading a C-2 aircraft and performed maintenance on 30 items of equipment.

PERSONAL

Offer well-developed mechanical and technical skills. Have a strong interest in continuing to grow and develop new abilities related to aviation. Logged 20 flight hours in a C-2.

Date

Exact Name of Person
Title or Position
Name of Company
Address (no., street)
Address (city, state, zip)

Dear Exact Name of Person (or Dear Sir or Madam if answering a blind ad):

I would appreciate an opportunity to talk with you soon about how I could contribute to your organization through my proven expertise in aircraft maintenance, production control, personnel supervision, and project management.

As you will see from my resume, I have gained valuable technical expertise and managerial abilities during my service in the U.S. Army, becoming highly skilled in the operation, repair, and maintenance of CH-47 Chinook, AH-64 Apache, UH-60 Blackhawk, OH-58 Kiowa Scout, and UH-1H Huey helicopters, while also troubleshooting, repairing, and replacing power plants, hydraulics, flight controls, power trains, and general airframe components.

During the War on Terrorism, many lessons were learned about how helicopters function in combat situations. On my own initiative, I designed and recommended several new items of equipment which will enable helicopter crews to fight fires which occur while helicopters are airborne. The equipment I designed is being field tested, and there is a good possibility that the Sikorsky corporation will install the equipment in all helicopters utilized by the U.S. military. Because of my expertise in the area of firefighting, I have been appointed as Sikorsky's Fire Marshal for the plant where I work.

With a reputation as a skilled leader and administrator, I am proficient in training, evaluating, and supervising personnel, scheduling and tracking work orders, and processing forms, documents, and corresponding paperwork. I also gained a reputation as a safety-conscious worker, earning two respected safety awards. I was instrumental in implementing a repair information computer system that significantly increased production and quality assurance level.

You would find me to be a hard-working and reliable professional who prides myself on giving 100% to every job I undertake. I can provide excellent references upon request.

I hope you will call or write me soon to suggest a time convenient for us to meet and discuss your current and future needs and how I might serve them. Thank you in advance for your time.

Sincerely,

Ivan A. Goode

IVAN ALAN GOODE

1110½ Hay Street, Fayetteville, NC 28305　　•　　preppub@aol.com　　•　　(910) 483-6611

OBJECTIVE

To benefit an organization that can use a safety-conscious rotary wing aircraft mechanic who offers hands-on technical experience, production control, and personnel supervision, as well as excellent motivational, planning, and time-management skills.

AIRCRAFT & FIREFIGHTING EXPERTISE

Can repair, troubleshoot, maintain, disassemble, and assemble a wide range of helicopters and other aircraft, including CH-47 Chinooks, UH-60 Blackhawks, OH-58 Kiowa Scouts, AH-64 Apaches, and UH-1H Hueys; am proficient in troubleshooting, repairing, and replacing power trains, power plants, hydraulics, flight controls, and general airframe components on various helicopters.

TRAINING & CERTIFICATIONS

Firefighter Level I & II
Hazardous Materials Level I Responder; Emergency Medical Technician (Defibrillation)

EXPERIENCE

Advanced in the following track record of promotion with Sikorsky Aircraft Corporation, Stratford, CT:
2000-present: HELICOPTER REPAIR SUPERVISOR & FIRE MARSHAL. Refined leadership skills after being rapidly promoted from mechanic to supervising four team leaders in the maintenance and repair of OH-58 Kiowa Scouts, UH-60 Blackhawks, CH-47 Chinooks, UH-1H Hueys, and other helicopters; control a $15 million tool room operation.
- Was appointed the organization's Fire Marshal; train 225 personnel in safety and fire prevention and received two awards for outstanding departmental safety record. Have earned credentials as a Firefighter, and have motivated 20 at the plants to also earn their firefighting credentials.
- Developed new equipment which gives flight crews tools for fighting fires in the air.
- Train, evaluate, and supervise 30 mechanics responsible for a $2 million Aviation Ground Unit MEP 360A. Earned praise for utilizing technical expertise and excellent time-management skills to reduce maintenance and repair time.

1999-00: HELICOPTER REPAIR SUPERVISOR. Polished technical expertise while handling maintenance and repairs for OH-58D's in addition to supervising five mechanics and a ground support equipment inventory worth $4 million.

1997-98: HELICOPTER REPAIR MANAGER. (1997-98). Rapidly promoted after being recognized by top-level management for my outstanding technical and managerial skills; served as team leader, ensuring quality of all OH-58D helicopter repairs and maintenance.
- Trained, supervised, evaluated, and directed six mechanics.
- Recognized by superiors for attention to detail and excellent decision-making.

1994-96: HELICOPTER MECHANIC. Learned the importance of teamwork while performing maintenance and repairs for OH-58A helicopters and preparing aircraft for missions; earned over 100 flying hours as a flight crewmember. Utilized avionic information computer systems, significantly increasing maintenance production output; trained other employees.

EDUCATION

Completed a wide range of technical training and continuing education courses, including leadership, management, safety, and over 1200 hours in helicopter repair.
- Honor Graduate, Helicopter Repair Supervisor Course, 1996.
- Distinguished Graduate, Helicopter Repair Course, 1995.

PERSONAL

Am an enthusiastic, hard-working professional who believes in always giving 100%.

Date

Exact Name of Person
Exact Title
Exact Name of Company
Address
City, State, Zip

Dear Exact Name of Person (or Dear Sir or Madam if answering a blind ad):

With the enclosed resume, I would like to make you aware of my interest in exploring employment opportunities with your organization.

Extensive technical background

As you will see from my resume, I served my country in the U.S. Navy and was promoted to management positions in charge of highly technical operations. I began my Navy service as a Damage Control Specialist, and I was named Junior Sailor of the Quarter. After my promotion to Shop Supervisor and Firefighting Instructor, I saved hundreds of dollars in taxpayer money through designing and fabricating new firefighting equipment which reduced costs and improved firefighting capability. Thanks to my Navy background, I am accustomed to managing multiple simultaneous tasks in environments in which there is "no room for error."

Outstanding communication and sales skills

Because of my outstanding communication skills and leadership ability, I was handpicked for the position as High-Risk Firefighting Training Instructor at the Naval Diving and Salvage Training Center in San Diego, CA. In that position, I trained Navy divers in high-risk firefighting operations, including explosive ordnance operations, and I received the prestigious Navy Achievement Medal in recognition of my technical and managerial accomplishments. I was evaluated in writing as an "inspirational leader" and was credited with rewriting significant portions of course curricula.

Educational accomplishments

Since leaving the Navy, I have worked in numerous part-time jobs while essentially working full-time to earn my Bachelor of Science degree in Safety Management.

I offer a reputation—backed up by solid accomplishments—as a highly resourceful individual who can "think outside the box" and develop cost-effective solutions to stubborn problems. If you can use a versatile top performer to contribute to the success of your organization, I would enjoy an opportunity to talk with you. I can provide outstanding references at the appropriate time.

Yours sincerely,

Keith Clarkson

KEITH CLARKSON

1110½ Hay Street, Fayetteville, NC 28305   •   preppub@aol.com   •   (910) 483-6611

OBJECTIVE
To benefit an organization that can use a versatile professional with expertise related to computer systems administration and business administration along with proven sales abilities and strong communication skills.

EDUCATION
Bachelor of Science in Safety Management, The University of Iowa, Iowa City, IA, 2004. GPA 3.92.
Technical training: Completed training sponsored by the U.S. Navy in these and many other areas:

Firefighting Team Training	Explosive Ordnance Disposal
Naval Explosive Hazards	Chemical Agents; Asbestos
Hazardous Material Control	Antiterrorism Training

CLEARANCE
Held one of the nation's highest clearances: Top Secret clearance for access to Critical Nuclear Weapons Design Information (CNWDI).

EXPERIENCE
FULL-TIME STUDENT. The University of Iowa, Iowa City, IA (2000-04). Have excelled while earning my B.S. in Safety Management.

SHOP SUPERVISOR & FIREFIGHTING INSTRUCTOR. U.S. Navy, Australia (1996-00). Supervised 12 Explosive Ordnance Technicians and firefighters. Received many Letters of Appreciation for technical and managerial accomplishments such as flawless management of $400,000 in firefighting equipment and expert training of military and civilian firefighters.
- Became accustomed to managing multiple simultaneous activities in an environment in which there was "no room for error" because one mistake could cost human lives.

HIGH-RISK FIREFIGHTING TRAINING INSTRUCTOR. U.S. Navy, Naval Diving and Salvage Training Center, San Diego, CA (1991-95). Because of my outstanding communication skills, was handpicked to teach high-risk training to a specialized firefighting division. Received the respected Navy Achievement Medal for accomplishments which included these: reorganizing and upgrading a major supply system; rewriting and implementing new curricula for Explosive Ordnance Disposal and Firefighting courses; developing and fabricating high quality training aids for use with the Firefighting course.
- Was evaluated in writing as a "top performer" and "inspirational leader" and was recognized for "superior leadership and material handling skills." Trained and supervised 60 personnel conducting 300 firefighting operations; planned and supervised dozens of explosive training operations.
- Saved hundreds of thousands of dollars in purchasing costs annually because of my creativity in designing new firefighting aids.

PROFESSIONAL FIREFIGHTER & DAMAGE CONTROL SPECIALIST. U.S. Navy, on board the U.S.S. Fox (1987-89). Selected Junior Sailor of the Quarter. Was commended for distinguished performance as a damage control maintenance man, firefighter, deck department welder, and fire emergency specialist.

PERSONAL
Outstanding references on request. Was the recipient of numerous medals and awards including the prestigious Navy Achievement Medal. Expert marksman. Am known for my resourcefulness and creativity.

Date

Exact Name of Person
Title or Position
Name of Company
Address (no., street)
Address (city, state, zip)

**LEAD FIREFIGHTER
& STATION CHIEF**

Dear Exact Name of Person: (or Dear Sir or Madam if answering a blind ad.)

I would appreciate an opportunity to talk with you soon about how I could contribute to your organization through my extensive experience in fire services.

I offer national certification in the following areas: Fire Officer I, Training Officer I, Inspector I, and Firefighter III. During my years of service I have developed a working knowledge of all military regulations pertaining to the fire protection career field as well as the 40 series which pertains to civilians.

Currently the Lead Firefighter and Station Chief with the 23rd Civil Engineers at Pope AFB, I also am the Training Chief for my reserve unit, the 915th CES. I am licensed as an Electrical Contractor.

I hope you will welcome my call soon to arrange a brief meeting at your convenience to discuss your current and future needs and how I might serve them. Thank you in advance for your time.

Sincerely yours,

Jorge Mercado

Alternate last paragraph:
I hope you will call or write soon to suggest a time convenient for us to meet and discuss your current and future needs and how I might serve them. Thank you in advance for your time.

JORGE MERCADO

1110½ Hay Street, Fayetteville, NC 28305 • preppub@aol.com • (910) 483-6611

OBJECTIVE
To contribute as a Fire Chief based on my experience in the fire service field, reputation as a leader, and knowledge of firefighting policies and procedure.

CERTIFICATIONS
Offer national certification as a **Fire Officer I**, **Training Officer I**, **Inspector I**, and **Firefighter III**. Certified by the State of NC as a **CPR Instructor** and **Self Aid and Buddy Care Instructor**. Hold an **Electrical Contractor's License** issued by the State of NC.

EXPERIENCE
LEAD FIREFIGHTER and **STATION CHIEF**. U.S. Government, 23rd Civil Engineers, Pope AFB, NC (1995-present). Provide leadership to a team of four firefighters while remaining aware at all times of military aircraft landing zones, and physical configurations of planes and their personnel so that my crews can be used most effectively.
- Controlled the activities of firefighting equipment, vehicles, and personnel.
- Directed crew response so they can be used to attack the fire rapidly and thoroughly.
- Contributed to the success of the Pope Emergency Response Team and directed the Hazardous Materials Team when the leader was unavailable.
- Schedule training and conduct classes for structural and crash drills in accordance with Air Force Reg. 92-1 and 93-3.
- Presented classes which prepared personnel to deal with any type of emergency.

Contributed professionalism and expertise to the 317th Civil Engineers, Pope AFB, NC.
1990-95: FIRE STATION CAPTAIN. Received a certificate and letter of appreciation for my contributions when called to active duty during the war in the Middle East.
- Directed 20 military firefighters and oversaw the operation of vehicles and equipment when responding to fire emergencies on the base.

1985-90: FIRE INSPECTOR. Inspected new construction for compliance with fire safety regulations, made recommendations on substandard findings, checked fixed fire suppression systems, and inspected potentially hazardous areas.
- Tested and performed minor maintenance on fixed systems.
- Learned fire codes and how they had to be integrated into buildings during construction.
- Became familiar with the physical layouts and locations of facilities by inspecting every building on base regularly.

1983-85: FIREFIGHTER and **DRIVER**. Gained knowledge of each of the P-series vehicles and their unique operating capabilities while driving and operating each.
- Became skilled in using manually operated and power extraction tools, emergency generators, axes, pike poles, ladders, winches, nozzles, and all other related tools.

EDUCATION
Completed **Associate's degree in Fire Science**, Central Texas College, Pope AFB, NC, 2003.

EQUIPMENT EXPERTISE
Offer experience with fire department equipment, vehicles, and communications systems including the following:
Fire equipment: Jaws of Life, Porta-Power, skin penetrator, and SCBA
Vehicles: all P-series vehicles -- 2, 4, 8, 10, 12, 18, 19, 20, 22, and 26
Communications systems: shortwave radio and two-way radio
Electrical equipment: multimeters, ohmmeters, voltage testers, and drills
Computers: FAMS system and Windows
Other equipment: gas detectors, heat gun, and safety winch for confined spaces

Date

Exact Name of Person
Exact Title
Exact Name of Company
Address
City, State, Zip

Dear Exact Name of Person (or Dear Sir or Madam if answering a blind ad):

    With this letter and the enclosed resume, I would like to express my interest in receiving consideration for employment opportunities within your organization. I am interested in discussing your need for an experienced Firefighting Supervisor. Although I am held in the highest regard in my current position, I am relocating with my wife to your area, and I am exploring opportunities with regional airports.

    In my current position as a Loadmaster and Firefighting Director for the Dayton Airport, I provide strong leadership for staffing, training, and planning with the goal of ensuring safety for passengers and cargo. In the aftermath of the terrorist attack of September 11, 2001, I played a key role in initiating numerous policies and procedures which have improved security and passenger safety, especially in the area of firefighting and fire prevention.

    I am proud of my reputation as a professional who is dedicated to safety and total quality management objectives. I have been selected for ever-increasing levels of managerial responsibilities because of my special skills related to managing resources for maximum productivity as well as my ability to develop and implement training designed to produce the most highly skilled firefighters. You will notice from my resume that I worked for one year as Firefighting Instructor at the National Firefighting School in Dallas.

    Through my experience and training, I have become widely recognized as a technical expert who sets high personal standards while leading others to maximum application of their own skills.

    If you can use a versatile and detail-oriented professional with special knowledge of aircraft support and airport firefighting operations, I hope you will call me soon for a brief discussion of how I could contribute to your organization.

    Sincerely,

Albert Finch

ALBERT FINCH

1110½ Hay Street, Fayetteville, NC 28305　　•　　preppub@aol.com　　•　　(910) 483-6611

OBJECTIVE　　To contribute through a track record of exceptional performance as a results-oriented resource manager who excels in ensuring proper aircraft loading operations while overseeing airport firefighting activities.

EDUCATION　　**Associate's degree in Aircrew Operations & Safety Management**, Community College of Chicago, Chicago, IL, 1999.
Excelled in extensive training which emphasized aircraft load-planning and inspection procedures, leadership, and instructional techniques; completed Volunteer Firefighter Course.

AREAS OF EXPERTISE　　*Clearance:* entrusted with a **Top Secret** security clearance.
Computers: working knowledge of Microsoft Windows, Word, and Excel.
Flight hours: logged in excess of 6,300 hours as an aircrew professional and am certified as an Instructor Loadmaster for the C-130 Hercules aircraft.

FIREFIGHTING CERTIFICATIONS　　**Certified Firefighter;** completed Fire Department Orientation/Safety I & II
Skilled in operating and utilizing equipment including the following:

Portable Extinguishers	Fire Hose, Appl. And Streams	Ladders I & II
Emergency Medical Care	Salvage — Level I & II	Fire Prevention
Sprinklers	Rescue — Level I & II	Fire Alarms
Fire Control	Hazardous Materials	Structural Burn
Ropes	Building Construction I & II	Fire Behavior
Safety	Forcible Entry I & II	Water Supplies
Wildland Fire Suppression	Incident Command Systems	

EXPERIENCE　　**LOADMASTER & FIREFIGHTING DIRECTOR.** Dayton Airport, Dayton, OH (2002-present). Am excelling in a position with three major areas of emphasis: acting as point of contact to ensure flights are adequately staffed with qualified personnel; ensuring the up-to-date training status of 28 people; and directing a team of firefighters in constant readiness to respond to emergencies.

FIREFIGHTING INSTRUCTOR. National Firefighting School, Dallas, TX (2000-01). Recognized as an expert on technical issues, taught classes on firefighting.

LOADING SUPERVISOR. Midway Airport, Chicago, IL (1999-00). Earned praise for my "meticulous attention to detail" while supervising and training several seven-person crews on loading, such as performing weight-and-balance computations, load planning, and inspections.

Highlights of military experience as a Loadmaster:
SUPERVISORY AIRCRAFT LOADMASTER. U.S. Air Force, Kadena AB, Japan (1995-99). Advanced to assist senior supervisors and personally oversee management and scheduling of up to 12 people; ensured quality control and conducted safety inspections of heavy equipment platforms and container delivery system bundles.
- Singled out to handle details of numerous multinational exercises and operations, provided support for such groups as Navy SEALS and Australian Special Air Services.

PERSONAL　　Volunteered as a firefighter and worked with the Big Brothers Program and Special Olympics. Earned honors including five Air Force Commendation Medals and two AF Achievement Medals. Excellent references on request.

Date

Exact Name of Person
Exact Title
Exact Name of Company
Address
City, State, Zip

Dear Exact Name of Person (or Dear Sir or Madam if answering a blind ad):

With the enclosed resume, I would like to make you aware of my expertise in designing firefighting enhancements for civilian and military aircraft.

As you will see from my resume, I have held supervisory roles in support of aviation firefighting operations throughout the world. In my current position with Raytheon, I managed a $9 million budget and supervised 32 people. Regarded as the company's subject matter expert on firefighting issues, I have been credited with improving firefighting capability onboard aircraft and have increased the number of firefighters and pilots involved in aircraft testing. I am particularly proud of the fact that, during the War on Terrorism, we made significant enhancements to aircraft used in combat environments that created a safer flying environment for our men and women in uniform.

In my previous position as an Inventory Control Manager with Boeing Aircraft, I handled planning for the transition to the newly designed facilities and reorganization of all supply operations and space. As the resident expert on aviation firefighting management, I controlled receiving, storing, issuing, and auditing of a $50 million inventory of specialized firefighting equipment.

With excellent time management, planning, and organizational skills, I have recently completed degree requirements for a B.S. in Aviation Management. I am familiar with automated data processing systems used to maintain documents and records of operations from the procurement and requisitioning stages on through all aspects of storage, issuing, and control. I offer a strong base of experience in providing firefighting support for both fixed- and rotary-wing aircraft which include C-130, P-3, F-14, FA-18, A-7, and S-3.

I hope you will call or write me soon to suggest a time convenient for us to meet and discuss your current and future needs and how I might serve them. Thank you in advance for your time.

Sincerely,

Allen E. Dumas

ALLEN E. DUMAS

1110½ Hay Street, Fayetteville, NC 28305   •   preppub@aol.com   •   (910) 483-6611

OBJECTIVE

To offer a distinguished background of accomplishments and extensive knowledge and experience related to inventory control management and firefighting to an organization that can benefit from my effectiveness in maximizing human, fiscal, and material resources.

EDUCATION & TRAINING

B.S. in **Aviation Management,** Rivier College, Spokane, WA, 2002.
Extensive training with an emphasis on aviation supply and maintenance material management, leadership development, program management, and financial operations. Completed approximately 1,200 hours of continuing education credit hours which led to **National Fire Protection Association Firefighter Professional Qualifications for Firefighter I and II.** Became knowledgeable of the following:

foam fire streams	ventilation	safety
portable extinguishers	fire control	rescue
emergency medical care	water supplies	ladders
CPR instructor training	forcible entry	salvage
fire department organization	fire behavior	streams
fire alarms and communication devices		

EXPERIENCE

MATERIAL CONTROL SUPERVISOR & FIREFIGHTING PRODUCT CHIEF. Raytheon Corporation, Spokane, WA (2000-present). Officially evaluated as the "consummate professional" and "most trusted advisor on all firefighting related issues," managed a $9 million budget while being credited with implementing improvements which improved aircraft firefighting capability and increased the number of firefighters and pilots in the testing program.
• Supervised 32 firefighters in a special testing operation which led to significant enhancements in firefighting capability onboard aircraft.
• Earned respect for my "positive and approachable demeanor."

INVENTORY CONTROL MANAGER. Boeing Aircraft, Seattle, WA (1998-00). Recognized as the company's firefighting materials management expert, supervised the receipt, storage, issue, location auditing, and inventory of material valued in excess of $50 million and which was located in ten separate warehouses.
• Provided support for a complex overhaul project in material management.

SUPPLY OPERATIONS SUPERVISOR. U.S. Navy, Naval Station, England (1990-97). Earned respect for my "astute management" while providing support for day-to-day operations and a wide range of special missions which received exceptional aircraft and administrative material support for a fleet air reconnaissance unit.
• Provided perfect accountability while issuing, controlling, and providing replenishment for a $4.5 million Weapons Replaceable Assembly pack up for a project in Crete.

Highlights of earlier U.S. Navy experience: Advanced in rank while building a reputation as a knowledgeable firefighter, aviation supply manager, and fiscal operations professional.

FIREFIGHTING DESIGN SKILLS

Experienced in designing firefighting support for C-130, P-3, F-14, FA-18, A-7, and S-3.

CLEARANCE

Top Secret security clearance with SBI

PERSONAL

Received several Joint Service and Navy/Marine Corps Achievement Medals in recognition of my accomplishments and expertise. Effective in dealing with culturally diverse teams.

CAREER CHANGE

Date

Exact Name of Person
Title or Position
Exact Name of Company
Address (no., street)
City, state, zip

Dear Exact Name of Person (or Dear Sir or Madam if answering a blind ad.):

With the enclosed resume, I would like to make you aware of my interest in exploring employment opportunities with your organization.

As you will see from my resume, I have served my country with distinction while gaining expert skills related to firefighting and the nuclear, biological, and chemical areas. In my most recent position, I designed and implemented a new firefighting training program which has assured the competence of every employee in utilizing basic firefighting equipment and practicing sensible safety habits. On numerous occasions, I have directed teams of professionals in responding to chemical spills and chemical fires, and I have learned that advanced training is critical to firefighting success.

While advancing in a track record of promotion ahead of my peers, I had many opportunities to utilize my safety knowledge and firefighting skills worldwide. Although I was strongly encouraged to remain in military service and assured of continued rapid advancement, I decided to leave the military and join an organization which needs experts in the safety and firefighting fields.

I hope you will welcome my call soon to arrange a brief meeting at your convenience to discuss your current and future needs and how I might serve them. Thank you in advance for your time.

Sincerely yours,

Harry Fontain

Alternate last paragraph:
I hope you will call or write me to suggest a time convenient for us to meet and discuss your current and future needs and how I might serve them. Thank you in advance for your time.

HARRY FONTAIN

1110½ Hay Street, Fayetteville, NC 28305 • preppub@aol.com • (910) 483-6611

OBJECTIVE   To benefit an organization that can use a versatile professional who offers proven skills related to managing resources, motivating personnel, and coordinating activities as well as the ability to solve tough problems in the environmental and firefighting fields.

EDUCATION   Completed courses in **English and Business Management**, Central Virginia Community College, Lynchburg, VA.

SECURITY TRAINING   Excelled in demanding college-level U.S. Army training courses related to:

Nuclear, Biological, & Chemical Warfare		Personnel Management
Stress Management	Communication	Strategic Planning
Employee Training	Security	First Aid
Reconnaissance	Surveillance	Counterterrorism

TECHNICAL SKILLS
- Operate automatic weapons, handguns, and shotguns; am familiar with foreign as well as U.S.-made weapons.
- Earned a **Leadership Award**, Noncommissioned Officer Development Course.
- Completed amphibious warfare and commercial vehicle operation courses.
- Operate radios; am knowledgeable of industrial security measures.

EXPERIENCE   **NBC OPERATIONS MANAGER** and **FIREFIGHTER**. U.S. Army, Fort Myer, VA (2004-present). Was handpicked to use my specialized knowledge of nuclear, biological, and chemical (NBC) operations to develop "from scratch" and manage a comprehensive NBC program for a newly formed 400-person operation.
- Designed and implemented a firefighting training program; earned a respected medal for my dedication and technical knowledge.
- Assessed organizational needs and obtained equipment valued at $1 million; created a maintenance program. Described as "setting the standard for others to emulate," have earned a reputation as a gifted instructor and counselor.

NBC OPERATIONS MANAGER. U.S. Army, Fort Drum, NY (2003-04). Was praised in writing for my ability to "communicate expert knowledge in a clear, concise, and enthusiastic manner" while directing four managers involved in overseeing activities for 450-person organization.
- Innovatively redesigned facilities to create an NBC center described as "uniquely practical and well organized."
- Developed a training program that raised personnel scores on knowledge test to 96%--the highest in the parent organization.
- Earned a distinguished award while leading activities in the politically sensitive demilitarized zone.

FIRST-LINE SUPERVISOR. U.S. Army, Fort Myer, VA (1999-02). Regarded as a charismatic leader, earned unusually rapid promotion to middle management roles; supervised up to 30 people while managing day-to-day and training operations.
- Was formally commended five times for my "unequalled" technical knowledge and willingness to "go the extra mile." Was praised for my "determination to succeed" in stressful situations during a major international mission.

PERSONAL   Am ambitious "self starter," take initiative whenever possible. Regarded as a "born motivator," excel in leading others to strive for and achieve high goals. Relate well to people.

Date

Exact Name of Person
Title or Position
Exact Name of Company
Address (no., street)
City, state, zip

**NUCLEAR
RESEARCHER
& FIREFIGHTING
TECHNICIAN**

This individual is
seeking an internal
promotion.

Dear Exact Name of Person (or Dear Sir or Madam if answering a blind ad.):

With the enclosed resume, I would like to make you aware of my interest in the position as Product Development Assistant which was recently advertised on the NIEHS website.

In my current position at the National Institute of Environmental Health Sciences, I have excelled in activities related to product design and have played a key role in the design of new fire resistant clothing which will be used by the next generation of firefighters. Known for excellent communication skills, I have performed extensive liaison with organizations including the Bureau of Indian Affairs, U.S. Fish and Wildlife Service, National Park Service, USDA Forest Service, and the National Association of Foresters to determine the latest thinking with regard to the need for updated and improved firefighting equipment and clothing. Because of the role I have played in product innovation within NIEHS, I was asked to present a paper at the 2004 international conference.

I feel that I am now ready for my challenge in the area of product development, and I respectfully request that I be considered for the position of Product Development Assistant on the highly respected NIEH team.

I hope you will welcome my call soon to arrange a brief meeting at your convenience to discuss your current and future needs and how I might serve them. Thank you in advance for your time.

Sincerely yours,

Vincent Haye

Alternate last paragraph:
I hope you will call or write me to suggest a time convenient for us to meet and discuss your current and future needs and how I might serve them. Thank you in advance for your time.

VINCENT HAYE

1110½ Hay Street, Fayetteville, NC 28305 • preppub@aol.com • (910) 483-6611

OBJECTIVE

I am seeking to benefit an organization that can use a creative and dedicated professional who offers excellent skills related to product design and firefighting support.

EDUCATION

Bachelor of Science degree in Physics with Minors in Nuclear Science and Math, Savannah State University, Savannah, GA, 2004.
- Presented a student paper at the Southeastern Section of the National Physical Society Conference on Fingertip Dosimeters and why they are used.
- Made the Dean's list for the spring semester of 2002.
- Earned 90% of my educational expenses.

Associate's Degree in General Education, Savannah State University, Savannah, GA, 1992. Graduated with honors.

EXPERIENCE

NUCLEAR RESEARCHER & FIREFIGHTING TECHNICIAN. National Institute of Environmental Health Sciences, Savannah, GA (2004-present). At this leading independent research laboratory, am involved in testing the current generation of firefighting equipment in order to assess their capabilities in the event of nuclear events and other disasters.
- Played a key role in the design of new fire resistant clothing which will be used by the next generation of firefighters.
- Performed extensive liaison with organizations including the Bureau of Indian Affairs, U.S. Fish and Wildlife Service, National Park Service, USDA Forest Service, and the National Association of Foresters to determine the latest thinking with regard to the need for updated firefighting equipment and clothing.
- On my own initiative, experimented in my spare time with fire-retardant material which could be used for aircraft passengers. This has the potential of dramatically protecting aircraft passengers in the event of fires.
- Presented a paper on new trends in firefighting clothing and equipment which was enthusiastically received at the international convention of the NIEHS, held in Sydney, Australia, in 2004.

PHYSICS LAB INSTRUCTOR. Savannah State University, Savannah, GA (2003-04). Taught three sections of introductory calculus-based physics laboratories.

SUMMER STUDENT INTERN. Keller Plant, Co., Columbus, GA (2003). Worked in the RF Power section of the Accelerator Division where I assisted in verifying proper installation of waveguides for cryostat modules. Built prototype of a device to present the appearance of a short or load to the klystrons to facilitate low power testing of the klystrons.

FIELD ENGINEER. Raymond Corporation, Charleston, SC (2000-02). Was assigned to a contract with Charleston Shipbuilding and Drydock Company; worked with a group that was tasked with verifying compliance to overhaul specifications of nuclear submarine shipboard systems.

NUCLEAR TRAINED MACHINIST MATE. U.S. Navy, Norfolk, VA (1992-00). Served on the U.S.S. George Washington and achieved the rank of First Class Petty Officer. Was responsible for maintenance and operation of the mechanical systems of the nuclear power plant. Collateral duties included Repair Parts Petty Officer, Diesel Petty Officer, Education Petty Officer, and QA Inspector.

PERSONAL

Outstanding references on request.

CAREER CHANGE

Date

Exact Name of Person
Exact Title
Exact Name of Company
Address
City, State, Zip

PARAMEDIC
&
FIREFIGHTER
Here you see
the resume and
cover letter of a
military
professional who
hopes to
become a
civilian
firefighter.

Dear Exact Name of Person (or Dear Sir or Madam if answering a blind ad):

I would like to take this opportunity to make you aware of the skills, experience, and knowledge I have gained while proudly serving my country in the U.S. Army in Special Forces and Ranger units where I contributed to the success of missions vital to national security.

As you will see from my enclosed resume, I have been serving with distinction as a Special Forces Medical Sergeant and Firefighter based out of Iraq and Bosnia for the past four years. I was selected for extensive training which led to certification in firefighting.

Currently focusing on training both American and allied forces personnel in medical and firefighting subjects, I am known for my ability to pass that knowledge on to others in an effective manner. One of my greatest accomplishments has been as part of a team which gave me the ability to reduce firefighting hazards in combat.

With the proven ability to work under intense pressure and deadlines, I am combat tested and was a member of a Ranger battalion which received the Valorous Unit Award for "gallantry in action" during Operation Desert Shield. I earned prestigious awards such as the National Defense Service Medal and the Expert Infantryman's Badge for my contributions during a period of intense urban combat against a "well armed and numerically superior enemy" in a battle considered to be among the ten most important in American military history.

If you can use a versatile and adaptable professional with well-developed leadership abilities, I hope you will call or write me soon to suggest a time when we might have a brief discussion of how I could contribute to your organization. I can provide excellent professional and personal references at the appropriate time.

Sincerely,

Kevin Y. Garcia

KEVIN Y. GARCIA

1110½ Hay Street, Fayetteville, NC 28305   •   preppub@aol.com   •   (910) 483-6611

OBJECTIVE

To offer a track record of accomplishments, honors, and experience to an organization that can benefit from my thorough knowledge of firefighting and security issues.

EDUCATION & TRAINING

College: Completed 18 semester hours of General Studies, University of South Carolina, Columbia, SC; was named to the **Chancellor's Honor List** in recognition of perfect 4.0 GPA.

Highlights of military training: Consistently placed at the top of each course and was named an **Honor Graduate** of nearly every military training program attended, which included the following:

- **Special Forces** Medical Skills Sustainment, Malaria Prevention and Control for Field Operations in Bosnia, Combat Tracking, Diver Medic Training and Emergency Medical Procedures, Special Forces Firefighting Courses, 2001
- **Individual Terrorism Awareness** Courses, 2000
- **Special Forces** Medical Sergeant Course Phase II, 2000, and Phase I, 1999
- **Special Forces** Assessment and Selection and Land Navigation, Ranger Team Leader, and Infantry Basic Refresher Training and Specialist Skills Courses, 1999
- **Assault Climbing,** Jungle Warfare, Toxic Agent Training, Jumpmaster Courses, 1998
- **Operator/Unit Level Maintenance** on the Improved Remotely Monitored Battlefield Sensor System (I-REMBASS), M1030 Military Motorcycle, Primary Leadership Development Course (PLDC), Advanced Firearms Tactics (U.S. Department of Treasury), and Pathfinder Courses, 1997
- **Ranger School**, Scout Swimmer, Pre-Ranger, Airborne, and Infantry Training, 1996

LICENSES & CERTIFICATIONS

National Registry of Emergency Medical Technicians Certification as an EMT and Paramedic, 2003

Paramedic License; Open Water Diver; Firefighter I and II; Advanced Cardiac Life Support

EXPERIENCE

Consistently singled out for recognition for my initiative and dedication as well as for my skills in training and mentoring others, U.S. Army Special Forces.

MEDICAL TECHNICIAN & FIREFIGHTER. Iraq (2002-present). Am building a reputation as a knowledgeable, proficient, and dedicated leader and model of professionalism while planning and carrying out firefighting training for military organizations throughout Iraq.

- Received a Certificate of Achievement for my efforts during a firefighting training initiative. Played a vital role in the development of a 90-day program of instruction which received praise from senior firefighters.

SPECIAL FORCES FIREFIGHTER. U.S. Army, Camp Tattum, 2-16th Ranger Battalion, Sarajevo, Bosnia (2000-02). Recruited to give the medical and firefighting support for a Ranger Battalion with its no-notice worldwide response mission.

- Received an Army Commendation Medal for my efforts in saving thousands of dollars by using internal resources for a live-fire complex construction project.

TEAM LEADER. U.S. Army, Delta Company, 4-23rd Infantry Division, Fort Hood, TX (1996-2000). Supervised, trained, and counseled members of a firefighting team charged with responding worldwide within 18 hours.

PERSONAL

Current military and civilian passports. All vaccinations up-to-date. Am extremely flexible, prepared to relocate globally, and fully capable of frequent or long-term travel. Have traveled to 15 countries. Am considered an expert in mountaineering and rock climbing.

Date

Exact Name of Person
Exact Title
Exact Name of Company
Address
City, State, Zip

Dear Exact Name of Person: (or Dear Sir or Madam if answering a blind ad)

With the enclosed resume, I would like to make you aware of my extensive background related to training management with particular emphasis on firefighting subjects. Although I have earned two masters degrees in Safety Management and Management, I discovered my appreciation of the firefighting field when I earned my Associate's degree in Firefighting Technology.

Presently excelling in a job which requires strong teaching, research, and writing skills, I provide academic and performance counseling for students in a firefighting course. In addition to instructing and counseling students, I write and revise lesson plans, update materials and equipment, and recruit subject matter experts to help develop and instruct sections of the course. Prior to this assignment, I worked in medical centers as a Medical Aide, which required extensive public contact as well as excellent communication skills, tact, and patience.

I have consistently been cited for my ability and willingness to give my time to mentor, train, and instruct others and for my effectiveness in working with people from varied backgrounds. I am fluent in Spanish. A member of the Society of Safety Managers, I am a versatile and highly self-motivated individual known for my ability to adapt to challenges, stress, and deadlines.

If you can use an articulate and self-motivated leader with experience related to human resources management as well as training program development and management, please contact me soon to suggest a time when we might have a brief discussion of how I could contribute to your organization. I will provide excellent professional and personal references at the appropriate time.

Sincerely,

Neville L. Montrose

NEVILLE L. MONTROSE

1110½ Hay Street, Fayetteville, NC 28305 • preppub@aol.com • (910) 483-6611

OBJECTIVE

To offer a broad base of experience in employee training, development, and instruction to an organization that can use a versatile professional with expertise related to firefighting.

AFFILIATION

Member of the **Society of Safety Managers.**

EDUCATION

M.A., Safety Management, California State University, Los Angeles, CA, 2003; 3.65 GPA.

M.A., Management, California State University, Los Angeles, CA, 2002; 3.65 GPA.

- *Thesis:* Evaluated the human resource program of Northern Arizona University; focused research on cost effectiveness of the program and how well it prepared students for "the real world".

Associate of Science in Firefighting Technology, Northern Arizona University, Flagstaff, AZ, 1994; 3.6 GPA.

SPECIAL SKILLS

Computers: Familiar with Microsoft Office Suite.

Languages: Speak, read, write, and understand Spanish.

Security clearance: Top Secret security clearance.

Medical: National Registry Emergency Medical Technicians, EMT Basic and Paramedic. Licensed in pediatric, advanced cardiac, advanced trauma life support, and EMT.

- Current EMT-B, EMT-P, BCLS, ACLS, PALS, and PHTLS; trained in ATLS.

Firefighting: Firefighting I and II Certified.

EXPERIENCE

FIREFIGHTING INSTRUCTOR & WRITER. Los Angeles Firefighting Training Center, Los Angeles, CA (2002-present). Provide a wide range of academic counseling and instruction along with technical consulting and support related to research, organization, and writing materials for a course for firefighting professionals.

- Act as **Primary Instructor** for subjects which include operation of firefighting equipment and firefighting techniques.
- Receive praise from students, peers, and subordinates for superior teaching skills as well as for my leadership style.

MEDICAL AIDE. Bayside Medical Offices, La Jolla, CA (2000-01). Working with four physicians, controlled inventories of supplies in order to provide treatment and care to patients; refined instructional and human resources management skills while working with nurses and dealing with patients in this busy medical setting. Assisted with treatment, and frequently was praised by patients for my skill and tact while treating them.

- Supported nurses by voluntarily taking over some of their duties when we were understaffed or very busy.
- Acted as a mentor for new personnel to train them on office requirements.
- Became adept at quickly establishing and setting up medical care facilities and controlling inventories of equipment and supplies in order to provide proper treatment.

MEDICAL AIDE. Beale Medical Center, Memphis, TN (1994-99). Gained and refined skills in providing routine and emergency medical treatment, assisting with nursing care, and maintaining medical records and files.

Highlights of earlier experience: Worked as an EMT for an ambulance company in Arizona.

PERSONAL

Excellent references on request.

Date

Exact Name of Person
Title or Position
Exact Name of Company
Address (no., street)
City, state, zip

Dear Exact Name of Person (or Dear Sir or Madam if answering a blind ad.):

With the enclosed resume, I would like to make you aware of my interest in exploring employment opportunities with your organization.

In my current position with Hewlett Packard as Supervisor of Quality Control Inspection and Firefighting Team Chief, I am responsible for a staff of 12-15 inspectors of P.C. board production, high quality electronic pads, and subassemblies to ensure quality standards are utilized. In response to the company's new emphasis on quality assurance in all areas, I have trained and now direct a team of firefighters who respond to firefighting problems and emergencies within all corporate plants.

Although I am held in high regard in my current position and can provide outstanding references at the appropriate time, I am selectively exploring opportunities with progressive major corporations that are committed to the highest level of quality and safety standards.

I hope you will welcome my call soon to arrange a brief meeting at your convenience to discuss your current and future needs and how I might serve them. Thank you in advance for your time.

Sincerely yours,

Kathryn Wright

Alternate last paragraph:
I hope you will call or write me to suggest a time convenient for us to meet and discuss your current and future needs and how I might serve them. Thank you in advance for your time.

KATHRYN WRIGHT

1110½ Hay Street, Fayetteville, NC 28305 • preppub@aol.com • (910) 483-6611

OBJECTIVE
To secure a position in quality inspection in order to utilize my knowledge of Total Quality Management (TQM) concepts and industrial firefighting techniques.

EXPERIENCE
Have excelled in the following track record of promotion with Hewlett-Packard Company, Orono, ME (1998-present).
2001-present: QUALITY CONTROL INSPECTOR & FIREFIGHTING TEAM CHIEF.
Responsible for a staff of 12-15 inspectors of P.C. board production, high quality electronic pads, and subassemblies to ensure quality standards are utilized.
- Trained support staff on inspection methodology and philosophy ensuring proper knowledge of blueprint reading in evaluating P.C. board quality.
- Trained and now direct a team of firefighters who respond to firefighting problems and emergencies within all corporate plants.

1998-01: INSPECTOR. Inspected incoming, first piece, in-process, personal computer boards, cables, chassis, harnessing, electronic assemblies, sub-assemblies, and systems.

Highlights of previous experience:
CHASSIS ASSEMBLER. Department of Defense, locations worldwide (1994-98). Responsible for mechanical assembly, soldering, wiring, wire wrapping, welding of electrical mechanical assemblies, quality control inspection (four years) government specifications on assemblies for radar for the U.S. Army and Navy.

INSPECTOR. YPR Corporation, Orono, ME (1989-94). Inspected electronic and time fuses and fuse-assembly devices for explosives. Inspected and adjusted electrical and mechanical switches.

EDUCATION
Earned a **Bachelor of Science degree in Industrial Safety,** University of Bridgeton, Bridgeton, ME, 1993. Completed this degree in my spare time while excelling in my full-time job.
Graduated from Bridgeton High School, Bridgeton, ME, 1989.

TRAINING & CERTIFICATIONS
Firefighter Level I & II
Hazardous Materials Level I Responder
Wildland Fire Suppression
Emergency Medical Technician (Defibrillation)-BLS
Emergency Vehicle Driving Certification
Driver/Operator Pumps: Trained as a Driver/Operator Aerials

EDUCATION
Completed the three-month Fire Academy, Orono Community College, and the three-month Emergency Medical Technician (Defibrillation) Course.
Training has included:
Driver/Operator (Aerials)
Driver/Operator (Pumps)
Hazardous Material Responder Level I
Incident Command (NFPA)
Flameout (Northwest Fire/Rescue College)

EQUIPMENT SKILLS
Use Firehouse software
Experienced in using personal protective equipment as well as portable extinguishers, ladders, hoses, and ropes. Experienced in operating heavy equipment including emergency vehicles.

Date

Exact Name of Person
Title or Position
Exact Name of Company
Address (no., street)
City, state, zip

SAFETY COORDINATOR

Dear Exact Name of Person (or Dear Sir or Madam if answering a blind ad.):

With the enclosed resume, I would like to make you aware of my interest in exploring employment opportunities with your organization.

In my current position as Safety Coordinator for Continental Airlines, I have made significant contributions to passenger safety and airport safety. In my spare time, I have aggressively sought out opportunities for further training in the safety area, and I have earned numerous firefighting certifications, including the Certified Airport Firefighter designation.

I hope you will welcome my call soon to arrange a brief meeting at your convenience to discuss your current and future needs and how I might serve them. Thank you in advance for your time.

Sincerely yours,

Noel T. McLaughlin

Alternate last paragraph:
I hope you will call or write me to suggest a time convenient for us to meet and discuss your current and future needs and how I might serve them. Thank you in advance for your time.

NOEL T. McLAUGHLIN

1110½ Hay Street, Fayetteville, NC 28305   •   preppub@aol.com   •   (910) 483-6611

OBJECTIVE

To contribute to an organization that can use an outstanding problem solver who offers extensive experience in troubleshooting and resolving quality assurance and safety issues in aviation environments, including airports.

EXPERIENCE

SAFETY COORDINATOR. Continental Airlines, Fond Du Lac, WI (2000-present). Meet monthly with the general manager of Continental Airlines to discuss areas needing improvement.

- Maintain cordial relationships with airport managers at major airports all over the world. Participate in annual conferences to discuss counterterrorism issues and firefighting problems.
- Report to the general manager of Continental Airlines on areas of potential hazard, especially fire hazards.
- Develop training programs for employees in all areas of safety including firefighting, and ensure proper maintenance of fire extinguishers.
- Through the use of the SABRE Systems access flight times and load weights.
- Maintain safe landing and take-off sights for aircraft approaching and leaving the ramp.
- Continuously refine the safety environment of Continental Airlines; safety and hazard changes are made upon my recommendations.

DATA ANALYST. National Aeronautics and Space Administration (NASA), Pensacola, FL (1996-99). Contributed to the development and refinement of the NASA office of the NASA Office of Space Flight, Human Resources Database Systems.

- Graphed and documented data for directors of the Office of Space Flight, Human Resources Division, based on raw data collected through survey.
- Performed minority and organizational health studies and converted into graphs.

TRAINING

Graduated from the following institutions and courses:
National Fire Academy (numerous courses)
First Responder Course
Hazardous Material Technician Course
Hazardous Materials Operations Course
Hazardous Material Awareness Course
Environmental Medicine Specialist Course
Munitions and Hazardous Materials Firefighting
Fire Protection Specialist Course

CERTIFICATIONS

Certified Airport Firefighter, International Fire Service Accreditation Congress
Certified Firefighter II, International Fire Service Accreditation Congress

EDUCATION & COMPUTER KNOWLEDGE

B.S. degree in Computer Science, Moraine Park Technical College, Fond Du Lac, WI, 2004.

Microsoft	Novell Network Administration
Web Server Administration	Programming with Java
Web Publishing Management	Web Programming
PC Hardware Repair and Installation	Principles of Networking

PERSONAL

Enjoy traveling, swimming, bowling, and reading.

REFERENCES

Outstanding references available upon request.

Date

Exact Name of Person
Title or Position
Name of Company
Address
City, state, zip

**SENIOR
FIREFIGHTING
INSTRUCTOR**

Dear Exact Name of Person (or Dear Sir or Madam if answering a blind ad.):

I would appreciate an opportunity to talk with you about how I could benefit your organization through my expert knowledge of firefighting techniques as well as nuclear, biological, and chemical (NBC) operations along with my proven skills in training, motivating, and managing others.

While earning rapid promotion to middle management roles in the U.S. Army, I became known for my unparalleled technical "know-how" and my ability to turn teams of workers into "top performers." Most recently I was chosen to "teach the teachers" who train Army personnel in firefighting and NBC operations, and I trained thousands of personnel in firefighting skills before they deployed to the Middle East to participate in the War on Terrorism. In previous jobs, I managed firefighting teams and NBC operations which were ranked as the "best of their kind," and I was chosen for administrative positions usually held by senior managers.

With an in-depth knowledge of firefighting equipment, I can operate and troubleshoot state-of-the-art equipment. Entrusted with a Secret security clearance, I am known for my reliability and "can-do" attitude.

You would find me to be a creative and enthusiastic professional who thrives on meeting new challenges.

I hope you will welcome my call soon to arrange a brief meeting at your convenience to discuss your current and future needs and how I might serve them. Thank you in advance for your time.

Sincerely yours,

Kevin Winther

Alternate last paragraph:
I hope you will call or write me soon to suggest a time convenient for us to meet and discuss your current and future needs and how I might serve them. Thank you in advance for your time.

KEVIN WINTHER

1110½ Hay Street, Fayetteville, NC 28305   •   preppub@aol.com   •   (910) 483-6611

OBJECTIVE	To benefit an organization that can use an energetic professional who offers expert skills in nuclear, biological, and chemical (NBC) operations and firefighting along with the proven ability to train, motivate, and supervise others.
EDUCATION	Completed courses in **Psychology and Police Science**, University of Southwestern Louisiana, Lafayette, LA.
	Excelled in U.S. Army training courses related to NBC operations and personnel management.
EXPERIENCE	**SENIOR FIREFIGHTING INSTRUCTOR**. U.S. Army, Fort Polk, LA (2004-present). Because of my technical "know-how" and communications skills, was selected to "teach teachers": train and supervise five instructors involved in training 770 people in NBC procedures, firefighting, and safety operations.

- Trained 2,600 personnel to fight fires and avoid fire hazards during the war in the Middle East.
- Led a team of 11 personnel operating firefighting and NBC decontamination equipment to be ranked best among Army, Air Force, Navy, and Marine teams during a large-scale training project; used my motivational skills to boost morale.
- Oversaw maintenance for vehicles and equipment valued at $600,000.

NBC MANAGER & FIREFIGHTER. U.S. Army, Fort Bragg, NC (2002-04). Excelled in wearing multiple "hats" while developing and implementing a comprehensive NBC program for a 250-person organization; oversaw a 22-person staff and managed maintenance of $1 million in equipment.

- Was handpicked for administrative roles usually held by senior managers; earned three respected medals for my technical and leadership skills.
- By improving NBC and firefighting training, increased the organization's scores on "hands-on" skills tests from 15% to 95%!
- Created an NBC operations center that "set the standard" for other centers.
- Trained NBC teams rated as the **best** in the parent organization.

FIRST-LINE SUPERVISOR. U.S. Army, Fort Drum, NY (2000-02). Was praised in writing for my "vast knowledge of NBC operations" while leading 11 personnel involved in operating sophisticated equipment.

- Dramatically improved my team's scores on intensive skills tests.
- Successfully led personnel through a transition in operational focus; trained dozens of personnel for NBC defense teams.

NBC SUPERVISOR. U.S. Army, Fort Jackson, SC (1998-00). Earned unusually rapid promotion to middle management roles while surveying areas for NBC contamination; trained NBC defense teams.

Other experience: Worked as a part-time volunteer firefighter during days I was not at work.

TECHNICAL EXPERTISE & CLEARANCE	

- Calibrate, operate, and troubleshoot radiological, chemical and biological test equipment.
- Hold a SECRET security clearance.
- Offer knowledge of decontamination procedures, protective materials usage, and techniques in calculating damage to people and the environment.

PERSONAL	A respected motivator, volunteer to help troubled teens and homeless.

Date

Exact Name of Person
Title or Position
Exact Name of Company
Address (no., street)
City, state, zip

VESSEL SAFETY SUPERVISOR & FIREFIGHTING COORDINATOR

Dear Exact Name of Person (or Dear Sir or Madam if answering a blind ad.):

With the enclosed resume, I would like to make you aware of my interest in exploring employment opportunities with your organization. I am responding to your advertisement for a Safety Supervisor for your cruise ship, and I understand that you are seeking an individual with firefighting experience and EMT credentials.

As you will see from my resume, I have excelled in a track record of promotion to increasing responsibilities with the Carnival Cruise Line. While working as Customer Service Representative, I worked as a Volunteer Firefighter for the city of Orlando. I was later handpicked for the job as Safety Supervisor & Firefighting Coordinator for the cruise line, and I am proud of the contributions I have made in that role. On my own initiative, I developed a new fire prevention and firefighting training program which was mandatory for all company employees, and that program has been credited with cutting in half the number of reported fire incidents.

Although I have enjoyed my experience with Carnival Cruise Lines, I am interested in exploring similar career opportunities with the Queen Elizabeth organization.

I hope you will welcome my call soon to arrange a brief meeting at your convenience to discuss your current and future needs and how I might serve them. Thank you in advance for your time.

Sincerely yours,

Bessie Norcross

Alternate last paragraph:
I hope you will call or write me to suggest a time convenient for us to meet and discuss your current and future needs and how I might serve them. Thank you in advance for your time.

BESSIE NORCROSS

1110½ Hay Street, Fayetteville, NC 28305 • preppub@aol.com • (910) 483-6611

OBJECTIVE

To contribute to an organization that can use a safety-conscious professional with a background in designing and implementing safety programs for customers and employees.

EDUCATION

Earned a **B.A. in English**, University of Oklahoma, Norman, OK, 2001.

EXPERIENCE

Have excelled in the following track record of promotion with Carnival Cruises, Orlando and Miami, FL:

2004-present. VESSEL SAFETY SUPERVISOR & FIREFIGHTING COORDINATOR. Orlando, FL. For this prestigious cruise line, oversee onsite management of all aspects of vessel safety support, including firefighting training.

- Strengthened the cruise line's emphasis on safety, and implemented new safety procedures which required that all cruise line employees, from cooks to captains, participate in fire prevention and firefighting training. This training program was conducted at all ships and is credited with cutting in half the incidence of fires onboard ships.
- Coordinate local provisioning, bookkeeping and turnaround support for four passenger vessel. Ensure excellent communication between boats and suppliers.
- Hire, supervise and schedule land crew.
- Responsible for timely deliveries of food, liquor, laundry and luggage to accommodate over 600 passengers a week.
- Schedule repairs and purchase parts and supplies for physical maintenance of vessels.
- Assist with customer service and sales.

2003: GALLEY LEAD. Miami, FL. Responsible for ordering and inventory of all ship's stores. Coordinated all food and beverage service for 180 passengers a week, including training crew in preparation and service. Maintained flexibility when working with weather.

2000-02: CUSTOMER SERVICE REPRESENTATIVE. Orlando, FL. Was part of nine person team working aboard a tour boat to ensure passenger safety and enjoyment. Responsible for a thorough knowledge of Florida, its wildlife, history and cities. Assisted with meal preparation and service.

- Worked as a Volunteer Firefighter for the city of Orlando.

Previous experience:

CIRCULATION ASSISTANT. Orlando Observer, Orlando, FL (1999-00). Administered all aspects of customer service for three publications. Maintained computer based circulation and billing records. Acted as liaison between publisher and post office. Assisted Marketing Director with designing promotional pieces. Managed Legal Publications division. Responsible for hiring and scheduling casual labor crew.

TRADE STAFF. Barnes & Noble Bookstore, Orlando, FL (1996-99). Evaluated and ordered trade books, handled customer service and maintained inventory.

INTERNSHIP. Orlando Office of Promotion and Tourism, Orlando, FL (1995). Wrote press releases and articles for tourism publications. Assisted with the coordination of special events.

CERTIFICATIONS

Fire Officer Level I; Public Fire Educator; Firefighter Level II; Hazardous Materials Level I

PERSONAL

Can provide excellent reference upon request.

Date

Exact Name of Person
Title or Position
Exact Name of Company
Address (no., street)
City, State, Zip

VOLUNTEER FIREFIGHTER

Dear Exact Name of Person (or Dear Sir or Madam if answering a blind ad):

I look forward to having the opportunity to talk with you soon about how I could contribute to the City of Colorado Springs as an experienced firefighter who offers outstanding technical, motivational, and communication skills.

As you will see from my resume, I have gained extensive expertise in firefighting techniques while answering over 250 calls yearly with one of the nation's busiest volunteer fire departments. Known for my ability to lead in stressful conditions, I was unanimously elected to be a part of this team serving 40,000 people. I hold a Colorado I and II Level firefighting certification, and I offer expert skills in using equipment, rescue and firefighting techniques, and fire safety. I will soon be completing my Level III certification and I am pursuing a National Firefighter certification.

A proven leader, I earned rapid promotion to "middle management" while supervising a team of ten mechanics in the U.S. Army. While expertly diagnosing and repairing automobiles and trucks, I was chosen for supervisory roles ahead of my peers and earned numerous commendations for my technical and leadership skills.

You would find me to be a dedicated and energetic professional with the ability to lead in life-or-death situations. Known for giving unselfishly of my time, I volunteer my time working for the Special Olympics.

I'm pleased to have the opportunity for us to meet and discuss your current and future needs and how I might serve them. Thank you in advance for your time.

Sincerely yours,

Michael Hess

MICHAEL HESS

1110½ Hay Street, Fayetteville, NC 28305   •   preppub@aol.com   •   (910) 483-6611

OBJECTIVE

To benefit an organization that can use a dedicated professional who offers outstanding technical ability, proven motivational and management skills, as well as specialized firefighting expertise.

CERTIFICATION

Am an NFPA certified Level I and II firefighter in Colorado.
* Am currently completing training for Level III certification.

EXPERIENCE

VOLUNTEER FIREFIGHTER. Denver Fire Department, Denver, CO (2000-present). At one of the nation's busiest volunteer fire departments, became highly skilled in firefighting techniques while testing and operating firefighting equipment; educate the public on fire safety and continuously "fine tune" my skills in weekly training.
* Play a key role in responding to over 250 fire calls yearly for this department serving a community of 40,000 people.
* Because of my ability to provide leadership in stressful situations, was unanimously elected by the department to be a volunteer fireman.

SHOP SUPERVISOR. U.S. Army, Fort Carson, CO (1996-00). Earned rapid promotion to "middle management" while supervising ten mechanics performing routine and unscheduled maintenance on over 160 vehicles; diagnose problems and make repairs on systems including:

braking systems	engines	body work
exhaust systems	steering components	electrical systems

* Earned numerous respected commendations for technical and leadership skills; was promoted to a supervisory role ahead of ten other mechanics.
* Was praised for my "attention to detail" while performing quality control checks and technical inspections.
* Became known as a skilled instructor and motivator.

FIREFIGHTING EXPERTISE & SKILLS

Am currently pursuing certification as a National Firefighter.
Am knowledgeable of a wide range of firefighting activities including:

scene evaluation	hazardous material control	building inspection
equipment inspection	nozzle design	advanced rescue tools

Offer expertise in using/maintaining firefighting equipment including:

hoses	advanced breathing apparatus	ladders
hydrants	salvage/overhaul equipment	

* Operate computers with various software.
* A highly skilled mechanic, maintain, troubleshoot, and repair a wide range of automobiles and trucks; operate and repair power generators.

EDUCATION & TRAINING

Completed courses in Level I, II, and III Firefighting, Community College of Denver, CO.
Completed course work in Industrial Engineering, Community College of Denver, CO.
Excelled in college-level Army training related to personnel management and leadership, automotive repair, and parachute operations.
* Was named Distinguished Honor Graduate, Basic Training and Advanced Automotive Training.

PERSONAL

Member, Colorado Firefighter Association. Known for my energy and dedication, have the ability to lead in life-or-death situations. Hold SECRET security clearance. Volunteer my time working with Special Olympics.

Date

Exact Name of Person
Title or Position
Name of Company
Address (no., street)
Address (city, state, zip)

VOLUNTEER FIREFIGHTER

Dear Exact Name of Person: (or Dear Sir or Madam if answering a blind ad.)

I would appreciate an opportunity to talk with you soon about how I could contribute to your organization through my firefighting skills and experience.

As you will see from my resume, I have excelled as a Volunteer Firefighter with the Ann Arbor Fire Department, and I have proudly contributed to the safety of my community. I have completed numerous courses related to arson detection, auto fire investigation, and other areas. I am particularly proud that I was named Rookie of the Year in my first year as a volunteer. Since then I have received a special award from the Fire Chief, and I have volunteered to travel to California to assisting in fighting wildfires. My certifications including Fire Officer Level I, Michigan Public Fire Educator, Michigan Firefighter Level II, and Hazardous Materials Level I.

Although I am excelling in my full-time paid employment as a Sales Manager, I have decided that I wish to make firefighting my full-time job. An outdoors person by nature, I previously worked as a lifeguard and park supervisor until I discovered the firefighting field.

I am confident that I could become a valuable asset to your station, and I hope you will call or write me soon to suggest a time convenient for us to discuss your needs and how I might serve them. Thank you in advance for your time.

Sincerely yours,

Bradley Hogan

Alternate last paragraph:
I hope you will welcome my call soon to arrange a brief meeting at your convenience to discuss your current and future needs and how I might serve them. Thank you in advance for your time.

BRADLEY HOGAN

1110½ Hay Street, Fayetteville, NC 28305   •   preppub@aol.com   •   (910) 483-6611

OBJECTIVE   I want to contribute to an organization that can use an experienced firefighter who offers a genuine commitment to making our communities safer and our citizens more secure.

EDUCATION   **B.S. degree in Criminal Justice, Law Enforcement Concentration**, University of Michigan, Ann Arbor, MI, December 2003.
Basic Law Enforcement Training Certificate, Washtenaw Community College, Ann Arbor, MI, April 2003
- Basic Certification in Impact Weapons, March 2003
- First Responder Certification, February 2003

EXPERIENCE   **VOLUNTEER FIREFIGHTER**. Ann Arbor Fire Department, Ann Arbor, MI (2000-present). Proudly contributed to the safety of my community. Completed courses including these:

Arson Ignition to Conviction	Firefighters Role in Arson Detection
Auto Fire Investigation	Salvage and Overhaul

Achievements and accomplishments:
- Was named Rookie of the Year, 2000.
- Received the Fire Chief's Award in recognition of outstanding service to the firefighting field.
- Volunteered to go to California to assist in fighting fires caused by natural wildfires.

Certifications:
Fire Officer Level I
Michigan Public Fire Educator
Michigan Firefighter Level II
Hazardous Materials Level I

Highlights of other experience:
SALES MANAGER. Mable's Antique Gifts & Furnitures, Troy, MI (2002-present). In my full-time job, am in charge of inventorying and displaying new merchandise. Assist customers with selections and purchases.
- Maintain stock. Open and close the store.

PARK SUPERVISOR. Ann Arbor Recreation Department, Ann Arbor, MI (2001). Maintained parks and ball fields.
- Operated concessions during tournaments.
- Umpired softball and baseball games.

LIFEGUARD. Michigan Water Park, Detroit, MI (1998-00). Opened and closed waterslide.
- Maintained pool pumps, slides, and yard.
- Supervised waterslide riders.

BUS DRIVER. Michigan Schools, Ann Arbor, MI (1997-98). Transported students to and from school.

Other experience includes: Service Attendant for Johnson Tire Company, Sales Clerk at The Crewland Company and Strickland Shop, and Shipping Clerk for Foreman, Inc.

PERSONAL   Outstanding references available upon request.

Date

Exact Name of Person
Title or Position
Exact Name of Company
Address (no., street)
City, state, zip

VOLUNTEER
FIREFIGHTER

Dear Exact Name of Person (or Dear Sir or Madam if answering a blind ad.):

With the enclosed resume, I would like to make you aware of my interest in exploring employment opportunities with your organization.

As you will see from my resume, I made the decision to become a firefighter while still in high school, and I spent all my time on the weekends and in the evenings earning certifications in the firefighting field. I hope the credentials shown on my resume will convince you of my dedicated nature and commitment to the firefighting field.

I hope you will welcome my call soon to arrange a brief meeting at your convenience to discuss your current and future needs for a full-time professional firefighter. Thank you in advance for your time.

Sincerely yours,

June Karl

Alternate last paragraph:
I hope you will call or write me to suggest a time convenient for us to meet and discuss your current and future needs and how I might serve them. Thank you in advance for your time.

JUNE KARL

1110½ Hay Street, Fayetteville, NC 28305   •   preppub@aol.com   •   (910) 483-6611

OBJECTIVE   I am seeking to contribute to a firefighting organization as a volunteer.

EDUCATION   Graduated from Nelson High School, Springfield, MO, Graduated, 1995
- Made the decision to become a firefighter when I was a youth. Spent all my spare time in the evenings and on weekends during my junior and senior year of high school earning certifications in the firefighting field

Completed Medical Technician's curriculum studying medical terminology, Webster University, Saint Louis, MO. 30 credit hours in general studies
Major Studies:
Emergency Medical Technician: 168 hours; received state certification
Nursing Assistant: 120 hours completed
Fire Academy: 244 hours; received state certification as Basic Rescue Technician
Emergency Rescue Technician
National Registry Emergency Medical Technician
Driver/Operator Pumps
Driver/Operator Aerials
Incident Command (NFPA)
E.M.T. Defibrillation
Arson Investigation
National Fire Academy Radiological Emergency Management
Forestry Wildland Fire Suppression
Arson Investigation
Radiological Emergency Management (National)
Firefighter Level I & II
Hazardous Material Responder Level I
Basic Rescue Technician
Incident Command (NFPA)

COMPUTER SKILLS   Proficient with software including Microsoft Word, Excel, and PowerPoint
Have utilized databases used in law enforcement. Use Firehouse software.

EMPLOYMENT   **VOLUNTEER FIREFIGHTER.** Springfield Fire Department, Springfield, MO (2003-present). Engage in fire suppression, and as an Emergency Medical Technician on the fire ground.

SHIPPING & RECEIVING MANAGER. Canfield Sporting Goods, Springfield, MO (2003-present). Responsible for all paperwork and payroll related to receiving truck shipments.

PHARMACIST ASSISTANT. Walgreens, Springfield, MO (2002). Performed monthly statements filing including insurance forms and recording accounts receivable, payments, and charges.

ASSISTANT SUPERVISOR. Linens and Things, Saint Louis, MO (1996-01). Scheduled employees' daily tasks and work schedule. Also responsible for eight employees and did the filing and documenting of all company shipments. Very knowledgeable of computer, and the programs.

PERSONAL   Outstanding personal and professional references upon request.

Exact Name of Person
Title or Position
Exact Name of Company
Address (no., street)
City, state, zip

VOLUNTEER
FIREFIGHTER
&
ELECTRICIAN

Dear Exact Name of Person (or Dear Sir or Madam if answering a blind ad.):

With the enclosed resume, I would like to make you aware of my interest in exploring employment opportunities with your organization.

As you will see from my resume, I am self-employed as an Electrical Contractor and, in my spare time, I volunteer as a Firefighter with the Bemidji Fire Department. It is now my desire to become employed full-time as a professional firefighter, and I feel I have much to offer a fire department through my vast electrical knowledge as well as my firefighting skills.

I hope you will welcome my call soon to arrange a brief meeting at your convenience to discuss your current and future needs and how I might serve them. Thank you in advance for your time.

Sincerely yours,

Martin Franklin

Alternate last paragraph:
I hope you will call or write me to suggest a time convenient for us to meet and discuss your current and future needs and how I might serve them. Thank you in advance for your time.

MARTIN FRANKLIN

1110½ Hay Street, Fayetteville, NC 28305   •   preppub@aol.com   •   (910) 483-6611

OBJECTIVE

To benefit an organization in need of a professional maintenance electrician through my expertise in commercial, industrial, and residential wiring and installation as well as through my firefighting skills and experience.

TRAINING

Completed **Code Review** program for State Electrician's License, Bemidji State University, Bemidji, MN, 1992. Passed exam for limited license.
Earned certification in **Basic Police Science**, Bemidji State University, Bemidji, MN, 1985.

FIREFIGHTING EXPERTISE & SKILLS

Certified National Firefighter.
Knowledgeable of a wide range of firefighting activities including:

scene evaluation	hazardous material control	building inspection
equipment inspection	nozzle design	advanced rescue

Offer expertise in using/maintaining firefighting equipment including:

hoses	advanced breathing apparatus
hydrants	salvage/overhaul equipment

EXPERIENCE

ELECTRICIAN & MANAGER. Martin's Electric Repair, Bemidji, MN (2003-present). As an independent electrical contractor, have developed and maintained long-standing service contracts with both residential and commercial accounts.
- Rewired and electrically remodeled a large grocery store.
- Troubleshoot and repair rare German equipment used in food/meat preparation.
- Maintain complete electrical tools and service truck.
- In my spare time, work as a **Volunteer Firefighter** for the Bemidji Fire Department.

MAINTENANCE ELECTRICIAN/MECHANIC. Northwest Manufacturing Company, Bemidji, MN (1999-03). Supervised up to six employees working with electrical equipment ranging from 600 volt 3 phase power to single phase while wiring wet and dry transformers, running pipe, and setting up/repairing panel boards.
- Scheduled work assignments and planned jobs including labor/materials costs.
- Became familiar with electronics maintenance such as replacing chips and changing boards.
- Performed mechanical services related to motors, bearings, and welding.
- Installed equipment and machines used in manufacturing processes wiring them according to schematics.
- Supervised and installed control wiring to blueprint specifications.

SUPERVISOR/ELECTRICIAN. Vester Electric Company, Bemidji, MN (1997-99). Led a four person team of electricians carrying out commercial, industrial, and residential single phase and three phase wiring in homes, businesses, and large stores.

COMMERCIAL/LINE ELECTRICIAN. Reynolds Electric Company, Bemidji, MN (1989-97). Worked with 277/480 volt equipment while wiring shopping centers, malls, and other commercial/industrial sites; completed line work as assigned.
- Gained additional experience in high voltage installation and repair.

PERSONAL

Have a great deal of experience in training people in electrical work. Lead by example as my managerial style. Keep current on advances in electrical technology and installation/repair techniques.

Exact Name of Person
Title or Position
Name of Company
Address (no., street)
Address (city, state, zip)

**VOLUNTEER
FIREFIGHTER**

Dear Exact Name of Person: (or Dear Sir or Madam if answering a blind ad.)

I would appreciate an opportunity to talk with you soon about how I could contribute to your organization through my experience in firefighting. My wife and I have just relocated to Dallas and I am seeking employment as a professional firefighter. I offer outstanding credentials and can provide superior references.

As you will see from my resume, I have excelled as a Volunteer Firefighter with the Chicago Fire Department and was offered paid employment by the city based on my excellent work. I respond to fires, handle emergencies, and motor vehicle accidents while working as a member of a firefighting team responding to emergencies involving hazardous materials.

I am confident that I could become a valuable part of your team, and I hope you will call or write me soon to suggest a time convenient for us to discuss your current and future needs. Thank you in advance for your time.

Sincerely yours,

Eric Tucker

Alternate last paragraph:
I hope you will welcome my call soon to arrange a brief meeting at your convenience to discuss your current and future needs and how I might serve them. Thank you in advance for your time.

ERIC TUCKER

1110½ Hay Street, Fayetteville, NC 28305   •   preppub@aol.com   •   (910) 483-6611

OBJECTIVE

To benefit an organization that can use a dedicated professional who offers a background related to criminal justice and sociology as well as superior analytical, communication, and management skills.

EDUCATION

Graduated **magna cum laude** with a **Bachelor of Science (B.S.) degree in Criminal Justice** and a **Bachelor of Arts (B.A.) degree in Sociology**, Columbia College, Chicago, IL, 2000.
- Member, National Dean's List, 1997-00
- Member, Beta Sugma Chi, an International Honor Society, March 1998-June 1999.

EXPERIENCE

FIREFIGHTER. Chicago Fire Department, Chicago, IL (2000-present). Excelled as a Volunteer Firefighter and was offered paid employment by the City of Chicago after my excellent work. Respond to fires, handle emergencies, and respond to motor vehicle accidents. Work as a member of a firefighting team responding to emergencies involving hazardous materials. Assist with all heavy and technical rescue operations.
- **Written communication:** Complete reports of emergency information. Maintain logs, records, and incident reports.
- **Advanced lifesaving skills and other training:** Became skilled in advanced lifesaving techniques. Maintain training in all areas of fire suppression and prevention.
- **Inspections and quality control:** Inspect, repair, and maintain equipment and facilities.
- **Communication systems:** Monitor communications systems including radios.

ADMISSIONS COORDINATOR. Illinois Health Care, Chicago, IL (2000-03). After college graduation, was recruited to direct this 80-bed long-term care facility offering three levels of care: skilled nursing beds, intermediate care beds, and domiciliary beds in addition to sub-acute Medicare beds for patients transferring from acute hospital care.
- Coordinated admissions by contacting local hospitals informing them of availability.
- Determined eligibility along with director of nursing and dietitian to determine appropriate placement.
- Explained patient rights and responsibilities according to IL law and federal statutes including advanced directives.
- Provided marketing assistance by implementing community involvement activities.
- Acted as liaison between facility and various government agencies.
- Determined psychosocial needs of each resident and developed/implemented an individualized care plan utilizing the R.A.I. (Resident Assessment Instrument).
- Monitored residents on psychotropic medications.

SECURITY OFFICER. Cornett Security Agency, Chicago, IL (1999-00). For this major security company, was "second-in-command" of security for American Roofing, Co., a multimillion-dollar, 1,000-employee roofing manufacturing facility operating 24 hours a day.
- Enforced personnel identification system; patrolled areas; checked vehicles; maintained lock and key system.
- Safeguarded equipment against loss and theft; performed instrumentation readings and maintained documentation.

AFFILIATION

Lifetime Member, National Eagle Scout Association

PERSONAL

Am a quick learner who thrives in challenging situations. Work well with people from all backgrounds. Have volunteered my time in the Special Olympics.

CAREER CHANGE

Exact Name of Person
Title or Position
Name of Company
Address (number and street)
Address (city, state, and zip)

**VOLUNTEER
FIREFIGHTER**

Dear Exact Name of Person: (or Dear Sir or Madam if answering a blind ad)

I would appreciate an opportunity to talk with you soon about how I could contribute to your organization through my experience in firefighting.

As you will see from my enclosed resume, I offer a history of success in positions that require the ability to think and react quickly. Both as a security/law enforcement professional and as a business manager, I have built a clean driving record while familiarizing myself with the geographical layout and locations throughout the city and county.

While excelling in full-time positions as a Deputy Sheriff and as General Manager of a fast-paced restaurant business, I have volunteered as a firefighter. I am now at the point where I have the experience necessary to become a full-time professional firefighter, and I am seeking an organization which can use a dedicated hard worker with extensive medical knowledge along with in-depth firefighting experience. I can provide outstanding references.

I hope you will welcome my call soon to arrange a brief meeting at your convenience to discuss your current and future needs and how I might serve them. Thank you in advance for your time.

Sincerely yours,

Daniel J. Pope

Alternate last paragraph:
I hope you will call or write me soon to suggest a time convenient for us to meet and discuss your current and future needs and how I might serve them. Thank you in advance for your time.

DANIEL J. POPE

1110½ Hay Street, Fayetteville, NC 28305   •   preppub@aol.com   •   (910) 483-6611

OBJECTIVE

To offer my experience and reputation for reliability, honesty, and dependability to an organization that can use a mature professional who offers a clean driving record, knowledge of the city and county, and a history of effectiveness with the public and coworkers.

VOLUNTEER EXPERIENCE

FIREFIGHTER & EMERGENCY MEDICAL TECHNICIAN (EMT)-DEFIBRILLATION. City of Austin, Station 5 at Queen Anne Hill Drive in Austin, TX (2002-present). Work on a shift with nine different firefighters. Worked on the pumper for the first year at this station.

- During my second year at this station, became a member of the two-person Rescue Squad and now operate the station's rescue vehicle.
- Provide rescue services while responding to EMS calls. Gained extensive experience in responding to emergencies which included stabbings, gun shootings, and car wrecks.
- Drive emergency response vehicle while handling varied responsibilities. Respond to medical and trauma emergencies.
- Function as primary care giver in basic and advanced life support. Took steps to prevent head, neck, and c-spine injuries.
- Gained extensive medical knowledge: Became knowledgeable of subjects including trauma and wound care.

EXPERIENCE

GENERAL MANAGER. Billy's BBQ, Austin, TX (2003-present). Refined my managerial abilities while handling a wide range of administrative functions in this busy family-owned restaurant:

    accounting — handle payroll and daily sales journals
    planning — make arrangements for parties and various catered events
    dealing with others — consult with vendors, supervise employees, and deal regularly
            with members of the public
    financing — handle the store's finances and business dealings

- Gained further experience in the areas of time management and scheduling.

DESK SERGEANT and **DEPUTY SHERIFF.** Jefferson County Sheriff's Department, Austin, TX (1999-2003). Handled a wide range of activities including using computers on a regular basis to prepare reports and maintain records, responding to complaints, and making decisions on how to respond to situations as they arose.

- Built a "clean" driving record while becoming familiar with the county and city's streets and geographical locations.
- As a Desk Sergeant, made daily briefings to personnel on activities and events they needed to have knowledge of.
- Earned a reputation as a patient and understanding person and good listener.
- Became effective in prioritizing demands on limited human resources and in organizing responses in order to get the most out of personnel.

SECURITY OFFICER and **COLLEGE STUDENT.** Austin Community College (ACC), Austin, TX (1993-99). Juggled the demands of attending college and working part time for the ACC campus security office.

EDUCATION

A.A., Law and Criminal Justice, Austin Community College, Austin, TX, 1999.
Certified EMT; certified Firefighter I, II, and III.

PERSONAL

Am proud of my reputation as a persistent and determined person who will not rest until the job is done. Always give 100% and believe in striving for one's best. Punctual and reliable.

CAREER CHANGE

Date

Exact Name of Person
Title or Position
Exact Name of Company
Address
City, state, zip

Dear Exact Name of Person (or Dear Sir or Madam if answering a blind ad.):

With the enclosed resume, I would like to make you aware of my interest in applying for the position as Fire Truck Mechanic for the city of Seattle.

As you will see from my resume, I am qualified by Wal-Mart to operate the RC, Slip, and Clamp forklifts, and I previously repaired, tested, and maintained 4K, 6K, and 20,000-lb. forklifts while serving my country as an Equipment Mechanic and Inspector in the U.S. Navy. As an Equipment Repair Specialist, Mechanic, and Inspector, I won numerous awards in recognition of my accomplishments in decreasing downtime, boosting organizational efficiency, and developing new systems that streamlined efficiency. I trained and developed personnel who became knowledgeable of operational inspection techniques, and I was singled out by the Navy for jobs as Work Center Safety Officer and Inspector because of my excellent technical knowledge and unquestioned reliability.

A skilled maintenance professional, I am proficient at maintaining hydraulic systems, reading schematics, and troubleshooting electrical systems. While in the Navy, I excelled in numerous schools and courses which refined my technical knowledge and troubleshooting abilities, and I became skilled in repairing, maintaining, and testing all types of firefighting equipment.

After leaving the Navy and prior to joining Wal-Mart, I worked as a Maintenance Mechanic for a private company where I was involved in building, installing, and repairing industrial equipment used in institutions such as jails and hospitals.

I am a responsible and hard-working individual who prides myself on my ability to make any activity function more efficient, and I would enjoy the opportunity to apply my strong technical knowledge for the benefit of the city of Seattle.

Sincerely,

Jackson Mitchell

JACKSON MITCHELL

1110½ Hay Street, Fayetteville, NC 28305   •   preppub@aol.com   •   (910) 483-6611

OBJECTIVE   I want to contribute to an organization through my skills related to the operation, maintenance, and repair of firefighting vehicles and equipment as well as my background in preventive maintenance, safety, training program management, and quality assurance.

LICENSES   Qualified and licensed to operate the RC, Slip, and Clamp forklifts

EDUCATION   Through training/experience while serving in the U.S. Navy, became skilled in repairing, maintaining, and testing **forklifts (4K, 6K, & 20,000-lbs.),** aircraft ground support equipment, and special use equipment such as firefighting vehicles. Routinely work on the following:

tow tractors	liquid oxygen carts	hydraulic units
gas turbine compressors	firefighting unit	mobile electric power plants

Completed ASE Class "A1" School; ASE GTC-85 Turbine Engine Course; ASE GTCP-100 Gas Turbine Engine Course.
Completed a six-week arc and gas welding course at a community college.
Skilled maintenance professional; maintain hydraulic systems; skilled in reading schematics; troubleshoot electrical systems

EXPERIENCE   **UNLOADER.** Wal-Mart, Hope Harbour, FL (2002-present). Began as a Staple Stock Unloader on 2A shift and then moved to DA Unloader on 1B.
   •   Safely and skillfully operate all three forklifts used by Wal-Mart.
   •   In my spare time, volunteer as a **Firefighter** with Hope Harbour Fire Department. Have saved the fire station money through my ability to maintain firefighting vehicles.

MAINTENANCE MECHANIC. X & Z Equipment, Tallahassee, Goldsboro, and Mt. Olive, FL (1999-02). For a private company, serviced and maintained coin-operated laundry equipment; built laundromats and installed large, commercial laundry equipment in institutions.
   •   Functioned as the company's mechanic, and troubleshot maintenance problems in multiple cities where the company installed and serviced equipment.
   •   Also maintained the owner's 49-unit trailer home park's plumbing system and well.
   •   Made regular visits to laundromats owned by the company to collect receipts, make bank deposits, complete maintenance and repair, and handle any customer service.

Served my country in the U.S. Navy and was promoted ahead of my peers because of my exceptional skills related to preventive maintenance, quality assurance, and safety:
EQUIPMENT MECHANIC & INSPECTOR. NAS Whidbey Island, WA (1995-98). Won several medals in recognition of my achievements in reducing downtime and boosting organizational efficiency, and cited as a major contributor to the air station's selection for the 1998 Installation of Excellence Award.
   •   Was selected to oversee a support activity in which 2,300 items of equipment for 22 customer units were properly issued, received, and accounted for.
   •   Trained personnel to be thoroughly knowledgeable of operational inspection techniques.
   •   Was singled out for the critical position of Work Center Safety Officer.

EQUIPMENT REPAIR SPECIALIST. NAS China Lake, CA (1993-95). Repaired and did preventive maintenance on gas turbine compressors and ground support equipment.

PERSONAL   Responsible and hard-working individual who excels in technical problem solving.

Exact Name of Person
Title or Position
Name of Company
Address (number and street)
Address (city, state, and zip)

VOLUNTEER FIREFIGHTER

Dear Exact Name of Person: (or Sir or Madam if answering a blind ad.)

I would appreciate an opportunity to talk with you soon about how I could contribute to your organization through my experience as a safety-oriented and dependable truck driver who has developed a strong interest in becoming more involved in firefighting activities.

You will see from my enclosed resume that I offer a strong background in trucking. However, in recent years I have become more involved in handling paperwork ranging from bills of lading, to collecting on COD shipments, to completing daily log keeping. A fast learner, I am known for my dedication to safety and service and in early 2004 received a safe driving award for eight consecutive years of safe driving as a Line Haul Truck Driver with Thompson Motor Lines. More recently I was transferred to City Pick-up and Delivery Driver for the southeastern portion of Alabama.

In addition to hauling general freight as well as hazardous materials, I have been certified as a Firefighter and Emergency Medical Technician. This has caused me to become interested in pursuing full-time employment as a firefighter.

I hope you will welcome my call soon to arrange a brief meeting to discuss your current and future needs and how I might serve them. Thank you in advance for your time.

Sincerely yours,

Peter K. Anderson

Alternate last paragraph:
I hope you will call or write me soon to suggest a time convenient for us to meet and discuss your current and future needs and how I might serve them. Thank you in advance for your time.

PETER K. ANDERSON

1110½ Hay Street, Fayetteville, NC 28305 • preppub@aol.com • (910) 483-6611

OBJECTIVE
To offer my strong interest in and knowledge of shipping and handling procedures to an organization that can use a hard worker, quick learner, and good listener with a reputation for strong personal qualities of honesty and dependability.

TRAINING
Completed training programs leading to certification in the following areas:
Level III Firefighter – Jefferson State Community College, Birmingham, AL — 2003
Emergency Medical Technician — Jefferson State Community College, Birmingham, AL — 2002
Truck Driver—graduated from the Truck Driving Academy at Bevill State Community College, Sumiton, AL—1992. Placed second in a class of 31 students.

EXPERIENCE
CITY PICK-UP AND DELIVERY DRIVER. Thompson Motor Lines, Birmingham, AL (2004-present). Am gaining increasing familiarity with all areas of Alabama while transporting general freight as well as shipments of hazardous materials.
- Handled bills of lading, collected on COD shipments, and completed daily logs.
- Work as a **Volunteer Firefighter** for Birmingham Station 345.

LINE HAUL TRUCK DRIVER. Thompson Motor Lines, Birmingham, AL (1995-04). Received a "Safe Driving Award" in January 2004 for my <u>excellent</u> safety record during eight years of safe driving in twin sets of trailers (doubles) on a regular route between Birmingham and Tuscaloosa.
- Hauled general freight safely, but transported hazardous materials as needed including ensuring that special "hazardous materials" signs were placed on each trailer.

LONG DISTANCE TRUCK DRIVER. Spenard Transports, Tuscaloosa, AL (1992-95). Transported shipments — consisting mostly of sheetrock, lumber, and steel — throughout the eastern U.S. Learned the proper procedures for loading and unloading tractor-trailers. Became familiar with the most effective ways of loading a trailer.

Highlights of earlier experience (Birmingham, AL):
FARM LABORER: learned how to bale hay and operate farm equipment as well as working with a team of people to construct an 80' by 120' barn in one summer job.
GENERAL LABORER: worked as part of a team constructing metal buildings including barns, horse stalls, garages, and retail centers for Woodland, Inc.
ASSISTANT MANAGER/DELIVERY MAN: learned customer service skills, light automotive maintenance, and how to deliver fuel oil at Alabama Oil Company.
- Handled station operations during absences of the manager including one scheduled day a week; accepted and processed payments.

SPECIAL SKILLS
Through training and experience, am familiar with vehicles and equipment including:
Tractor-trailers: Volvo FE-7, Freightliner, Kenworth, Mack, and White road tractors as well as city pick-up and delivery tractors
Forklifts: Komatsu, Caterpillar, Hyster, and TCM
Farm equipment: Massey-Ferguson, Ford, Case, and John Deere
Other: backhoes and fire apparatus as well as most common hand tools

PERSONAL
Am known for my good listening skills and soft-spoken manner. Feel a great deal of personal satisfaction from helping people as a **Volunteer Firefighter and** EMT. Am a family-oriented Christian who is involved in church activities.

You may already realize that applying for a federal government position requires some patience and persistence in order to complete rather tedious forms and get them in on time. Depending on what type of federal job you are seeking, you may need to prepare an application such as the SF 171 or OF 612, or you may need to use a Federal Resume, sometimes called a "Resumix," to apply for a federal job. But that may not be the only paperwork you need.

Many Position Vacancy Announcements or job bulletins for a specific job also tell you that, in order to be considered for the job you want, you must also demonstrate certain knowledge, skills, or abilities. In other words, you need to also submit written narrative statements which microscopically focus on your particular knowledge, skill, or ability in a certain area. The next few pages are filled with examples of excellent KSAs. If you wish to see many other examples of KSAs, you may look for another book published by PREP: "Knowledge, Skills & Abilities for Federal Government Jobs."

Although you will be able to use the Federal Resume you prepare in order to apply for all sorts of jobs in the federal government, the KSAs you write are particular to a specific job and you may be able to use the KSAs you write only one time. If you get into the Civil Service system, however, you will discover that many KSAs tend to appear on lots of different job announcement bulletins. For example, "Ability to communicate orally and in writing" is a frequently requested KSA. This means that you would be able to use and re-use this KSA for any job bulletin which requests you to give evidence of your ability in this area.

What does "Screen Out" mean? If you see that a KSA is requested and the words "Screen out" are mentioned beside the KSA, this means that this KSA is of vital importance in "getting you in the door." If the individuals who review your application feel that your screen-out KSA does not establish your strengths in this area, you will not be considered as a candidate for the job. You need to make sure that any screen-out KSA is especially well-written and comprehensive.

How long can a KSA be? A job vacancy announcement bulletin usually does not specify a length for a KSA, but each of your KSAs should probably be 1-2 pages long. Remember that the purpose of their requiring this KSA is to microscopically examine your level of competence in a particular area, so you need to be extremely detailed and comprehensive. Give examples and details wherever possible. Your written communication skills might appear more credible if you provide the details of the kinds of reports and paperwork you prepared. For example, a Legal Secretary might mention her specific reports.

KSAs are extremely important in "getting you in the door" for a federal government job. If you are working under a tight deadline in preparing your paperwork for a federal government position, don't spend all your time preparing the Federal Resume if you also have KSAs to do. Create "blockbuster" KSAs as well!

CAPTAIN & FIREFIGHTER

JUAN J. ONSTOTT
SSN: 000-00-0000
ADDRESS: 1110½ Hay Street, Fayetteville, NC 28305
HOME PHONE: (111) 111-1111
TELEPHONE: (222) 222-2222

Position, Title, Series, Grade:
Announcement Number: DN-00-000
Veteran's Preference:

CAPTAIN & FIREFIGHTER

This firefighter is seeking a federal position in his field.

EXPERIENCE

Am excelling in four simultaneous positions:
April 2002-present. **CAPTAIN & FIREFIGHTER.** Up to 40 hours per week (2-3 days a week on 12-hour shifts). $8.75 per hour. Scottsdale Fire Department. Scottsdale, AZ. Eric Simmons, Supervisor, (333) 333-3333. Began as a Firefighter in April of 2002 and was promoted in April of 2003 to Shift Captain. Serve as a **member of a firefighting crew** engaged in the protection of life and property. Respond to major emergencies, and respond to alarms. Combat fires while performing the full performance of firefighting tasks involving structures, equipment, facilities, as well as fuel and chemical fires. When combating structural fires, wear self-contained breathing apparatus and move through dark interior corridors and stairways to locate the origin of the fire. Control and extinguish fires while performing rescues.

- **Management Responsibilities as Shift Captain:** Responsible for the supervision of all daily, weekly, and monthly activities of shift members. Establish and document public fire awareness programs. Supervise live fire/rescue calls and conduct after-action debriefings of firefighters. Supervise up to 30 personnel on small and large-scale emergency situations.

- **Hazardous Material Incident Management:** As Shift Captain, handle supervisory responsibilities related to medical emergencies, fire suppression related emergencies, and Hazmat incidents. Respond to hazardous material incidents. Detect and identify hazardous materials. Make proper risk assessments. Understand and interpret basic hazards of a chemical incident. Identify safety and health hazards encountered at hazardous materials incidents. Play a key role in determining and implementing response plan and termination of the incident. Utilize advanced control containment and/or confinement procedures, cleanup, decontamination, and related operations.

- **Crosstraining:** On as needed basis, am skilled in performing the duties of hoseman, ladderman, hydrantman, rescueman, nozzleman, salvageman, and hand lineman. Am skilled at technical duties including unreeling connects, laying and operating hose lines, placing and raising ladders, and operating portable and stationary firefighting apparatus.

- **Safety, First Aid, and Rescue Operations:** Evacuate and rescue occupants. Administer first aid and protect fellow firemen during firefighting.

- **Detection, Reduction, and Elimination of Potential Fire Hazards:** Perform fire protection inspections. Check fire alarms and sprinkler systems in buildings to ensure operability. Prepare reports of fire inspections.

- **Operation of fire communications equipment:** Operate computerized telecommunications equipment. Operate communication alarm center and monitor sprinklered buildings and alarm systems. Receive administrative and emergency telephone calls.

March 1999-2002. **SEARCH AND RESCUE (S.A.R.) TEAM MEMBER.** Maricopa County Sheriff's Department, Glendale, AZ. Up to 10 hours per week (am on call, 24 hours a day for two weeks at a time). $11.00 per hr. Issac McDouglas, Supervisor (444) 444-4444. Am a member of a highly skilled search and rescue team. Assist with all tactical search and rescue operations. Provide swiftwater and dive rescue operations. Play a key role in land searches and high angle rescues on statewide response areas. Was instrumental in planning and implementing all aspects of rescue training for S.A.R. team members.
- **Emergency Services Coordinator:** Was honored by selection as Glendale Emergency Services Seminar Equipment Coordinator in May of 1999. Was the youngest person ever chosen for this role which involved setting up classes for law enforcement and public service officials. Planned and managed the Glendale Emergency Services Seminar in September 2001 which was attended by hundreds of people from many states. Work closely with more than 45 instructors at Glendale Community College to coordinate training in fire protection, counterterrorism, Hazmat, and public fire education.

December 1996-May 1999. **CAPTAIN & TRAINING OFFICER (Volunteer).** Up to 10 hours per week as a volunteer, Flagstaff Volunteer Fire Department, Flagstaff, AZ. Rudolph, Dugle, Supervisor (555) 555-5555. Am the Officer in Charge in the absence of the chief and deputy chiefs. Responsible for recordkeeping of all training and continuing education hours for firefighting personnel. Schedule and instruct classes pertaining the state certifications.

February 1994-December 1996. **EMERGENCY MEDICAL TECHNICIAN (DEFIBRILLATION).** 48 hours per week. $10.00 per hour. Flagstaff Emergency Medical Services, Flagstaff, AZ. Jimmy Bullock, Supervisor (666) 666-6666. Function as primary care giver in basic and advanced life support. Responsible for defibrillating and intubating patients in an attempt to sustain life. Take steps to prevent further head, neck, and c-spine injuries.
- **Extensive medical knowledge:** Became knowledgeable of subjects including trauma and wound care.

VOLUNTEER RESCUER. January 1993-February 1994. 15 hours per week. Pinal County Rescue, La Palma, AZ. Katie Fadden, Supervisor (777) 777-7777. Assisted with all BLS/ALS medical calls. Assisted with all heavy and technical rescue operations.
- **Advanced lifesaving skills:** Became skilled in advanced lifesaving techniques.

HONORS & AWARDS

September 6, 2003: Named **Glendale Emergency Services Seminar Equipment Coordinator** for Maricopa County. Was the youngest person ever to receive this honor.
April 14, 1999: Flagstaff Fire Department Chief's Award. For outstanding service to the firefighting field "above and beyond the call of duty."
September 12, 1998: Flagstaff Fire Department Chief's Award. For outstanding service and in recognition of contribution to the firefighting field.
July 5, 1998: Flagstaff Distinguished Service Award. Volunteered to go to Colorado to assist in fighting fires caused by natural wildfires.

CERTIFICATIONS

Fire Officer Level I, October 15, 2004, 180 hours
Arizona Public Fire Educator, July 12, 2004, 80 hours
Arizona Firefighter Level II, February 23, 2003, 260 hours
Arizona Hazardous Materials Level I, January 3, 2003, 40 hours

CAPTAIN & FIREFIGHTER

Arizona Basic Rescue Technician, November 9, 2002, 160 hours

Arizona Emergency Rescue Technician, March 19, 2002, 180 hours

National Registry Emergency Medical Technician, October 2, 2002, 230 hours

Arizona Driver/Operator Pumps, April 11, 2001, 30 hours

Arizona Driver/Operator Aerials, April 11, 2001, 50 hours

Incident Command (NFPA), August 21, 2000, 20 hours

Arizona E.M.T. Defibrillation, January 17, 2000, 48 hours

Arizona Arson Investigation, March 28, 1999, 40 hours

National Fire Academy Radiological Emergency Management, June 7, 1998, 40 hours

Arizona Forestry Wildland Fire Suppression, May 28, 1998, 40 hours

EDUCATION

Graduated from D.E. Lakes High School, 1997.

- Made the decision to become a firefighter when I was a youth. Spent all my spare time in the evenings and on weekends during my junior and senior year of high school earning certifications in the firefighting field.

At institutions which included the Arizona Justice Academy, Maricopa Technical College, Scottsdale Community College, Arizona National Fire Academy, the University of Arizona, and Glendale Community College, completed courses and training programs including these:

Fire Officer I, October 2003

A.R.F.F., October 2003

Driver/Operator (Aerials), September 2001

Driver/Operator (Pumps), September 2001

Emergency Medical Technician (Defibrillation), June 2001

Emergency Rescue Technician, June 2001

Emergency Medical Technician (National Registry), August 2000

Arson Investigation, August 2000

Radiological Emergency Management (National), August 2000

Wildland Fire Suppression, NC Forestry, June 1999

Arizona Firefighter Level I & II, June 1999

Hazardous Material Responder Level I, January 1998

Basic Rescue Technician, January 1998

Incident Command (NFPA), December 1998

COMPUTER SKILLS

Proficient with software including Microsoft Word, Excel, and Powerpoint Have utilized databases used in law enforcement. Use Firehouse software.

CLEARANCE

Nonsmoker and nondrinker. Can pass the most rigorous background investigation.

FIREFIGHTER & EMT

ADAM GARRETT

SSN: 123-45-6789

Date of Birth: 01/01/1973

1110½ Hay Street

Fayetteville, NC 28305

Citizen of US

(910) 483-6611

E-mail: PREPPub@aol.com

HONOR   Was named **FIREFIGHTER OF THE YEAR, 2003**. Was selected for this honor by the community at large.

EXPERIENCE   Have excelled in the following track record of advancement with the City of Seattle, WA, while working in three different fire stations (June 1999-present).

April 2004-present. **FIREFIGHTER & EMERGENCY MEDICAL TECHNICIAN (EMT)**. 40 hours per week. Salary: $27,000. City of Seattle, Station 11 on Chinook Road, Seattle, WA. Supervisor: Gary Edwards, Captain. Serve as a member of a firefighting crew engaged in the protection of life and property. Respond to major emergencies, and respond to alarms. Respond to and combat fires in wooded areas and on structures which potentially contain ammunitions, fuels, gases, and volatile chemicals. Combat fires while performing the full performance of firefighting tasks involving structures, equipment, facilities, as well as fuel and chemical fires. When combating structural fires, wear self-contained breathing apparatus and move through dark interior corridors and stairways to locate the origin of the fire. Control and extinguish fires while performing rescues.

- **Communication and Public Relations:** Organize and implement activities related to ensuring the public safety and educating the public about fire safety in the community. Work with schools in order to educate the public about fire safety and to perform demonstrations by firefighters. Personally give speeches to youth groups about fire prevention and fire safety.
- **Hazardous Material Incident Management.** Utilize my training in incident response management while performing the above responsibilities. Have been trained to utilize advanced control containment and/or confinement procedures, cleanup, decontamination, and related operations.
- **Crosstraining:** On as-needed basis, am skilled in performing the duties of hoseman, ladderman, hydrantman, rescueman, nozzleman, salvageman, and hand lineman. Am skilled at technical duties including unreeling connects, laying and operating hose lines, placing and raising ladders, and operating portable and stationary firefighting apparatus.
- **Safety, First Aid, and Rescue Operations:** Evacuate and rescue occupants. Administer first aid and protect fellow firemen during firefighting.
- **Detection, Reduction, and Elimination of Potential Fire Hazards:** Perform fire protection inspections. Check fire alarms and sprinkler systems in buildings to ensure operability. Prepare detailed assessments and reports of potential fire problems in commercial buildings. Brief building owners and others on potential problems and suggest remedies. Prepare reports of fire inspections.
- **Operation of fire communications equipment:** Operate communication alarm center and monitor sprinklered buildings and alarm systems. Operate computerized telecommunications equipment. Receive administrative and emergency telephone calls. Serve as an emergency driver of a pumper and tanker fire truck.

May 2001-March 2004. **FIREFIGHTER & EMERGENCY MEDICAL TECHNICIAN**. City of Seattle, Station 4 at Space Needle Road. Seattle, WA. 40 hours per week, Salary: $26,000. Supervisor: Gary Edwards, phone unknown. Perform essentially the same duties as in the previous job.

June 1999-April 2001: **FIREFIGHTER & EMERGENCY MEDICAL TECHNICIAN (EMT)-DEFIBRILLATION**. City of Seattle, Station 5 at Queen Anne Hill Drive in Seattle, WA. 40 hours per week. Salary: $25,000. Supervisor: Joshua Cregar, phone unknown. Worked on a shift with nine different firefighters. Worked on the pumper for the first year at this station. During my second year at this station, was a member of the two-person Rescue Squad and operated the station's rescue vehicle. Provided rescue services while responding to EMS calls. Gained extensive experience in responding to emergencies which included stabbings, gun shootings, and car wrecks. Drove emergency response vehicle while handling varied responsibilities. Responded to medical and trauma emergencies. Functioned as primary care giver in basic and advanced life support. Took steps to prevent head, neck, and c-spine injuries.

- Extensive medical knowledge: Became knowledgeable of subjects including trauma and wound care.

FIREFIGHTER
&
EMERGENCY
MEDICAL
TECHNICIAN
(EMT)

March 1998-June 1999. **VOLUNTEER FIREFIGHTER**. Tacoma Fire Department, Puget Road, Tacoma, WA. Supervisor: Francis Roberts, Captain. Excelled as a Volunteer Firefighter and was offered paid employment by the City of Seattle after my excellent work in Tacoma. Responded to fires, handled emergencies, and responded to motor vehicle accidents. Worked as a member of firefighting team responding to emergencies involved hazardous materials. Assisted with all heavy and technical rescue operations.

- Written communication: Completed reports of emergency information. Maintained logs, records, and incident reports.
- Advanced lifesaving skills and other training: Became skilled in advanced lifesaving techniques. Maintained training in all areas of fire suppression and prevention.
- Inspections and quality control: Inspected, repaired, and maintained equipment and facilities.
- Communication systems: Monitored communications systems including telephone and radios.

March 1998-June 1999. **WINDOW REPAIRMAN**. Callahan Window Repairs, Co., 987 Glassmen Avenue, Seattle, WA 98987. 40 hours per week. Salary: $10.00 per hour. Supervisor: John Glassmen, phone unknown. Expertly installed new windows and tore old roofs off commercial and residential buildings.

August 1994-March 1998. **WINDOW REPAIRMAN**. Packert Floors and Windows, Inc., 123 Pane Road, Seattle, WA 98123. Salary: $10.00 per hour. Supervisor: Mark Panes, phone unknown. Installed new windows and tore old roofs off commercial and residential buildings.

MILITARY EXPERIENCE: U.S. Army. Rose to the rank of E-4 while excelling in the following positions:
November 1993-August 1994: **RIFLEMAN**. 82nd Airborne Division, Fort Bragg, NC. 40 hours per week. Salary: E-4. Trained for combat duty as an infantry soldier while utilizing my skills as an expert marksman with the M-16 rifle.

November 1992-November 1993. **DRAGON GUNNER**. 82nd Airborne Division, Fort Bragg, NC. 40 hours per week. Salary: E-2. Was trained to fire wire guided missiles as part of a nine-person squad.

November 1991-November 1992. **MORTARMAN**. 82nd Airborne Division, Fort Bragg, NC. 40 hours per week. Salary: E-1. Performed with distinction as an infantryman.

TRAINING &	Seattle Firefighter Level I & II	August 1997
CERTIFICATIONS	Seattle Hazardous Materials Level I Responder	August 1997
	Wildland Fire Suppression, WA Forestry	April 1997
	Emergency Medical Technician (Defibrillation)-BLS	July 1997
	Washington Emergency Vehicle Driving Certification	Nov 2001
	Washington Driver/Operator Pumps	March 2001
	Trained as a Washington Driver/Operator Aerials	March 2001
	A.R.F.F.	February 2002

EDUCATION   Completed the three-month Fire Academy, Seattle Community College, and the three-month Emergency Medical Technician (Debrillation) Course, 1997.
Training has included:
Part 1 of 4 parts: Driver/Operator (Aerials)
Part 1 of 8 parts: Driver/Operator (Pumps)
Hazardous Material Responder Level I
Incident Command (NFPA)
Flameout (Northwest Fire/Rescue College)
- Completed three months of firefighting training as well as training in EMT-BLS. Graduated from Puget Sound High School, Bellevue, WA, 1990.
- In my senior year, attended Bellevue Vocational School and completed police security classes.

COMPUTER   Use Firehouse software
SKILLS

EQUIPMENT   Experienced in using personal protective equipment as well as portable extinguishers, ladders,
SKILLS   hoses, and ropes. Experienced in operating and driving heavy equipment including emergency medical vehicles, fire trucks, tractors, trenchers, backhoes, front end loaders, track hoes, and bulldozers. Also operate small equipment including weed eater, chain saw, mowers, blowers, and edgers. Operate handtools such as axes, positive pressure and negative pressure fans, hurst extraction tools, K12 saws, and ventilation saws.

DIRECTOR OF FIREFIGHTING

HARVEY T. BELLMAN

1110½ Hay Street, Fayetteville, NC 28305
Home: (111) 111-1111
Work: (222) 222-2222
SSN: 000-00-0000

Announcement number: BC 6548-900
Firefighting Management Positions:
Series/Grade: GS-0000-00-00
Country of Citizenship: U.S.A.
Veteran Preference: 30%
Highest Federal civilian grade held: GS-00 (_____ job series & dates held)

EDUCATION

High School: Mulholland High School, Los Angeles, CA 90545, 1986.
College: University of California, Los Angeles CA, 90200, 2002.
Major: Firefighting
Completed one year towards Associate degree. Total credit hours: 84.

TRAINING &
CERTIFICATIONS

Firefighter Level I & II
Hazardous Materials Level I Responder
Wildland Fire Suppression
Emergency Medical Technician (Defibrillation)-BLS
Washington Emergency Vehicle Driving Certification
Driver/Operator Pumps
Driver/Operator Aerials

EDUCATION

Completed the three-month Fire Academy, Seattle Community College, and the three-month Emergency Medical Technician (Debrillation) Course, 1997.
Incident Command (NFPA)
Flameout (Northwest Fire/Rescue College)
- Completed three months of firefighting training as well as training in EMT-BLS.
  Graduated from Puget Sound High School, Bellevue, WA, 1990.
- In my senior year, attended Bellevue Vocational School and completed police security classes.

EXPERIENCE

FIREFIGHTING CHIEF. (series, grade). Angus Beef Corporation (USDA), 8521 Reseda Boulevard, Los Angeles, CA 90784.
Supervisor's name and phone number: Phillip Lusane, (333) 333-3333. (You may contact him.)
Starting and ending dates: 10/2004-present
Hours per week: 40
Salary: $42,000
In a red meat plant which employs 4000 employees, direct safety programs and firefighting activities. Serve as a **member of a firefighting crew** engaged in the protection of life and property. Respond to major emergencies, and respond to alarms. Combat fires while performing the full performance of firefighting tasks involving structures, equipment, facilities, as well as fuel and chemical fires. When combating structural fires, wear self-contained breathing apparatus and move through dark interior corridors and stairways to locate the origin of the fire. Control and extinguish fires while performing rescues.

SAFETY INSPECTOR. (series, grade). Angus Beef Corporation (USDA), 5801 Permastone Road, Portland, OR 91860.
Supervisor's name and phone number: Curtis Meyers, (444) 444-4444. Starting and ending dates: 04/2001-10/2004
Hours per week: 40
Salary: $39,500
Performed the duties of a slaughter inspector as described in the previous job. Transferred to Los Angeles plant.

For a federally regulated beef-producing plant which employs 1,000 people, developed and implemented safety regulations in order to protect the general public as well as plant employees. Responded to major emergencies, and respond to alarms. Fought fires while performing the full performance of firefighting tasks involving structures, equipment, facilities, as well as fuel and chemical fires. When combating structural fires, wore self-contained breathing apparatus and moved through dark interior corridors and stairways to locate the origin of the fire. Controlled and extinguished fires while performing rescues.

FOOD SERVICE MANAGER. (rank). Portland Veterans Hospital, 8151 Billingsworth Hwy, Portland, OR 91706.
Supervisor's name and phone number: Robert Williams, (555) 555-5555.
Starting and ending dates: 11/1998-04/2001
Hours per week: 40+.
Salary: $37,000
Supervised a staff of five consisting of cooks and food service workers. Developed a rotating menu consisting of five-day weeks, four-week months based on USDA meal guidelines appropriate to the needs of children ages six weeks to six years old. Managed food supplies in excess of $200,000 within strict budgetary guidelines. Managed accountability of government purchase card worldwide of up to $300,000.

*   Developed an international logistics and procurement network which lowered food costs while boosting quality.
*   Supervised food service operation for the annual Veterans Health Fair sponsored by Proctor & Gamble.
*   Organized, planned, and directed a pancake breakfast for a 8-mile run in Seattle, WA.
*   Developed a preventive maintenance schedule which improved productivity.
*   On my own initiative, directed and implemented food service sanitation training; provided leadership in formulating new food menus based on product availability.

SHIPPING AND RECEIVING AGENT. Hargray Contractors, 5689 Maas Boulevard, Reedley, CA 90542.
Supervisor's name and phone number: Carlton Foley, (666) 666-6666.
Starting and ending dates: 04/1996-11/1998
Hours per week: 40+.
Salary: $32,335
Managed a budget of $2.75 million utilized by 19 geographically separate recreation facilities. Supervised a staff of five individuals involved in conducting and maintaining monthly inventories while also distributing supplies to the 19 facilities. Developed an accounting spreadsheet which greatly improved financial control.

KITCHEN SUPERVISOR. Orleans Restaurant, 1039 Affinity Road, Reedley, CA 90542.
Supervisor's name and phone number: Jason Dennison, (777) 777-7777.
Starting and ending dates: 09/1994-04/1996
Hours per week: 40+.
Salary: $30,787
Supervised a staff of 15 cooks and bakers involved in a large kitchen

DIRECTOR OF FIREFIGHTING

operation which prepared 3 meals a day for at least 60 customers per week.

- Supervised monthly scheduled banquets for local businesses and organizations throughout the Reedley Community.

HOTEL MANAGER. The Courtyard, Marriott, 1937 Sardonyx Lane, Reedley, CA 90542.
Supervisor's name and phone number: John Forbis, (888) 888-8888.
Starting and ending dates: 08/1992-09/1994
Hours per week: 40+.
Salary: $29,400
Managed a 42-room hotel and supervised the professional maintenance of accommodations for the surrounding Reedley area.

SHIPPING AGENT. U.S. Navy, Naval Station Pearl Harbor, 850 Ticonderoga Street, Ste 100, Pearl Harbor, HI 96860-5102.
Supervisor's name and phone number: Captain Antonio Tyler, (999) 999-9999.
Starting and ending dates: 01/1989-08/1992
Hours per week: 40+.
Salary: $25,870
Supervised a staff of 36 people involved in ordering base food store items valued at $1.9 million.

- Developed and organized logistics of food provisions to support Naval Station of 180,000 personnel sailors and officers in Pearl Harbor.

ACCOUNTANT. U.S. Navy, Navy Region North East, Box 100 Groton, CT 06349-5100.
Supervisor's name and phone number: Brian Devanney, (000) 000-0000.
Starting and ending dates: 03/1986-01/1989
Hours per week: 40+.
Salary: $21,000
Managed accounting records for a food service operation.

Highlights of other U.S. Navy experience:
CATERING CHIEF. Organized and catered special meals for military and civilian social functions including retirement ceremonies, promotion parties, weddings, funerals, employee get-togethers, and social gatherings of all types.

TRAINING CHIEF. Trained apprentice-level cooks in food preparation.

REMOTE FACILITIES MANAGER. Organized and supervised operation of field mess operations serving hundreds of soldiers three meals a day in remote locations.

TRAINING

Graduated from U.S. Navy training programs including the following:
Management Food Operations, 1992.
Advance Management Food Operations, 1992.

Advance Food Preparation, 1991.
Accounting for Food Service, 1991.
Health and Sanitation Instructor Course, 1991.
FDA certification, 1991.
Restaurant Cost Control Course, 1991.
Helo Crash Crew, 1990.
Firefighting, 1990.
Preventive Maintenance Coordinator Course, 1990.

CERTIFICATES   FSP qualified, 1990.
Certified Preventive Maintenance Coordinator, 1990.
Certified Health and Sanitation Instructor, 1990.
Certified in First Aid and CPR, 1990.

AWARDS   Received Unit Commendation in Pearl Harbor, HI
Honorable discharge from the U.S. Navy

CLEARANCE   Held Secret security clearance

LANGUAGE   Speak, read, and write Italian.

LEADERSHIP ACTIVITIES   Elected President of California Firefighters Association, Los Angeles, CA 2003.

OTHER SKILLS   **Organizational abilities:** Extensive experience in organizing and playing team sports; have coached junior varsity basketball girls and boys team. Have participated in team sports including flag football, softball, volleyball, and other sports.
- Offer exceptionally strong organizational skills, and have organized sports and morale-boosting activities for people of all ages, ranging from children to adults.

Writing skills: Am experienced in the marketing and promotion of athletic and recreation activities through my ability to develop and produce brochures, pamphlets, and flyers which explain and market team sports and other programs.

Fundraising and marketing skills: On numerous occasions have successfully solicited funding from private industry, local communities, and individuals in order to set up recreation activities for youth and adults. Have also raised funds which were donated to the United Way of Los Angeles, CA other charities.

Teaching and public speaking skills: Have gained strong oral communication skills while teaching firefighting skills to small groups and giving speeches to large groups while serving as a volunteer leader of sports/recreation activities.

Computers: Skilled in utilizing computers with Microsoft Word. Have used spreadsheets for financial analysis. Have used automated systems for purchasing.

PERSONAL   Highly motivated individual with an outstanding personal and professional reputation. Can provide outstanding references.

FIREFIGHTING TRAINING COORDINATOR

FRANK P. IVEY

1110½ Hay Street

Fayetteville, NC 28305

Day: (910) 483-6611

SSN: 000-00-0000

Announcement No: 123456-1234

Position: Firefighting Safety Coordinator GS-00

FIREFIGHTING TRAINING COORDINATOR

This civilian firefighting officer seeks an executive position in the federal government.

OBJECTIVE

To serve the National Safety Administration as a Firefighting Training Coordinator through my demonstrated knowledge of firefighting as well as through my vast experience in developing, evaluating, and administering firefighting safety programs and other safety programs.

PUBLICATIONS

Currently responsible for the development, evaluation, revision, and marketing of the following publications:

The Firefighting Training Instructors' Manual

Firefighting Manual for Firefighters

Firefighting Driver Training Curriculum for Basic Firefighting Training

SUMMARY OF EXPERIENCE

In the following track record of career advancement, have earned a reputation as one of the leading experts in Florida in firefighting program administration; on a daily basis am utilizing my written and oral communication skills as well as my ability to plan, budget for, implement, and administer firefighting safety and firefighting operational programs. At national levels, am widely regarded as an expert in the development and administration of firefighting safety programs, including programs pertaining to the licensing and training of firefighting equipment and vehicle operators.

EXPERIENCE

FIREFIGHTING TRAINING COORDINATOR. Florida Department of Justice, Attorney General's Office, 8322 Palau Street, Miami, FL, 33344, John Griffin, Supervisor, phone: (111) 111-1111. (2002-present). Am responsible for program development and implementation of programs related to firefighting and handle key responsibilities in these and other areas:

Technical Assistance: Ensure that technical assistance is accurate and conforms to currently accepted practices; keep the Florida Firefighting Academy, Firefighting Training Standards and Firefighting Standards Divisions and their staff informed on issues which have impact on firefighting effectiveness.

Course Coordination: Ensure that training environment is appropriately organized and that students' training needs are appropriately facilitated while coordinating the following courses:

Firefighter I Training Course

Firefighter II Training Course

Firefighter III Training Course

Re-Certification Training for Firefighters

Re-Certification Training for Firefighting Vehicle Operators

Driver Training Modules

Firefighting Curriculum Development: Ensure that curricula are job-related and applicable, reflect current information and practices, employ appropriate training methodology, and accurately measure student achievement while developing or redeveloping courses including firefighting training needs and resources.

Teaching: Ensure that materials are applicable and job-related while instructing in 12 different courses for firefighters at various levels of experience.

* Develop, evaluate, coordinate, and deliver training programs to firefighting officers throughout FL seeking certification in training programs conducted within the state.
* Prepare program materials and translate firefighting issues into cohesive programs which are understood, accepted, and utilized by the firefighting community.
* Provide guidance to develop, promote, and market program concepts and materials for use by firefighting leaders, national associations, and state and local governments.
* Gather the results of program findings and evaluations and incorporate these findings into materials which can be used in functional areas of firefighting services.
* As School Director for the Florida Firefighting Academy's Specialized Instructor Training Course, have trained 350 officers currently certified as Firefighting Instructors.
* Have developed and implemented a revised firefighting vehicle training curriculum for the Basic Firefighting Training Program which increased the training of basic recruits from 16 hours to 44 hours while also mandating training in emergency response.
* As School Director for the Academy's Firefighter Instructor Training Courses, am responsible for development, revision, coordination, and delivery of training for firefighting officers seeking certification to instruct in Firefighter Training courses in the state (have personally trained all of the approximately 150 current instructors).
* Am staffed to the Florida Firefighting Education and Training Standards Commission, and am responsible for monitoring firefighting curriculums.
* Since 2004, have planned and budgeted for more than 40 separate programs; during a normal year, am simultaneously budgeting for and administering more than 10 separate programs, which are mandated by the Firefighting Commission.
* Am proud of the contributions I have made to firefighting and consumer safety in FL; am indirectly responsible for decreasing deaths due to fires. Am also proud of the reduction in fatalities projected to occur because of the improved Firefighter Training Program.

PRESIDENT. Dunlap Independent (self-employed), Florida Department of Justice, Attorney General's Office, 945 Sycamore Lane, Tallahassee, FL, 33344 (1998-02). Served as an independent traffic accident/collision reconstruction consultant and training coordinator.

Firefighting Certifications:

* In my spare time, made a career transition into the firefighting field and achieved numerous certifications and credentials during this period of time. At institutions which included the Florida Justice Academy, Tallahassee Technical College, Merced Community College, Florida National Fire Academy, the University of Florida, and Miami Community College, completed courses and training programs including these:

  Fire Officer I, October 2002   A.R.F.F., October 2002
  Driver/Operator (Aerials), September 2001   Driver/Operator (Pumps), Sept 2001
  Emergency Medical Technician (Defibrillation), June 2001
  Emergency Rescue Technician, June 2001
  Emergency Medical Technician (National Registry), August 2000
  Arson Investigation, August 2000
  Radiological Emergency Management (National), August 2000
  Wildland Fire Suppression, NC Forestry, June 1999
  Firefighter Level I & II, June 1999
  Hazardous Material Responder Level I, January 1998
  Basic Rescue Technician, January 1998
  Incident Command (NFPA), December 1998

FIREFIGHTING TRAINING COORDINATOR

INSTRUCTOR/COORDINATOR. Florida Department of Justice, Florida Justice Academy, 2299 Breezewood Hwy, Tallahassee, FL 32585, Jason Greenburg, Supervisor, phone: (333) 333-3333. (1988-1998). Was responsible for coordination and instruction of training programs to law enforcement officers throughout Florida.

- Submitted training budgets for approval, and became known for my resourcefulness in stretching training dollars to their maximum effectiveness.
- Selected instructors to assist in training courses; formulated and revised lesson plans.
- Served on advisory committees for training programs such as the Basic Law Enforcement Training Course mandated by the Training and Standards Division of the Florida Department of Justice.
- Served as President for the Florida Law Enforcement Training Officers Association, responsible for providing training programs to law enforcement trainers throughout the state. Acted as a consultant to law enforcement agencies. Florida Department of Crime Control and Public Safety, Division of State Highway Patrol, 1561 Eastern Blvd, Tallahassee, FL 32445, Michael Brisbane, Supervisor, (444) 444-4444. (1988-1995). Excelled in these varied assignments:
- **April-September 1995** assigned to Jefferson County. Patrolled state highways within assigned area to monitor traffic, to arrest or warn persons guilty of violating motor vehicle law, criminal law, or safe driving practices; provided road information and assistance to motorists; directed traffic in accident or disaster areas and at special events, such as races and ball games; rendered emergency medical treatment to injured; investigated conditions and causes of accidents and prepared written reports; performed general police work by keeping order and apprehending criminals; appeared in court as witness in traffic violation and criminal cases; maintained records and reports of activities; spoke to civic organizations and school groups concerning programs supported by the highway patrol; broadcast taped and live radio safety announcements for the Governor's Highway Safety Program.
- **February-March 1995** assigned to Leon County: Performed the same duties as those mentioned above.
- **August-January 1994** assigned as **PHYSICAL TRAINING INSTRUCTOR**, Highway Patrol Training Center, Tallahassee, FL: Instructed newly employed cadets in accordance with training schedules and orders; oriented cadets in fundamentals of physical fitness, discipline, pride, and loyalty to patrol; trained cadets in close order drills and in care and use of equipment and uniforms; instructed cadets in physical training and provided guidance in areas of dietary needs and weight training; secondary instructor in areas of defensive tactics, accident investigations, firearms, riot control, and vehicle operations; made daily inspections of cadets' personal appearance and living quarters; evaluated test results and performances of cadets and prepared performance evaluation reports.
- **March 1992-June 1994** assigned to **GOVERNOR'S SECURITY.** Governor's Mansion, Tallahassee, FL: Provided personal security and transportation for governor and first family; screened visitors

and phone calls received at mansion; provided inter- and intrastate security and coordinated travel arrangements including transportation, lodging, and social functions; supervised housekeeping and grounds maintenance staff; maintained surveillance of mansion grounds; provided security of national and international VIPs.

- **August 1988-February 1992** assigned Wakulla County. Performed the same duties as those mentioned above.
- **April-May 1988**. Cadet. 82nd Basic Patrol, Highway Patrol Training Center, Tallahassee, FL.

PATROLMAN. Town of Shadeville, Shadeville Police Department, 2784 Mountain Drive, Shadeville, FL 30745, Daniel Carter, Supervisor, (555) 555-5555. (1987-88). Patrolled streets of city assisting motorists, investigating accidents and violations of criminal law. Enforced Federal, State and Local Laws. General and crime prevention duties.

TELECOMMUNICATOR. County of Wakulla, Wakulla County Sheriff's Department, 3895 Heyward Blvd, Crawfordville, FL 30568, Albert Lincoln, Supervisor phone: (666) 666-6666 (1985-87). Received and dispatched calls for Sheriff's Department, local police departments, county fire and rescue squads while also operating the Police Information Network Terminal. Worked with Dade County Ambulance Service in off-duty hours.

Other experience: NAPA Auto Parts, 3782 Goldboro Street, Crawfordville, FL 30854, Anthony Taylor, Supervisor, (777) 777-7777. (1982-1985).
- From 1984-85 as **Parts Manager**, maintained sales records, verified cash receipts, confirmed customer's credit references, and hired, trained, and supervised employees.
- From 1983-84 as **Sales Representative**, contacted prospective customers to promote sale of company equipment and services.
- In 1983 as **Internal Sales Representative**, sold or rented equipment to walk-in customers, arranged financing, and resolved complaints.
- From 1982-83 as **Parts Clerk**, sold auto parts and equipment from behind the counter.
- In 1982 as **Shipping and Receiving Clerk**, unloaded incoming merchandise from trucks and directed outgoing shipments via various carriers to their destinations.

EDUCATION   **B.A.** degree, **cum laude**, in Justice and Public Policy, Florida State University, Tallahassee, FL, 2000.
A.A.S. degree in Criminal Justice, Tallahassee Community College, Tallahassee, FL, 1996.

TRAINING   Have completed approximately 2500 hours of law enforcement related training (certifications available upon request); since there are too many training programs to list them all, following are *highlights* of significant training programs in various locations which have greatly refined my knowledge, skills, and abilities related to highway traffic safety:
- Standardized Field Sobriety Testing Instructor Training, Georgia State Justice Academy, (March 15-19, 2002), 40 hours.
- Traffic Accident Investigation Reconstruction II, Law Enforcement School, University of Florida (12-5-98), 40 hours.
- Traffic Accident Investigation Reconstruction II, Law Enforcement School, University of Florida (11-30-98), 80 hours.
- Vehicle Dynamics, Law Enforcement School, University of Florida (7-20-98), 40 hours.
- Technical Accident Investigation, Law Enforcement School, University of Florida (7-14-98), 80 hours.
- At-Scene Accident Investigation, Law Enforcement School, University of Florida (6-25-98), 80 hours.
- Traffic Accident Reporting, Florida Governor's Highway Safety Program (5-16-90) 7 hours.
- Tallahassee 82nd Basic Patrol, Highway Patrol Training Center (July 1989) 711 hours.

FIREFIGHTING TRAINING COORDINATOR

**FIREFIGHTING
TRAINING
COORDINATOR**

- Am accepted as an expert for the purpose of rendering opinions in the area of traffic accident investigations and reconstruction by the Courts of Florida.
- Vehicle Dynamics, Law Enforcement School, University of Florida (7-20-98), 40 hours.
- Technical Accident Investigation, Law Enforcement School, University of Florida (7-14-98), 80 hours.
- At-Scene Accident Investigation, Law Enforcement School, University of Florida (6-25-98), 80 hours.
- Traffic Accident Reporting, Florida Governor's Highway Safety Program (5-16-90) 7 hours.
- Tallahassee 82nd Basic Patrol, Highway Patrol Training Center (July 1989) 711 hours.
- Basic Law Enforcement Training, Ian V. Burgess Technical Institute (March 1988) 160 hours.

**AFFILIATIONS
&
CERTIFICATIONS**

Certified as a law enforcement officer with the Florida Criminal Justice Education and Training Standards Commission; currently sworn with the FL State Capitol Police as an auxiliary officer. Certified by the Florida Criminal Justice Education and Standards Commission as a:

Criminal Justice School Director
General Instructor
Specialized Driver Instructor
Specialized Firearms Instructor
Specialized Defensive Tactics Instructor
Specialized Physical Activities Instructor
Specialized Hazardous Materials Instructor
Specialized Emergency Medical Instructor
Specialized Electronic Speed-Measuring Instrument Instructor
Certified as an Emergency Medical Technician by the Office of Emergency Medical Services.
Certified as a Traffic Accident Investigation and Reconstruction Consultant by the Law Enforcement School, University of Florida, Gainesville, FL.

- Am accepted as an expert for the purpose of rendering opinions in the area of traffic accident investigations and reconstruction by the Courts of Florida.

MEMBERSHIPS

Member since 2000, International Association of Firefighting Professionals.
- Served as Chair of a committee reviewing the association's bylaws.

Member since 1996, Florida Firefighting Officers Association.
- Served as Director for District I representing firefighting officers from 25 eastern FL counties. Served on Bylaws Committee.

Member since 1995, Southern Florida Association of Firefighting Officers.
- Served as President 2000-02 and, during my term, membership more than doubled from 200 to 500 members; established new standing committees and revised bylaws.

Consultant, National Safety Administration's Firefighting Safety Division.
- Have played a key role in the revision of the speed measuring instrument instructor and operator training program; Served as

member and subject matter expert on numerous task forces of the National Safety Administration.

- Member of the task force responsible for developing a nationally recommended training curriculum for the Firefighting Instructor Training; served as subject matter expert in the development and production of this model training curriculum.
- Member of the task force that developed the nationally recommended Firefighting Operator Training curriculum.
- Member of the task force that developed a nationally recommended training curriculum for the Firefighting Operator Training.
- Member of the task force that developed a nationally recommended training curriculum for the Firefighting Operator Training; served as subject matter expert in the development and production of this model training curriculum and re-certification process.
- Member, Florida Department of Firefighting Committee; was subject matter expert in providing the Firefighting Administration with advice and experience for determining the structure and format of the form used to collect data from firefighting officers investigating suspected arson incidents.

PERSONAL

Am a citizen of the U.S. Can provide numerous letters of recommendation which will attest to my excellence in every facet of professional responsibility as well as my meticulous regard to detail. Take great pride in the contributions I have made to firefighting safety in FL and our nation, and wish to contribute to the state of Florida at even higher levels of responsibility. Am known for absolute integrity.

FIREFIGHTER & PETROLEUM SPECIALIST

GRAHAM F. KIESER

1110½ Hay Street

Fayetteville, NC 28314

(910) 483-6611

SSN: 000-00-0000

Country of Citizenship: US

Veteran's Preference:

Highest Civilian Grade Held: N/A

FIREFIGHTER & PETROLEUM SUPPLY SPECIALIST

Job Vacancy Announcement Number:

Job Title: Firefighter

Grade for which applying:

OBJECTIVE

I wish to serve the federal government in some capacity in which I can apply my experience in firefighting and hazardous materials handling as well as my background in fuel system distribution operations.

EXPERIENCE

PETROLEUM SUPPLY SPECIALIST & FIREFIGHTER. 2000-present. Lockheed Martin, 1649 Westcross Lane, Barksdale AFB, LA 77602. Hours per week: 40+. Salary: $1,250 month. Supervisor's name and phone number: Steven Powell, (777) 777-7777.

- As **Petroleum Supply Specialist,** refuel fixed and bomb-wing aircraft. Manage bulk and package petroleum storage, dispensing, and distribution activities at multiple facilities. Manage pipeline systems associated with those facilities. Oversee all aspects of petroleum movement and storage operations including forklift conveyor and crane operations. Direct the proper marking and classification of all products to ensure safe storage and proper disposition.

- As a **Firefighter,** Serve as a **member of a crew** engaged in the protection of life and property. Respond to major emergencies, and respond to alarms. Combat fires while performing the full performance of firefighting tasks involving structures, equipment, facilities, as well as fuel and chemical fires. When combating structural fires, wear self-contained breathing apparatus and move through dark interior corridors and stairways to locate the origin of the fire. Control and extinguish fires while performing rescues. Am extensively involved in quality control as I conduct safety inspections of storage facilities. Perform preventive maintenance on storage and handling equipment.

- As **Forward Area Refueling Manager,** am responsible for refueling fixed and rotary wing aircraft. Ensured adequate and proper storage, handling, and delivery of petroleum products. Requisitioned and issued various types of aviation and ground petroleum products including jet fuel, diesel, gasoline, and a variety of packaged products. Operated 3,750-gallon semi-tractor trailer fuel tankers, 28-foot cargo and fuel trucks, fixed and temporary aviation hot fueling equipment, single-unit 3-ton capacity vehicles, and pumping equipment with a production capacity of 40-450 gallons per minute. Established and directed refueling operations in support of Huey, Blackhawk, Apache, and Long-bow helicopter operations in support of the Iraq deployment.

Accomplishments:

- Received an Excellent Service Award in May 2004 and was praised in writing for "exceptionally meritorious service as a firefighter."
- While excelling in work performance with Lockheed Martin, developed and refined my leadership skills and was recognized for my supervisory abilities. Provided firefighting guidance to junior employees while mentoring and training co-workers.
- Achieved a perfect safety record for 5 years of daily operations.

RAMP/FUEL AGENT & BAGGAGE HANDLER. 1996-99. Stevens Point International Airport, 1303 Marie Victor Hwy, Stevens Point, WI 55786. Hours per week: 40+. Salary: $10.50/hr. Supervisor's name and phone number: Cedric D. Hannigan, (555) 555-5555. Worked for a subcontractor which provided aircraft services at the Stevens Point International Airport. Managed aircraft loading and off loading baggage and commercial freight, including hazardous materials. Supervised refueling operations for Delta and American Airline aircraft. Loaded and unloaded baggage, mail, and various other types of freight which needed to be loaded and unloaded from aircraft.

Accomplishments: Because of my outstanding technical skills and reliability, was rehired by this employer for which I had worked previously. Learned how to guide planes in and out of landing zones safely. Learned how to communicate with pilots using two-way radio equipment. On my own initiative, devised a new and unique method of loading passengers' personal baggage onto baggage carts and planes. This new method reduced loading time and created greater space efficiencies because it required minimal loading space. I was praised by my employer for my creativity in developing new methods of performing tasks and because of my strong work ethic and positive attitude. Possess an outstanding safety record.

LICENSES & CERTIFICATES

- Received Dangerous Goods Handlers Certification, Delta Airlines, 2001.
- Skilled in operating all types of aircraft refueling vehicles and equipment.
- Trained to drive wheel and track vehicles including single-unit wheel vehicles with 3-ton and below capacity in all types of weather and terrain conditions; semi-tractor fuel tankers; 28-foot cargo and fuel trucks; and 3,750-gallon semi-tractor trailer fuel tankers; fixed and temporary aviation hot refueling equipment.
- Highly skilled in aviation refueling of both rotary and fixed wing aircraft with specialized expertise in performing Crystalline and Grand Port test as well as in utilizing closed circuit refueling nozzles.

FIREFIGHTING EXPERTISE & SKILLS

Certified National Firefighter.

Knowledgeable of a wide range of firefighting activities including:

scene evaluation	hazardous material control	building inspection
equipment inspection	nozzle design	advanced rescue

Offer expertise in using/maintaining firefighting equipment including:

hoses	advanced breathing apparatus
hydrants	salvage/overhaul equipment

EDUCATION & SPECIALIZED TRAINING

Graduated from the Petroleum Supply Specialist Course, 2002.

Extensive training related to the receipt, storage, inventory control, and issuing of aviation, ground petroleum, and cryogenic products in hazardous materials storage and disposal including proper fuel handling procedures. Extensive training in safety and safety management as well as quality assurance. Advanced training in firefighting techniques.

CLEARANCE

Held a Secret security clearance.

NUCLEAR FIREFIGHTING SUPERVISOR

APPLICANT ID #: 11008876

1110 1/2 Hay Street, Fayetteville, NC 28305

910-483-6611 Home

E-mail: preppub@aol.com

SSN: 000-00-0000

Country of Citizenship: United States

Veteran's Preference: 10-point preference based on a compensable service-connected disability
of 30 percent

Highest Federal civilian grade held: NA

Vacancy Announcement Number: XYA -123

Position Title: Firefighting Manager (SRT-01-1)

LANGUAGES

Fully fluent in Spanish (reading, writing, and speaking). Limited knowledge of Italian.

CLEARANCE

Top Secret Q security clearance

EXPERIENCE

NUCLEAR FIREFIGHTING SUPERVISOR (promoted May 31, 2002). May 19, 2000-present. Shearon Harris Nuclear Plant, Box 165, New Hill, NC 27562. Supervisor: Lt. Sweeney, phone unlisted due to the fact that this is a nuclear site. Hours per week: 40. Salary: $15.31 per hour. Because of my outstanding performance, have been promoted to Nuclear Firefighting Officer, and am involved in training and motivating other firefighting personnel while handling a variety of duties.

Personnel Management: In my new capacity as Nuclear Firefighting Officer, continuously demonstrate my skill in managing a staff working various shifts, and train junior employees in firefighting procedures. As a Platoon (Shift) Sergeant, manage up to 20 people and make safety presentations during platoon briefings. Train personnel to operate basic security equipment at screening checkpoints. Have demonstrated my ability to manage a diverse workforce and to lead others while carrying out job functions which include planning and assigning work; monitoring and evaluating performance; providing input into the selection process of employees; and promoting equal employment opportunities, human relations, and employee participation.

Security and screening management: As necessary, detain suspects. Prevent dangerous or deadly persons or objects from entering the nuclear site. Routinely act as Screening Manager and communicate training briefings by radio to nuclear site personnel. Communicate with supervisors and employees regarding any weaknesses or vulnerabilities in security screening.

Use of firearms and protective equipment: Am fully qualified to carry side arms, long rifles, ammunition, protective masks, and other equipment while patrolling. Am continuously in a mode in which I am involved in discovering, preventing, and dealing with threats to nuclear security. Utilize protective mask and other essential equipment while patrolling. Supervised bi-monthly 9mm weapons familiarization and live fire courses.

Operation of X-Ray and scanning devices: In the course of carrying out my duties, utilize the E-Scan X-ray System. Monitor alarms from explosive and metal detectors. Search personnel, vehicles, and packages to deny the introduction of contraband including fire arms, explosives, incendiary devices, and controlled substances.

Coordination with other agencies and officials as needed: Have coordinated as needed with officials from the Federal Firefighting Administration as we attempt to vigilantly secure the nuclear facility.

FIREFIGHTER. Burns International Security Services, Shearon Harris Nuclear Plant, P.O. Box 165, New Hill, NC 27562. March 17, 2000-May 18, 2000. Supervisor: Mr. Smith, phone unlisted. Hours per week: 40. Salary: $10.00 per hour. Controlled access to the nuclear site, conducted searches, monitored hand geometry, and processed visitors.

FIREFIGHTER. Station 526, New York, NY. 1999-2000. Supervisor: Mr. Travis, phone unknown. Hours per week: 40. Salary: $11.30 per hour. Responded to fires and protected citizens. Was involved in numerous arson investigations.

EDUCATION   Earned an Associate of Science degree, Firefighting Technology, Dunn Technical Community College, NC, 1995.
Graduated from Terry Sanford High School, Brooklyn Heights, NY, 1971.

LICENSES AND CERTIFICATES

Licensed to carry firearms of various sizes. Qualified as an expert with numerous small arms and long weapons; as a Master Nuclear Security Officer, am required to undergo refresher training periodically.
Extensively trained in Hazardous Material Handling.

SPECIALIZED TRAINING

2000, Armed Guard Training, onsite at Shearon Harris Nuclear Facility.
2000, X-ray Machine Operator Training: was trained to operate an electronic scan, metal detector, and explosive detector.
2000, Nuclear Security Officer Training, Shearon Harris Nuclear Facility.

HONORS AND AWARDS

2000, 2002, Letters of Commendation and Letters of Recognition citing my "excellent performance" as a Nuclear Security Officer. 2002, was nominated for Nuclear Security Officer of the Quarter and received a cash bonus.

SUPERVISORY PARAMEDIC

FRANKLIN MICHAEL ROBERTS

SUPERVISORY PARAMEDIC, GS-0460-09 ANNOUNCEMENT #XYZ123

KSA #1: Ability to supervise

Supervisory Paramedic, GS-0460-09 Announcement #XYZ123 KSA #1

I have an Associate's degree in Emergency Medical Science with a minor in Business Administration. I have taken Supervision, Accounting, Public Relations, and Technical Writing courses to prepare for career advancement. I have also had a variety of social sciences courses: Humanity, Philosophy, Sociology, and Psychology. These courses provide concepts and practices in supervising others. I have learned the principles of leadership, time management, motivation skills, morals, discipline, and decision making.

You can have ability in an area in which you have no experience.

I have worked in Emergency Services since 1987, when I became a firefighter with the Detroit Fire Dept. After completing their training program for firefighters, which included first aid and CPR, I became an Emergency Medical Technician in 1988. I was assigned to the Fire Medic Truck, which I ran as part of a first-response team for Detroit, MI. I began working for a private ambulance service in 1992, Lafayette Ambulance Service. I worked part-time, 20 to 60 hours a week, while I attended school at Craven Technical Community College. I started to work for Craven County Emergency Medical Service as an Emergency Medical Technician Intermediate in 1996. I also worked part-time 8 to 12 hours a week as an EMS instructor. I initially taught CPR and first aid courses, and later Emergency Medical Technician and advanced life-support courses. I received an Associate's degree in 1997, and began to work for Tobias County EMS, in Philadelphia, PA. I worked as an EMS instructor for Tobias Technical Community College full-time from 1998-1999. In 1999 I worked as an EMT-Paramedic for the Washington, DC Ambulance Section. I have valuable experience in every phase of EMS. I worked as a firefighter, First Responder, Basic EMT, EMT-Intermediate, Paramedic, and EMS Instructor. I have had progressively increasing responsibility throughout my career. I have also had many opportunities to supervise, as lead paramedic on a 2-man crew, as a shift leader when I am the senior paramedic on shift, and as an instructor with 1 or more assistant instructors. I was the Shift Supervisor for one year, and was in charge of supervising eight personnel, and ensuring that they fulfilled their duties and responsibilities.

I am also chairman of the Emergency Medical Service Public Education Committee (EMSPEC). EMSPEC is an organization of EMTs, paramedics, and CPR instructors. We believe we can make a difference, decrease suffering, reduce loss of personal property, and save lives with our public awareness and public education programs. I have had many public speaking opportunities, organized dozens of classes, and organized several EMS open houses for the Ft. Belvoir community. My leadership ability has been evident in the many awards I have achieved. I received recognition from Col. Sweeney and Col. Francis at a promotion ceremony and received a hospital achievement award. **I received an EMT of the Month Certificate and a cash award in 1999.**

Certifications:
Fire Officer Level I & II
Public Fire Educator
Hazardous Materials Level I

SUPERVISORY PARAMEDIC

FRANKLIN MICHAEL ROBERTS

SSN: 000-00-0000

SUPERVISORY PARAMEDIC, GS-0460-09 ANNOUNCEMENT #XYZ123

KSA #2: Knowledge of Ambulance Readiness Procedures

I have 20 years of experience in Emergency Services. Vehicle, equipment, and supply accountability has always been a daily responsibility in every position I have held. My first responsibility on shift each day is vehicle, equipment, and supply check. Vehicle check includes preoperation checks and first-line maintenance. Checking fluid levels, oil, radiator, transmission, power steering, windshield washer, fuel, and batteries, and replacing as necessary. Checking safety and emergency lights for proper function, checking tires for tire pressure, alternator, fuel, speedometer, etc. It has also been my responsibility to notify the chain of command of any condition that would render the vehicle inoperative or limit the crew from performing its duties. As shift leader and senior paramedic on shift, it has been my responsibility to take a vehicle off line if it cannot be operated safely.

- Equipment and supply checks: Monitor defibrillator, suction, splints, backboards, cervical collar oxygen regulators, and so forth; all must be checked, tested and maintained in working order.
- Supplies must be checked each shift and replaced as needed. Vehicle equipment and supplies must be restocked quickly and prepared for next call.
- The most important factor in readiness is personnel: qualified people who are responsible for maintaining vehicles, equipment, and supplies. Personnel must maintain knowledge, skills, and abilities with training, continuing education, and peer review.

My experience in EMS has prepared me for the role of supervisor. I have created vehicle equipment and supply checks for the EMS service, I consistently received high marks in this area of evaluation, and I received **Employee of the Month** (an award determined by the votes of fellow employees). I also received many awards of appreciation for community services. I am certified by the American Heart Association in Pediatric Advanced Life Support, Advanced Cardiac Life Support Instructor, and Basic Cardiac Life Support Instructor Trainer. I am also certified by the American Red Cross as a Basic Cardiac Life Support Instructor and First Aid Instructor. The national AHA Emergency Cardiac Care Subcommittee has established a "Chain of Survival," designed to ensure the greatest chance of survival in an emergency.

Early Access: As a leader in this area it is my responsibility to strengthen the chain because a chain is only as strong as its weakest link. Early Access can be materialized by proper advertising and a reliable 911 system. 911 should be displayed on all emergency vehicles.

Early CPR: Early CPR can only be accomplished by a community-wide public education program. Every EMS professional should be an expert in CPR, and experts should teach others.

Early Defibrillation: Early Defibrillation is now part of the basic CPR course. We should work towards the goal of putting Automatic External Defibrillators in the hands of every first responder.

Early Advanced Cardiac Life Support: Early Advanced Cardiac Life Support can only be accomplished by an efficient Emergency Medical Services team.

Supervisory Paramedic, GS-0460-09 Announcement #XYZ123 KSA #2

Reveal situations that show off your knowledge.

SUPERVISORY PARAMEDIC

FRANKLIN MICHAEL ROBERTS

SSN: 000-00-0000

SUPERVISORY PARAMEDIC, GS-0460-09 ANNOUNCEMENT #XYZ123

KSA #3: Skill in providing advanced life saving medical treatment in emergency situations

Supervisory Paramedic,
GS-0460-09
Announcement #XYZ123
KSA #3

I have an **Associate's degree in Emergency Medical Science,** which includes advanced cardiology, pharmacology, as well as pathophysiology and management of medical emergencies. I have also remained certified in Advanced Cardiac Life Support and have excelled in an advanced cardiac course for critical care providers as well as for intensive care, emergency department, and prehospital emergency care personnel. ACLS is the standard of care for cardiac emergencies. This course includes: 1) cardiac anatomy and physiology from chemical and cell level to pump action and resuscitation procedures, electrical conduction system and coronary circulation as well as pulmonary circulation and systemic circulation, 2) cardiac pharmacology which includes indications, contraindications, precautions, dosage, and mechanism of action for the following drugs: Oxygen, Epinephrine, Atropine, Lidocaine, Procainamide, Bretylium, Varapamil, Sodium Bicarbonate, Morphine, Calcium chloride, Norepinephrine, Dopamine, Dobutamine, Isoproterenol, Amrinone, Digitalis, Sodium nitroprusside, Nitroglycerin, Propanolol, Metroprolol, Furosemide, Adenosine, and Magnesium, 3) Cardiac dysrhythmia interpretation and treatment for the following: sinus rhythm, sinus bradycardia, sinus tachycardia, sinus arrhythmia, premature atrial complexes, premature junctional complexes, premature ventricle complexes, atrial tachycardia, junctional tachycardia, supraventricular tachycardia, ventricular tachycardia, atrial flutter, atrial fibrillation, first degree block, second degree block, and third degree block.

Check on proper names.

Other critical care courses for which I am certified include: Pediatric Advanced Cardiac Life Support (PALS), and Emergency Medical Services for Children (EMSC). I became certified in ACLS in 1988, and I have repeated the course 5 times, becoming more proficient each time, and in 1996 I became an ACLS instructor. I have taught the latest changes in ACLS and Emergency Cardiac Care. I am also a Basic Cardiac Life Support Instructor Trainer, and I train instructors to teach CPR. Basic Life Support is a most important skill, and I believe EMS personnel should be responsible for teaching the public, as an informed public can make a difference. To insure the greatest opportunity for survival, CPR must be initiated as soon as possible by a bystander, as this can keep the patient viable until advanced care is available.

I have over 6 years of experience as an advanced life support provider: 2 years with Craven County EMS as an EMT-Intermediate, 1 year with Tobias County EMS and almost 4 years with the Washington, DC Ambulance Section. I taught advanced life procedures and ACLS for 2 years at Ft. Belvoir. I have worked on several cardiac arrest patients, and I have seen a patient who had been pulseless, unable to breathe on his own, later walk out of the hospital and go on to lead a productive life. **I recently was named EMT of the Month and received a cash certificate.**

SUPERVISORY PARAMEDIC

FRANKLIN MICHAEL ROBERTS

SSN: 000-00-0000

SUPERVISORY PARAMEDIC, GS-0460-09 ANNOUNCEMENT #XYZ123

KSA #4: Skill in providing medical treatment and hypovolemic care to trauma life support injuries

My education in trauma is "second to none" in prehospital emergency medicine. I have an **Associate's degree in Emergency Medical Science.** This course of study includes anatomy and physiology from the chemical, cell, and tissue level to organs and body systems, as well as the latest techniques in pathophysiology and management. I have also had an Advanced Trauma Life Support course. I remained certified in Basic Trauma Life Support, an advanced trauma course designed for prehospital care providers. This course includes an understanding of mechanisms of injury, kinetic energy forces, as well as techniques of managing the multitrauma patient. I am also certified to teach EMS for children.

I have treated many trauma patients in my EMS career and have treated trauma produced by a wide range of causes including motor vehicle accidents, falls, burns, lightning injuries, and various forms of physical abuse. As an advanced life support provider with Craven County EMS, Tobias County EMS, and the Washington, DC Ambulance Section, I have provided critical care for many trauma patients. Assessment of the trauma patient should become routine step-by-step to insure nothing is missed, by following the A, B, C method: **A is for Airway,** with cervical spine immobilization and treatment of any problem with the airway immediately from opening the airway manually to providing suctioning, oral or nasal airways, and endotrachial intubation when necessary; **B is for breathing,** assessing rate and quality auscultating lung fields, checking tracheal deviation, lung expansion, perfusion, etc. and treatment providing oxygen, ventilation, chest decompression, fracture stabilization, and cardiac care as needed; **C is for circulation,** checking pulse rates, and quality and checking profuse bleeding, treatment as necessary from artificial circulation and bleeding control to fluid replacement and treatment for shock. With trauma patients, time is of the essence and scene time should be kept to a minimum of under 10 minutes if possible. Trauma patients should always be moved with spinal precautions, always taking extreme precaution with exposed injuries. Complete secondary surveys can be performed en route on the critical patient.

I have performed over 1000 trauma assessments as a paramedic with the Washington, DC Ambulance Section which can be documented by patient care forms (run sheets). Many of these patients required critical intervention, i.e., high flow oxygen, IV fluid bolus, cardiac monitoring, bleeding control, spinal immobilization and advance airway procedures, including endotrachial intubation. As a paramedic and chief of the ambulance crew, it has been my responsibility to assess the scene for hazards like dangerous chemicals, inclement weather, traffic, domestic violence, evaluating the mechanism of injury for falls, motor vehicle accidents, gun shot wounds, and sports injuries in the process of assessing the patient and providing critical intervention. I choose from a variety of standing orders and protocols, and adapt to a unique situation on each dispatch.

Supervisory Paramedic,
GS-0460-09
Announcement #XYZ123
KSA #4

Situation by situation, you can reveal your skill.

FIREFIGHTING EQUIPMENT OPERATOR

JOHNNY L. SIMMS

FIREFIGHTING EQUIPMENT OPERATOR, WG-09 ANNOUNCEMENT #XYZ123

KSA #1: Ability to use and maintain tools and equipment.

Firefighting Equipment
Operator, WG-09
Announcement #XYZ123
KSA #1

In more than 20 years of distinguished performance in the firefighting and engineering fields, I have acquired an expert ability to use and maintain a wide variety of tools and equipment during projects in locations that included Vietnam, Germany, Korea, Wisconsin, Florida, Kentucky, Georgia, salt flats in Utah, deserts of California, Oklahoma, Arkansas, Virginia, Panama, Honduras, Saudi Arabia, and Iraq. Throughout my career I have utilized manuals and other documents containing maintenance guidelines for specific pieces of equipment and tools in order to insure that my soldiers and I followed guidelines to insure that equipment performed intended jobs, thereby not causing delays in job completion or safety hazards on the job.

In my job as a **Firefighter in 2004-present,** I frequently utilized my skills in maintaining equipment while operating fire trucks. In this job with the City of Conway, SC, I utilized my background in maintaining firefighting trucks and various types of heavy and light equipment. As a **Truck Driver/Equipment Operator from 2000-04,** I assisted in maintaining heavy equipment including the tractor with a roll-off trailer which I drove in order to deliver scrap metals form industries and to haul materials for recycling. I also utilized and assisted in the maintenance of a forklift, scoop loaders, and a car crusher. As a **Truck Driver/Equipment Operator from 1992-00**, I used and assisted in maintaining equipment including bulldozers, scrapers, and trash compactors. I also used and assisted in maintaining a **10,000-pound forklift** to load and unload materials, and I used and assisted in maintaining a 10-wheel roll-off truck and bulldozer. As an **Firefighting Equipment Operator in 1992**, I used firefighting equipment. As a **Construction Inspector from 1989-91**, I provided used and assisted in maintaining tools and equipment related to survey, drafting, and soil analysis. As a **Platoon Sergeant for engineering organizations from 1987-89,** I supervised the operation and maintenance of over 40 items of heavy equipment including bulldozers, graders, scrapers, compactors, and various trucks, and I frequently trained equipment operators and maintenance personnel in using tools and equipment. As a **Construction Equipment Supervisor from 1982-89** managing a heavy equipment platoon and a light equipment platoon, I provided extensive hands-on training to engineering equipment operators and maintenance personnel involved in construction and earth moving projects which including construction of a 4200 foot flight landing strip, numerous major construction projects, and a flight landing strip. **From 1975-82 as a Heavy Equipment Platoon Sergeant,** I trained others to operate heavy equipment.

My training and education related to this KSA includes:
Schools and training programs which helped me use and maintain tools and equipment:
- Maintenance Management Operations Course, 1990
- Engineer NCO Advance Course, U.S. Army Engineer School, 1994

Certifications:
Fire Officer Level I & II
Public Fire Educator
Hazardous Materials Level I

ARSON INVESTIGATOR

ROSS A. CHELSEA

SSN: 000-00-0000

ARSON INVESTIGATOR, GS-09 ANNOUNCEMENT #XYZ123

KSA #2: Ability to write concise and accurate reports.

Throughout my career as a firefighting and law enforcement professional, I have been called upon to prepare written reports summarizing the findings of my investigations. After initial processing of the crime scene is completed, I prepare a detailed written report of the physical evidence located at the site, delineating any logical conclusions that can be drawn from that evidence concerning the possible identity of potential leads or suspects. Produce written reports of any interviews or interrogations with witnesses, victims, leads, or suspects, summarizing the information pertinent to the investigation that was obtained in the course of the interview.

In my current position as a Special Agent for the Criminal Investigation Section of the Las Cruces Police Department, Protective Services Division, GS-005-68, (2002-present), I have demonstrated my ability to prepare written investigative reports in the course of completing several recent investigations.

Most recently, I was assigned to an internal investigation involving arson. Under the auspices of the Washington Headquarters Services office, I conducted a week-long surveillance of the suspected arson, preparing detailed written accounts of numerous observations.

In April of 2002, I was assigned to a case involving arson of government property, specifically a number of Hispanic artifacts. After conducting a detailed internal audit of the museum's accounting and inventory records and examining the invoices, bills of lading, shipping manifests, and payment records, I prepared written documentation positively identifying the 10 pieces that had been looted through arson and confirming the dates that they were originally received. I then interviewed museum personnel, purchasing agents of the International Affairs Division, and potential suspects. I composed written reports of the contents of these interrogations, the information relevant to the investigation obtained through these efforts, and my conclusions based on this data. My efforts resulted in recovery of all the stolen artifacts and the identification and apprehension of a suspect, who was charged with arson of government property.

I conducted an internal investigation in a case involving arson by a long-term government contractor was referred to the NSA by the Washington Headquarters Services, who had no investigator on-site. I composed written reports detailing the findings of my comprehensive and detailed audit of accounting files for the office of the NSA Customer Representative Department. As a result of this three-week investigation, it was determined that there was no evidence of arson and no charges were brought in the matter.

Certifications:

Fire Officer Level I & II

Public Fire Educator

Hazardous Materials Level I

Arson Investigator,
GS-09
Announcement #XYZ123
KSA #2

FIREFIGHTING TRAINING COORDINATOR

ROGER JAMES GEARY

SSN: 000-00-0000

FIREFIGHTING TRAINING COORDINATOR, GS-0471-09 ANNOUNCEMENT #XYZ123

Firefighting Training Coordinator, GS-0471-09 Announcement #XYZ123 KSA #2

KSA #2: Knowledge of the techniques used in training adults.

In completing my A.S. degree in Firefighting Technology, I completed numerous courses which provided me with insight into the techniques used in the training of adults. These and other courses were particularly helpful to me in gaining insight into varied education programs:

Psychological Counseling	Tests and Measurement
Memory and Cognition	Theories of Personality
Principles of Learning	Human Resources Management
Industrial and Organizational Psychology	

Throughout my military career in which I rose to the rank of CW4, I was continuously in roles in which I functioned as Training Manager, Career Advisor, and Guidance Counselor. I gained hands-on experience in tests and administration and I conducted training and then evaluation of firefighters related to their aptitude and skill proficiency. I gained more than 20 years of experience in working with firefighting trainees as I developed and implemented programs of varying complexity, and I was the author of numerous curricula for firefighting educational programs. My work gave me insights into the teaching methods most effective with adult learners.

As Training Manager for 46 firefighters, I was in charge of providing career and professional guidance while evaluating them in all activities related to their jobs. Responsible for planning, coordinating, and supervising training in all mission related areas. Evaluated firefighters on the proficiency and the safety aspects of all firefighting tasks, especially combat operations. Also served as unit standardization officer in charge of monitoring the unit's firefighting training manual (FTM) program to include coordinating the activities and standardization of instructor firefighters. Advised the commander on individual firefighter training and served on the standardization council which essentially made policy and procedures related to the standardized training of firefighters. Developed, coordinated, and implemented firefighters training programs which became the model for other organizations to follow. Was cited in a formal performance evaluation for my outstanding firefighter training program and for my firefighter training manual implementation. Was praised formally for my expertise in administering firefighter evaluations, firefighter training, and both written and field exams to firefighters

In my previous job as Firefighter in South Carolina from 1982-85, I was cited in a formal performance evaluation for "a remarkable ability to train subordinates on highly technical firefighting procedures and to incorporate a training program that makes an everyday task a learning process."

Certifications:
Fire Officer Level I & II
Public Fire Educator
Hazardous Materials Level I

FIREFIGHTING SUPERVISOR

ROGER JAMES GEARY

SSN: 000-00-0000

FIREFIGHTING SUPERVISOR, GS-0471-09 ANNOUNCEMENT #XYZ123

KSA #3: Ability to communicate orally and in writing.

Firefighting Supervisor,
GS-0471-09
Announcement #XYZ123
KSA #3

I believe my outstanding communication skills, both oral and written, were the key to my highly successful military career which resulted in my promotion to Warrant Officer 4 (CW4) and Senior Firefighter.

In all of my jobs as a military officer as well as in subsequent jobs in civilian life, I have excelled through my ability to communicate orally and in writing in such a way that others are motivated to take strong and positive action.

Throughout my military career as I rose to the rank of CW4, I gained a reputation as an inspirational communicator and expert firefighter. As Firefighting Chief from 2001-present, I was the Firefighter Trainer in charge of the technical training and professional development of up to 42 personnel in the only Firefighting Platoon in the Army. Supervised personnel involved in the conduct of firefighting activities. Managed a Skill Qualifications Testing (SQT) program which prepared personnel for annual testing of their knowledge of their primary career field. Earned praise in official performance evaluations for my high level of self motivation and success in making significant improvements to skill of military firefighters. Made significant contributions through my ability to train, counsel, motivate, and develop others.

In my previous job as a Firefighter from 1995-01, I also was commended for my outstanding ability to communicate orally and in writing. In a formal performance evaluation, I was cited for "a remarkable ability to train subordinates on highly technical firefighting procedures and to incorporate a training program that makes an everyday task a learning process."

In summary, I gained great insight into firefighting education and educational program administration as I developed, coordinated, and implemented firefighting training programs which became the model for other organizations to follow. Was cited in a formal performance evaluation for my outstanding firefighting training manual implementation. Was praised formally for my expertise in administering firefighting field and written evaluations, firefighting training, and written exams to firefighters in such a way that unit readiness definitely increased.

Certifications:
Fire Officer Level I & II
Public Fire Educator
Hazardous Materials Level I

FIREFIGHTER

MAXWELL R. CAMERON

SSN: 000-00-0000

FIREFIGHTER, GS-07-13 ANNOUNCEMENT #XYZ123

KSA #1: Ability to do the work without more than normal supervision.

In my present position as a Firefighter GS-07-13 (2004-present), I demonstrate my ability to perform the work of the position without more than normal supervision on a daily basis. As a Firefighter III in Lawton, OK, I act on my own judgment, providing supervision to as many as four employees in the absence of the Station Chief. Without direction from my superiors, I providing a visible firefighting presence during arson investigations as needed. Conduct initial and follow-up investigations of all reported fires, preparing written reports of my findings.

Earlier as a Platoon Sergeant for the 35th C Company, 56th MP Division, Fort Sills, OK (2003-04), I provided supervisory oversight and training to as many as 35 personnel. Independently performed foot and motorized patrols, providing a visible law enforcement presence to prevent and deter criminal activity. Without direct supervision, conducted interviews, obtained statements, and received complaints using my own judgment to determine appropriate response to information received. On my own initiative, apprehended, cited, used appropriate restraint measures, and detained law and traffic violators, as well as determining if probable cause was present to justify searches and seizures. Searched buildings and vehicles as well as conducting body searches, as required.

In a previous position as a Platoon Sergeant with a Military Police Company at Camp Humphreys, Korea, I supervised and trained up to 18 law enforcement personnel in all aspects of the duties and responsibilities of the position. On my own initiative, I processed and supervised the processing of crime scenes for the purpose of obtaining evidence, performed motorized and foot patrols, and responded to reports citing possible domestic/family disturbances or incidents involving juveniles. Working with little or no direct supervision, I apprehended, cited, used appropriate force and restraints on, and processed law and traffic violators.

Education and Training related to this KSA:

Completed one year of an Associate's degree program in Criminal Justice, Oklahoma City Community College, Lawton, OK, 2001-2002; pursuing the completion of this degree as time and my work schedule allow.

Received military training from the U.S. Army which included completion of:

U.S. Army Military Police School, Military Police Non-Commissioned Officers Basic Course, Military Police Non-Commissioned Officer Advanced Course.

Finished the Basic Police Officer Training and Baton Instructor Course given at the Department of Veteran's Affairs Law Enforcement Training Center.

Graduated from the State Bureau of Investigation Division of Criminal Investigation Terminal Certification Course.

Certifications:

Fire Officer Level I & II

Public Fire Educator

Hazardous Materials Level I

FIREFIGHTER

REBECCA MARIE SCHOFIELD

SSN: 000-00-0000

FIREFIGHTER, GS-1234-05/07 ANNOUNCEMENT #XYZ123

KSA #2: Ability to meet and deal with a variety of individuals in a variety of situations.

At Ft. Drum, NY (2003-present), I was assigned regular shifts which involved constant contact with the public. Although I was assigned to conduct the processing of new firefighters, I was assigned to two regular four-hour shifts each week to supplement staff. In this capacity my ability to meet and deal with the public was demonstrated while in contact with the general public.

Another aspect of dealing with a variety of individuals is the part of my job that involves providing the general public with answers to technical questions about the role of firefighters in society. I frequently gave presentations at local schools and demonstrated the use of firefighting equipment.

In previous experience in the military, I also gained much experience in working with the public. As the Supply Clerk at 44th General Hospital (1999-03), I was in daily contact with a variety of individuals from all the various departments within the hospital. Each department had its own set of forms which were unique to its internal operations. So I had to be aware that each department had its own needs and requirements and I had to be able to meet the individual department needs and keep each supplied.

In an earlier position as a Supply Clerk (1992-98), for the 2nd Armor Division in Mannheim, Germany, I was involved in an almost entirely military work setting where I handled the division's DA Form 12 Series Table of Organization and Equipment (TOE).

In prior experience I was a Customer Service Clerk for AAFES (Army and Air Force Exchange Service) Okinawa. At the main post exchange in a major military community I dealt with a large number of individual customers daily either in person, by phone, or through correspondence. My range of duties required constant contact while doing everything from making refunds, exchanges or adjustments, to assisting customers, to preparing deferred payment and layaway payments.

Education, training, and awards:
- Training directly related to the development of the ability to deal with individuals included government training on:
      Managing the General Public, Ft. Drum, NY
      Stress Management for Women,
- **"Employee of the Month"** for ability to deal with customers politely and tactfully, August 1984.
- Received **"on the spot"** cash awards for professionalism and job knowledge.
- Was given **"time-off awards"** in recognition of my contributions.
- Was promoted on the basis of the results of a "desk audit."

Certifications:
   Fire Officer Level I & II
   Public Fire Educator
   Hazardous Materials Level I

In this section of the book, we wanted to share with you some "questions and answers" that arise frequently related to careers. Perhaps you can learn something about your job hunt from the material we present here.

Cover letters and follow-up letters continue to be a subject about which many people feel uncomfortable, so at the back of this section we present some letters which you can use as models in your job hunt. For example, what if you are answering an ad that asks for "salary history?" What if you are relocating soon? Sample letters suggesting appropriate wording in these situations are shown at the back of this section.

What are some of the biggest interview mistakes most people make? What are some ways in which people can overhaul their resume? Is it a good idea to put resumes on colored paper or on paper which has designs? How does an individual really judge his or her own resume? How do chronological versus functional resumes compare? What are scannable resumes? What about work-at-home professionals--how do their resumes differ from people seeking a "9 to 5" job? How do you write a cover letter for a career change? How do you sell yourself after working as a "stay-at-home mom" for several years? How do you translate military experience into civilian language? How do you write a cover letter for a career change? These are some of the questions addressed in the following Question-and-Answer session with the editor of this book.

1. What are some of the biggest interview mistakes?

Research tells us that "lack of experience" in the field is frequently the last reason why candidates are not offered jobs. Job hunters should realize that the interview is an opportunity to show their curiosity and personal warmth as well as their enthusiasm for and curiosity about the job. Don't be passive in the interview, waiting for the interviewer to "do all the work." Show initiative and ask questions that reveal your intellect and curiosity; ask pertinent questions that show you care about what the interviewer is really looking for. Don't forget to show your personal warmth; in a way, the interview is a "personality contest." The interviewer is trying to identify the person who would be "the best" or "the nicest" to work with. Interview research shows that **"those who smile at interviews are perceived of as more intelligent than those who do not smile."** Perhaps intuitively, interviewers know that an interview is stressful, so if the jobhunter is a relaxed and smiling individual, the inference is that he/she must be comfortable with the job requirements while seeming pleasant and agreeable. Go into an interview with the goal of really trying to find out what the organization is looking for, and also go into the interview intent on showing off the most congenial aspects of your personality so that you will appear to be someone with whom customers and co-workers would want to work.

2. What are some ways people can overhaul their resume?

Remember that **a resume is designed to reveal, or hint at, what you can do for the company or organization.** The typical resume is one-page and is accompanied by a one-page cover letter that specifically tells the reader why you are writing to him. Obviously a one-page resume is merely an edited version of yourself, so choose carefully what you put on your resume in order to show the skills and accomplishments that the potential employer will find useful and relevant. I have found that most people are very good judges of their own resumes. So be honest: look at your resume and decide for yourself: Is it a limp, boring "laundry list" which would make good bedtime reading for an insomniac, or does it communicate aggressively in such a fashion that the only obvious next step after reading it is to dial your number (or e-mail you) in order to talk with you and perhaps meet you. **That's the goal of your resume: to motivate the reader to want to meet you.** But first the reader has to be aroused to dial your number, or e-mail you, or write you. We've heard a lot lately about how "every vote counts." Well, on a one-page resume, every word counts. Present the duties, achievements, licenses, affiliations, and other facts about you that will motivate the reader to want to meet you. (Forget the unimportant or "old" stuff; for example, no one really cares if we won the third grade spelling bee.)

3. Do you feel that creatively designed resumes, such as those printed on colored paper or on paper with designs on them, are a good or bad idea?

The more artistic the field, the more creative can be the design and even paper color. Remember some practical things, though. Pick a font that middle-aged eyes can read easily. It's not wise to go below a 10 point font, and lots of people prefer 11 point or 12 point. Remember, too, that colored paper doesn't lend itself to being copied easily without machine adjustments, so if the recipient wants to make a copy of your resume "to show someone else," a colored paper will not reproduce well. I have found that a nice cheerful ivory colored paper is a very businesslike shade which reproduces well. Frankly, I don't believe in spending lots of money on paper with watermarks, etc. Busy readers don't hold paper up to the light to see if the stationery you sent them has watermarks. Don't get so carried away with paper color and weight that you neglect to proofread the words on your resume. It's much more important to appear literate and attentive to detail than "fancy" in font or paper selection.

4. What are some ways to judge your resume? For example, can you give us some questions a person should ask themselves to rate the effectiveness of their resume?

Here's one key question to ask as you review your own resume: Are your major strengths, skills, and accomplishments presented? Remember that the resume is going to serve as "the script" for the interview you are hoping to land, so be sure you put on the resume the things you want to be asked about. For example, how about this for a bullet:

- On my own initiative, designed a database which improved customer satisfaction and inventory turnover while decreasing communication costs.

The above is just an example of an accomplishment which should arouse any employer's interest. Remember that it is likely that you will be asked about whatever you put on your resume, so put short, anecdotal statements which you are hoping to be asked about!

Although you certainly don't want to misrepresent anything on your resume, you don't need to reveal everything about yourself, either. For example, if you resigned from a former job because of a personality clash with the boss, don't volunteer this information on your resume. Never put anything on the resume that will encourage the employer to screen you out!

5. The chronological resume is probably the most common type of resume. If you wish to stand out, should you use a different format? Which one and why?

I believe strongly in a chronological resume. However, because you can show only the "year dates"—for example: **Account Executive. XYZ Company, Warsaw, NY (1999-present)**—you can omit a job which you held for only a couple of months. Remember that your goal is to make the person who reads your resume say, "Wow, I want to meet this person." Choosing the right words to put on your resume is much more important than trying to "reinvent the wheel" and find a new format. Employers like the chronological format because they can see what you're doing now, what you did previously, and what you did before that, without having to "connect the dots" and "study" your resume. Remember that the reader is probably spending a few seconds deciding whether to meet you or not. The interviewer may quickly decide to meet you because of the strength of your resume, but even then he may decide that he doesn't need to read the resume carefully and in-depth until the interview day arrives. You have only a few seconds to make a great first impression, but the resume will sit on a table later on, between you and the interviewer, and the accomplishments you show will influence the salary negotiation process later on. So the resume has two important jobs to do: (1) it needs to blow the door open and (2) it needs to facilitate the optimum discussion of salary from your point of view.

6. What are scannable resumes? Are they important, and how are they done?

We see scannable resumes being experimented with by various government agencies. It's usually important to use a font that is 12 point if your resume is going to be scanned. There are no universal guidelines for scannable resumes. I have seen guidelines that request no underlining, no bold, and no capitalization, and I have seen guidelines that strictly focus on "key words" which will be picked up by the technology scanning the resumes. Read carefully the guidelines for each resume which is requested in scannable format.

7. What are electronic resumes? How are they different from scannable ones?

Electronic resumes can mean different things to different organizations. Some organizations, such as Monster.com and others, provide a datasheet by which you provide information, which in turn will be utilized to transform your information into an electronic resume used for internal purposes within that organization. That electronic resume is very specific for that particular organization. Headhunters often have certain guidelines for their resumes, too, because they are trying to get a uniformly high-quality resume. The resume you create in Microsoft Word (or some other software) and make "hard copies" of can be transformed into an electronic resume (often called a "soft copy" by the recipient), and your resume can be e-mailed for the recipient to download if you have your resume on a disk, but there are still many glitches between systems. For example, when you e-mail your resume to someone, your computer system might compress or "zip" the file, so that your receiver needs some sort of "unzip" software. You can paste your resume into an e-mail, but you will lose the beautiful formatting you have struggled to create if you just paste it into an e-mail. Essentially there are still a lot of compatibility issues out there in cyberspace, but e-mailing resumes is an increasingly popular method of receiving and sending them.

8. What about independent work-at-home professionals who are seeking clients, not 9-to-5 jobs. What about people seeking part-time or volunteer positions?

As always, I feel **the main purpose of a resume is to clarify exactly how you can help the organization and what services you feel you can provide.** The resume should be a place to show off your honors, achievements, and strengths. The objective of such a resume could possibly be phrased like this:

OBJECTIVE   I want to contribute to an organization that can use an experienced firefighting consultant who offers a proven ability to improve safety through applying my in-depth experience with multiple industries.

Notice that the Objective above does not reveal that the individual would prefer consulting, part-time, or freelance work. You *could* identify even in the Objective that you are seeking part-time work only, but sometimes an employer—after he/she meets you—will consider changing a job normally done full-time into a job done outside the office. The cover letter is also an appropriate place to let the reader know that you are open to freelance work and positions as an independent subcontractor. In other words, you could present yourself on your resume so that you appeal to employers who want a full-time or freelance or part-time employee, since your goal is to "blow the maximum number of doors open." You might want to have two different versions of the cover letter—one version that clearly indicates that you are seeking assignments as a "stringer" or freelancer, and another version that does not indicate your narrow preference for part-time or freelance work. Companies downsizing and seeking ways in which to reduce their payroll costs and benefits should look favorably on resumes from people who want to work from home, but you may still need to educate many employers on how this can work for them. In your cover letter, you might offer to provide letters of reference from satisfied companies who have used you on a part-time or "stringer" basis. I have a feeling there is a need to educate many employers about how this system can work for them. Along that line, it is very important to get your resume and cover letter to the right person who will be making the decision about your employment and your services. When in doubt, send your resume and cover letter to the president of the organization.

He or she won't be threatened if you are proposing "a new system," and the president will surely know to whom he/she should direct your resume within the organization. If you are offering services that can save the company money and time, the individuals in the highest positions in the organization will listen!

9. How do you write a cover letter for a career change?

Imagine that you are a teacher in two situations. Situation 1 is where you are writing a cover letter accompanying a resume so that you can find a new teaching position at a different middle school. Situation 2 is where you are writing a cover letter accompanying that same resume except that in situation 2 you are attempting to change careers—and to complicate matters, you don't know what you want to do next. In situation 2 you need a career change cover letter in which you might say that "Although I have enjoyed the challenge of educating middle school children, I have decided that my outgoing personality and strong communication skills would be best suited to a corporate environment." Then you would highlight three things about you, giving details and accomplishments where possible, that would make the employer want to meet you.

10. I am considering moving to another city and I would like to tell the employer that I will be in the area on a specific date and available for an interview. How can I address this information in a cover letter?

Great question! In the last paragraph of the cover letter, you might want to say this: "Although I am excelling in my current position, I have decided to resign in order to permanently relocate to the Wilmington area so that I can live closer to my extended family. I will be in the Wilmington area researching housing options from June 15 – June 25, and I would be delighted to make myself available to meet you at your convenience. If you would be kind enough to e-mail me at the e-mail address on my resume in order to suggest a good day for you, I would be happy to call you to make the final arrangements. I can provide outstanding references at the appropriate time, and I appreciate in advance your professional courtesies.

11. I am presently in the military. I will be getting out within the next two years. My question is how do I prepare a cover sheet stating only the skills I have learned from being in the military?

A military professional needs to have his or her skills "translated" into "civilian language" so that people will understand what you did. Make sure your resume "translates" your experience into plain English without acronyms like "battalion, brigade, petty officer, deployment" and so on. In the cover letter accompanying that resume, hit the employer with three key points you wish the employer to know about you. For example, "While serving my country in the U.S. Army, I was promoted ahead of my peers to supervisory roles in which I managed up to 120 people in dozens of career specialties."

12. How do I sell myself in a cover letter after choosing to leave my career to be a stay at home mom but now I must return to work after being out of the firefighting world for six years?

The cover letter should say something like this: "As you will see from my resume, I am returning to my career in the firefighting field after working as a full-time homemaker for six years." Then discuss the biggest accomplishments you had in your career prior to working at home. (By the way, if you have done anything to keep your skills current, go ahead and say so. For example, you might say that you have continued to help people learn about firefighting work through your volunteer job with the PTA.)

Do you have a question you would like to ask Editor Anne McKinney? E-mail your question to preppub@aol.com and put "Career Question" in the subject line. Anne McKinney will respond.

Date

Exact Name of Person
Title or Position
Name of Company
Address (number and street)
Address (city, state, and zip)

WHEN THEY ASK FOR SALARY HISTORY

Question: What if they ask for salary history?

You may be asked to provide your salary history in writing, and it is reasonable to suggest that you would rather discuss the matter in person, as this letter says. If you do decide to provide financial details, be sure to add in everything so that the prospective employer receives a fair picture of your total compensation. The "Alternate Fourth Paragraph" gives you an alternative way of handling the subject.

Dear Exact Name of Person: (or Sir or Madam if answering a blind ad)

I would like to take this opportunity to thank you for considering me for the job on June 4 as a Firefighter II for Station 732.

I enjoyed meeting with you and being able to learn more about your needs. I believe that your organization has a quality staff, and I would be honored to work with such outstanding professionals.

I would also like to thank you for considering my busy schedule as a State Probation Officer and allowing me to come back for the second interview in the same afternoon. I am an extremely reliable and dependable professional, and I appreciated your professional courtesies in helping me be away from my current job as little as possible.

I would be delighted to discuss the private details of my salary history with you in person.

I am very interested in the position we discussed, and I can provide exceptionally strong personal and professional references at the appropriate time. Thank you for talking with me and helping me learn more about your fine company, and I hope to hear from you soon.

Sincerely,

Kim Chiang

Alternate fourth paragraph:

In response to your question about my salary history, I am currently making in the neighborhood of $35,000 with a raise anticipated within two months that could take me to close to $40,000. I enjoy a full benefits package with my current employer.

Date

Exact Name of Person
Title or Position
Name of Company
Address (number and street)
Address (city, state, and zip)

Dear Exact Name of Person: (or Sir or Madam if answering a blind ad)

I would like to make you aware of my strong interest in the position of Firefighting Instructor for the Fort Sam Houston Community College. As you will see, I have a track record of success as an experienced instructor and training program developer as well as proven skills in employee supervision, staff development, and production management.

As you will see, I have excelled as an instructor, course developer, and technical writer. Training and counseling junior personnel have always been key responsibilities.

With a versatile background which includes experience in the firefighting field as well as law enforcement, I offer numerous credentials in the firefighting field as shown in detail on my resume. I offer a reputation as a skilled communicator who has been especially effective in providing instruction in individual and group situations. I am especially proud of the associate's degree I earned while excelling in my full-time job.

With regard to my salary requirements, I would be delighted to discuss the private details of my salary history with you in person. I can assure you that I can provide excellent references at the appropriate time.

If you can use an experienced professional who is dedicated to setting and achieving high standards in all areas of performance, I hope you will contact me to suggest a time when we might meet to discuss your needs. I am confident that I could become an asset to Dickinson Associates.

Sincerely,

Chico Flores, Jr.

WHEN THEY ASK FOR SALARY REQUIREMENTS

Question: What if they ask for salary requirements?
It's not in your best interests to provide your salary requirements in response to an ad. It's better to discuss that subject in person with the employer, and always let the employer bring the subject up. If the employer brings up salary, he or she is probably interested in you and you'll be able to negotiate your best package. See the fourth paragraph for the exact wording in handling this delicate matter.

Date

Exact Name of Person
Title or Position
Name of Company
Address (number and street)
Address (city, state, and zip)

Dear Exact Name of Person: (or Sir or Madam if answering a blind ad)

Question: If I'm relocating soon, how do I say that?
Employers are nosy people! If they receive a resume from someone whose last (or current) job was in another town or state, they wonder why you've relocated. Go ahead and satisfy their curiosity in the cover letter you send in advance of your arrival in town.

With the enclosed resume, I would like to initiate the process of being considered for employment within your organization. Because of family ties, I am in the process of relocating to the Houston area by a target date of December 5. Although I already have a Houston address which is shown on my resume, it is my brother's home and I would prefer your contacting me at the e-mail address shown on my resume or at my current telephone number if you wish to talk with me prior to December 5th.

Since graduating from the National Firefighters Academy, I have a track record of loyal and dedicated service with the Miami Beach Fire Department, Station 234. On numerous occasions I have trained and mentored junior firefighting professionals, and I have gained a reputation as someone who will "go the extra mile" to assist his colleagues as well as the general public.

In my job, rapid change is a daily reality, and I have become accustomed to working in an environment in which I must make rapid decisions. I have earned a reputation as a persuasive communicator while visiting local schools to make presentations on subjects that include careers in firefighting, firefighting techniques, and what to do in case of fires.

I can provide excellent personal and professional references, and I assure you in advance that I am a hard worker who is accustomed to performing to the best of my ability in all areas.

Yours sincerely,

Dale P. Jensen

Date

Exact Name of Person
Title or Position
Name of Company
Address (number and street)
Address (city, state, and zip)

Dear Exact Name of Person: (or Sir or Madam if answering a blind ad)

With the enclosed resume, I would like to make you aware of my background in firefighting. My husband and I have relocated back to Rochester, where our respective families are from.

While recently completing my Associate of Science degree in Firefighting Technology, I excelled academically and was named to the Dean's List seven times. Prior to earning my degree, I excelled in both military and civilian environments.

In my most recent job in North Carolina, I began as a Firefighter I and was promoted to the job of Captain in less than two years.

With my husband's retirement, we are eager to replant our roots in New York, and I am seeking employment with a station that can use a highly motivated hard worker who is known for excellent decision-making, problem-solving, and organizational skills. If you can use a resourceful and versatile individual with excellent firefighting and communication skills, I hope you will contact me to suggest a time when we can discuss your present and future needs and how I might meet them. I can provide outstanding personal and professional references, and I thank you in advance for your time and consideration.

Sincerely,

Antoinette Pardue

RECENTLY RELOCATED

Question: If I've recently relocated, what do I say in the cover letter?
Employers like the sound of the fact that you have relocated permanently back to the place where you're from. That fact tends to communicate that you might be a permanent and stable employee in the work force of a local employer.

Date

Exact Name of Person
Title or Position
Name of Company
Address (number and street)
Address (city, state, and zip)

FOLLOW-UP LETTER

Dear Exact Name of Person: (or Sir or Madam if answering a blind ad)

Question: How do I write a follow-up letter after an interview?
Notice the last paragraph. A follow-up letter is an excellent opportunity to send your requests for reimbursement for any out-of-pocket expenses you incurred in connection with the interview.

I want you to know how much I enjoyed talking with you in Sioux Falls on Friday, January 12th.

I am intensely interested in working with you to develop fire safety programs for the convenience store industry. I believe you are aware that I performed essentially that job for the construction industry in a previous position. With Newcombe Construction Systems, I rose from Firefighter to Director of Safety Development as I transformed a substandard operation into an efficient one.

In my current job as Safety Director and Fire Prevention Chief, I have played a key role in making many changes within FashionPlus, a major retail chain, which made the company an acquisition target. Now that we are a part of a larger retail company, I am directing safety programs for this vastly larger organization. I understand your company's growth goals, as you explained them to me, and I feel I could become a valuable part of your strategic planning and implementation process.

One of my strengths is that I have a vast knowledge of many different areas, ranging from employee interface, to the continual troubleshooting of problems and refinement of systems. It has been my responsibility to sit with technical experts in all functional areas and be able to assure the attainment of specific goals in their area of operation. I am very proud of the fact that I have developed employee safety programs that have reduced the incidence of fires by 86%.

Thank you for giving me so much of your time and for letting me become better acquainted with your needs. I am enclosing a copy of my mileage statement (423 miles) and a copy of the hotel statement. I believe I could become a valuable member of your management team.

Sincerely,

James W. White

Date

Exact Name of Person
Title or Position
Name of Company
Address (number and street)
Address (city, state, and zip)

Dear Exact Name of Person: (or Dear Sir or Madam if answering a blind ad)

It is with genuine sadness and many mixed feelings that I must inform you that I will be resigning from my position as Station Chief at Station 632, effective July 26.

Station 787 in Duluth, MN, has offered me a position as a Station Chief at a salary of $10,000 more annually than I am making now, and I feel I must accept that offer.

Leaving the station is very difficult for me professionally and emotionally. After I earned my Firefighter I & II certifications, you gave me my first job in the firefighting field, and I have thoroughly enjoyed the family atmosphere coupled with the professional style of the station. You have taught me so much about how to solve problems, how to work more efficiently, and how to handle people. I am deeply grateful for your encouragement, professional mentoring, and strong personal example.

Although the decision to leave the station is difficult, I really feel that I have no choice. As a single parent who provides full financial support of my daughter, I am driven by the desire to provide a gracious standard of living for my small family. I will be placing her in a Christian school in Duluth so that she can continue learning in the same Christian environment as she has had in Tacoma.

I hope you know that I have always given 110% to your firm in terms of my financial knowledge, intelligence, and problem-solving ability, and I hope you feel that I have made contributions to its reputation. I feel I am separating more from a family than from an employer, and I felt I wanted to put this information in writing to you as a first step because getting the words out verbally would be a difficult emotional experience for me.

Thank you from the bottom of my heart for all you have done for me professionally and personally.

Yours sincerely,

Elizabeth J. Ritchie

LETTERS OF RESIGNATION

Question: How do I resign—gracefully?
Here's an example of a letter that will be an emotional experience for the people receiving it as it was for the person who signed it. Employers are often not happy when you leave them, so a great letter of resignation can ease the hurt.

ABOUT THE EDITOR

Anne McKinney holds an MBA from the Harvard Business School and a BA in English from the University of North Carolina at Chapel Hill. A noted public speaker, writer, and teacher, she is the senior editor for PREP's business and career imprint, which bears her name. Early titles in the Anne McKinney Career Series (now called the Real-Resumes Series) published by PREP include: *Resumes and Cover Letters That Have Worked, Resumes and Cover Letters That Have Worked for Military Professionals, Government Job Applications and Federal Resumes, Cover Letters That Blow Doors Open,* and *Letters for Special Situations.* Her career titles and how-to resume-and-cover-letter books are based on the expertise she has acquired in 25 years of working with job hunters. Her valuable career insights have appeared in publications of the "Wall Street Journal" and other prominent newspapers and magazines.

PREP Publishing Order Form

You may purchase our titles from your favorite bookseller! Or send a check, money order or your credit card number for the total amount*, plus $4.00 postage and handling, to PREP, 1110 1/2 Hay Street, Fayetteville, NC 28305. You may also order our titles on our website at www.prep-pub.com and feel free to e-mail us at preppub@aol.com or call 910-483-6611 with your questions or concerns.

Name: _____

Address: _____

E-mail address:_____

Payment Type: ☐ Check/Money Order   ☐ Visa   ☐ MasterCard

Credit Card Number: _____ Expiration Date: _____

Put a check beside the items you are ordering:

☐ $16.95—REAL-RESUMES FOR RESTAURANT, FOOD SERVICE & HOTEL JOBS. Anne McKinney, Editor

☐ $16.95—REAL-RESUMES FOR MEDIA, NEWSPAPER, BROADCASTING & PUBLIC AFFAIRS JOBS. Anne McKinney, Editor

☐ $16.95—REAL-RESUMES FOR RETAILING, MODELING, FASHION & BEAUTY JOBS. Anne McKinney, Editor

☐ $16.95—REAL-RESUMES FOR HUMAN RESOURCES & PERSONNEL JOBS. Anne McKinney, Editor

☐ $16.95—REAL-RESUMES FOR MANUFACTURING JOBS. Anne McKinney, Editor

☐ $16.95—REAL-RESUMES FOR AVIATION & TRAVEL JOBS. Anne McKinney, Editor

☐ $16.95—REAL-RESUMES FOR POLICE, LAW ENFORCEMENT & SECURITY JOBS. Anne McKinney, Editor

☐ $16.95—REAL-RESUMES FOR SOCIAL WORK & COUNSELING JOBS. Anne McKinney, Editor

☐ $16.95—REAL-RESUMES FOR CONSTRUCTION JOBS. Anne McKinney, Editor

☐ $16.95—REAL-RESUMES FOR FINANCIAL JOBS. Anne McKinney, Editor

☐ $16.95—REAL-RESUMES FOR COMPUTER JOBS. Anne McKinney, Editor

☐ $16.95—REAL-RESUMES FOR MEDICAL JOBS. Anne McKinney, Editor

☐ $16.95—REAL-RESUMES FOR TEACHERS. Anne McKinney, Editor

☐ $16.95—REAL-RESUMES FOR CAREER CHANGERS. Anne McKinney, Editor

☐ $16.95—REAL-RESUMES FOR STUDENTS. Anne McKinney, Editor

☐ $16.95—REAL-RESUMES FOR SALES. Anne McKinney, Editor

☐ $16.95—REAL ESSAYS FOR COLLEGE AND GRAD SCHOOL. Anne McKinney, Editor

☐ $25.00—RESUMES AND COVER LETTERS THAT HAVE WORKED. McKinney. Editor

☐ $25.00—RESUMES AND COVER LETTERS THAT HAVE WORKED FOR MILITARY PROFESSIONALS. McKinney, Ed.

☐ $25.00—RESUMES AND COVER LETTERS FOR MANAGERS. McKinney, Editor

☐ $25.00—GOVERNMENT JOB APPLICATIONS AND FEDERAL RESUMES: Federal Resumes, KSAs, Forms 171 and 612, and Postal Applications. McKinney, Editor

☐ $25.00—COVER LETTERS THAT BLOW DOORS OPEN. McKinney, Editor

☐ $25.00—LETTERS FOR SPECIAL SITUATIONS. McKinney, Editor

☐ $16.95—REAL-RESUMES FOR NURSING JOBS. McKinney, Editor

☐ $16.95—REAL-RESUMES FOR AUTO INDUSTRY JOBS. McKinney, Editor

☐ $24.95—REAL KSAS--KNOWLEDGE, SKILLS & ABILITIES--FOR GOVERNMENT JOBS. McKinney, Editor

☐ $24.95—REAL RESUMIX AND OTHER RESUMES FOR FEDERAL GOVERNMENT JOBS. McKinney, Editor

☐ $24.95—REAL BUSINESS PLANS AND MARKETING TOOLS ... Samples to use in your business. McKinney, Ed.

☐ $16.95—REAL-RESUMES FOR ADMINISTRATIVE SUPPORT, OFFICE & SECRETARIAL JOBS. Anne McKinney, Editor

☐ $16.95—REAL-RESUMES FOR FIREFIGHTING JOBS. Anne McKinney, Editor

☐ $16.95—REAL-RESUMES FOR JOBS IN NONPROFIT ORGANIZATIONS. Anne McKinney, Editor

☐ $16.95—REAL-RESUMES FOR SPORTS INDUSTRY JOBS. Anne McKinney, Editor

☐ $16.95—REAL-RESUMES FOR LEGAL & PARALEGAL JOBS. Anne McKinney, Editor

_____ **TOTAL ORDERED**

_____ **(add $4.00 for shipping and handling)**

_____**TOTAL INCLUDING SHIPPING *PREP** *offers volume discounts on large orders. Call us at (910) 483-6611 for more information.*

Would you like to explore the possibility of having PREP's writing
team create a resume for you similar to the ones in this book?

For a brief free consultation, call 910-483-6611
or send $4.00 to receive our Job Change Packet to
PREP, 1110 1/2 Hay Street, Fayetteville, NC 28305. Visit our
website to find valuable career resources: www.prep-pub.com!

QUESTIONS OR COMMENTS? E-MAIL US AT PREPPUB@AOL.COM